Asset–Liability Management for Financial Institutions

Balancing Financial Stability with Strategic Objectives

Asset–Liability Management for Financial Institutions

Balancing Financial Stability
with Strategic Objectives

Edited by
Bob Swarup

qatar
FINANCIAL CENTRE
AUTHORITY

BLOOMSBURY

First published in 2012 by

Bloomsbury Information Ltd
50 Bedford Square
London
WC1B 3DP
United Kingdom

Bloomsbury Publishing, London, Berlin, New York, and Sydney
www.bloomsbury.com

A CIP record for this book is available from the British Library.

Standard edition
ISBN-10: 1-84930-041-0
ISBN-13: 978-1-84930-041-4

Middle East edition
ISBN-10: 1-84930-048-8
ISBN-13: 978-1-84930-048-3

E-book edition
ISBN-10: 1-84930-058-5
ISBN-13: 978-1-84930-058-2

Project Director: Conrad Gardner
Project Manager: Ben Hickling
Project Editor: Lizzy Kingston

Typeset by Marsh Typesetting, West Sussex, UK
Printed and bound by CPI Group (UK) Ltd, Croydon, CR0 4YY

MIX
Paper from responsible sources
FSC www.fsc.org FSC® C013604

Contents

Introduction

The Essence of Asset–Liability Management

In the aftermath of the credit crunch of 2007–09, a new joke has begun to do the rounds in the rarefied community of asset–liability managers. According to this joke, the real reason behind the financial crisis was that financial institutions forgot the basics of ALM. On the left, you have liabilities. On the right, you have assets. Unfortunately, on the left, nothing was right. And so, on the right, eventually nothing was left.

If you are new to the world of asset–liability management (or ALM, to use its less clunky acronym), you may worry at what passes for humor among your peers. If you are steeped in this world, it may bring a smile to your lips.

Regardless, the witticism encapsulates a fundamental truth. For any institution, assets and liabilities are inextricably bound and must be viewed as a holistic whole. This is particularly true for financial institutions such as banks and insurance companies, where the balance sheet is typically highly leveraged and often complex. Here, ALM becomes a delicate balancing act and any failure can rapidly lead to contagion. As the recent financial crisis has shown us, failing to appreciate and manage the mismatches between assets and liabilities that arise can have a devastating impact on the institution and, *in extremis*, on the wider economy.

Simply put, good asset–liability management is the key to the continued health and longevity of any financial institution. This is true irrespective of geography, specialization, size, regulatory environment, or business model. All of these are just nuances that are reflected in the refinement and precise nature of the ALM models adopted by institutions.

In the chapters that follow, a range of distinguished experts lay out some of the challenges for ALM practitioners and give their perspective on different approaches as well as regulatory regimes. They supply some much-needed meat on what has historically been a neglected and somewhat skeletal exhibit. It is all the more important in today's world, where regulatory scrutiny of financial institutions is on the increase and ALM has once again taken center stage.

However, before we dive into the detail, there are some simple fundamental principles to bear in mind.

First, *understand all your assets and liabilities before you begin to manage them*. It may seem a truism, but plenty of institutions have forgotten this to their painful cost, and assets and liabilities are fundamental inputs that underpin every model. In particular, all financial institutions have two types of liabilities they need to manage. There are the tangible liabilities that are captured in endless models—be it customer deposits, insurance liabilities, and so on. And there are the often ignored intangible liabilities, in the form of customer expectations and the wider perception of the institution in the market place. It is very important to understand that these are fundamentally interrelated. Confidence is the key to every successful leveraged business model, but it is also a double-edged sword. In the financial world particularly, reputation is everything, and nothing can kill a business as quickly as a loss of confidence.

Second, *ALM and risk management are synonymous*. All financial institutions are first and foremost businesses. That means they exist to make money, and ALM is vital to creating value for investors and shareholders. But they are also leveraged businesses. Although this is fundamental to how they generate their returns, this leverage also places huge demands on understanding the complex interplay between assets and liabilities. Get it wrong and the impact is very painful, as has been amply demonstrated by recent experience. That makes ALM vital to controlling risks and the judicious allocation of economic capital.

Third, *good ALM is not about the avoidance of risk but rather the art of learning how to live with it*. You need to take risks to make money, and the Eurozone sovereign crisis has taught us that risk-free is nothing more a theoretical construct. The goals of any effective ALM program are simple: avoid the catastrophic losses that can come through taking unintended risks, and remove all of those unwanted risks wherever possible. By protecting the downside, opportunities can be exploited to maximize the upside.

Fourth, *have a proactive and dynamic approach*. Changing markets mean changing risks. And while long-term return expectations may have a sound basis, you still have to navigate through the short-term and its associated volatility to survive long enough to harvest those returns. Good asset–liability management is a constant and evolving trade-off between risk, return, and capital employed. There are also many hidden risks—such as counterparty risk, interest rates, inflation, data risk, regulatory change, and so on—that need to be factored in. It is important to know them all and focus on accepting only those risks you understand. Actively manage, and hedge out the rest.

Fifth, *all models are broken*. Humans have a propensity to fall in love with precision, no matter how illusory it may be. If there is one thing we can be certain of, it is that the future is unpredictable. Models do have valuable uses as they give us an indication of potential outcomes and where stresses may lie. However, it is also important to know their limitations. For example, correlations can be spurious and subject to selection bias. Assumptions are important and need to be actively challenged as garbage in will inevitably mean garbage out. Most importantly, models are not microcosms of the wider world. They are—by definition—simplifications, and their roots in past behavior mean that you are always at risk in tail events.

Sixth, *the big risks are not everything*. AIG is a lesson for those who might otherwise forget. One of the largest insurance companies in the world was brought down by one small division—AIG Financial Products—that sold credit protection and turned out to stand behind some US$441 billion worth of structured products. The rest of the businesses were profitable, but it took just one little bad apple that was overlooked to undo decades of hard work. Far too many people focus on just the big nominal risks, which means that the true risks can go on slipping through unnoticed until it's too late. In particular, there is a bias toward those risks, such as market risk, that are easy to quantify to the detriment of other equally important areas, such as operational and counterparty risks.

Seventh, *always watch the outside world*. No business is an island, and this is especially true of financial institutions. Financial markets are not static entities. They are collective nouns representing the actions born of the hope, greed, and fear of countless human participants. Though we may prey on each other, we still herd together, and this herd behavior can both enhance and mitigate risks. In the modern globalized world, we are all interconnected far more than ever before. Even hedging does not remove risk—it merely transmutes it into a lesser one that is harder to quantify and draws us deeper into an intertwined web of interdependency.

Eighth, *understand what will kill you*. This may seem anathema to many practitioners and an admission of failure, but it is a vital exercise. No business can survive everything, and understanding where your business model breaks down irretrievably is perhaps the most valuable input of all into your ALM approach. There has been a growing fallacy over the last decade or two that confuses good risk management with 25,000 Monte Carlo simulations and 867 scenarios. But people forget that their best tool is not the supercomputer round the corner. It's their mind, and thinking is the best deterrent we have against complacency and failure. Once you know what your ultimate tail risk is, you can start managing your assets and liabilities to minimize that outcome.

These core principles are all interrelated and run as an undercurrent through the ALM universe. Like most truisms, they are obvious when expounded but forgotten in practice all too often. They have held true through a multitude of markets and they will continue to hold true, even as financial innovation progresses and models evolve. It helps, therefore, to commit them to memory as we plunge into an increasingly complex world, where detail can often overcome the bigger picture. Properly applied, they can help to create a sustainable business with stable and visible returns, which is all that any of us can aspire to.

Dr Bob Swarup
Editor

Contributors

Marius Bochniak was educated at the Technical University of Kaiserslautern. From 1995 to 2000 he worked at the Technical University of Stuttgart, specializing in the development and implementation of mathematical models in continuum mechanics. After receiving a PhD in mathematics in 2002, he moved to the Faculty of Mathematics and Economics at the University of Ulm, where he was appointed junior professor in applied mathematics in the same year. In 2006 he moved to the Risk Methodology and Analytics Department of the HypoVereinsbank in Munich, where he worked on the development of various market risk models. Since January 2011 he has been working on the risk standards and methods team of Lloyds TSB Bank in London.

Alex Canavezes is the managing director and founder of Quant Analytics, a consultancy firm that offers financial solutions ranging from risk management to derivatives modeling and litigation advisory. Before that, he was a structurer with the corporate solutions team of BNP Paribas and an associate of the insurance and pensions solutions group of Dresdner Kleinwort in London. His expertise includes pricing complex structured products encompassing all asset classes; asset–liability modeling of large pension funds; design, pricing, and marketing of variable annuity guarantees for insurance and reinsurance companies; optimization of debt composition for corporations after a merger or acquisition; and advising investment banks undergoing litigation. Canavezes holds a PhD in astrophysics from Imperial College, London, and a certificate of advanced study in mathematics from the University of Cambridge.

Giorgio Consigli has been professor of applied mathematics in economics and finance at the University of Bergamo since 2004. He has a PhD in mathematics, a diploma in the economics of financial intermediaries, and an honors degree in economics from the University of Rome La Sapienza. After a postdoctoral position at the Centre for Financial Research, University of Cambridge, in 1995–97, he was appointed vice president at UBM, the investment bank of the UniCredit banking group, and later worked as a consultant on advanced quantitative developments in the finance industry. Since 2006 he has been a visiting professor at the University of Svizzera Italiana in Lugano, and since August 2007 an elective member of the International Committee on Stochastic Programming (COSP). He is a fellow of the UK Institute of Mathematics and Applications since 2011.

Kambiz Deljouie is liability and multiasset solutions director at Aviva Investors, which he joined in 2009. He has 20 years of experience in investment and banking, spanning trading, structuring, investment, and strategic consulting. Before joining Aviva, he was a senior investment consultant at Watson Wyatt Worldwide, and prior to that global head of structured risk finance at ABN AMRO. He spent three years at McKinsey & Company as a principal associate serving global financial institutions, and before that he spent a number of years as a quantitative proprietary trader and desk head, trading different asset classes. Deljouie has a PhD in numerical analysis from Kings College, London, and an MBA from the London Business School.

Jean Dermine is professor of banking and finance at INSEAD, Fontainebleau. Graduating with a doctorat ès sciences économiques from the Université Catholique de Louvain and with an MBA from Cornell University, he has been a visiting professor at New York University, the Wharton School, and the Stockholm School of Economics. As a consultant he has worked with international banks, auditing and consulting firms, national central banks, the European Central Bank, the Bank for International Settlements, HM Treasury, the OECD, the World Bank, and the European Commission. Professor Dermine is coauthor of the ALCO Challenge, a banking simulation used on five continents. His work has been quoted in the international press, such as *The Economist*, the *Financial Times*, the *New York Times*, and the *Wall Street Journal*.

Gary M. Deutsch is founder and president of BRT Publications LLC, a professional education and training company that has served the financial industry for over 10 years. He has written numerous publications for Sheshunoff and A. S. Pratt on topics such as risk management, credit management, asset and liability management, and accounting and internal auditing. He also consults on credit risk management and allowance for loan and lease loss regulatory compliance and accounting issues. Prior to founding BRT Publications, Deutsch worked extensively in management positions with regional financial institutions and community banks in audit, lending, financial, and operational areas. He is a licensed CPA in Maryland and has a BA in accounting and an MBA in finance from Loyola University Maryland. He holds certified management accountant, certified internal auditor, and certified bank auditor designations.

Massimo di Tria is property and casualty chief investment manager at Allianz Investment Management Milano SpA and contract professor of equity portfolio management and financial economics at Bocconi University, from which he gained a master's degree in economics. He is a member of the CAIA (Chartered Alternative Investment Analyst Association) and SIdE (Italian Econometric Association). Before joining the Allianz Group, he worked for Fineco Investimenti SGR SpA and for the Paolo Baffi Center at Bocconi University. He has extensive knowledge of the insurance and investment management business at the international level and is the author of several publications in the field of asset allocation, risk management, ALM, and asset pricing.

Jens Hagendorff is the Martin Currie professor of finance and investment at the University of Edinburgh. Previously, he was an economist in the regulation department of the Bank of Spain and a lecturer in finance at the University of Leeds. His research examines the impact of bank regulation and corporate governance on bank behavior. Professor Hagendorff's work has appeared in the *Journal of Banking and Finance*, the *Journal of Corporate Finance*, and other highly ranked international journals.

Markus Krebsz is a strategic management consultant with expert knowledge in the spheres of securitization and rating agencies and nearly two decades of experience in global financial markets. A well-regarded speaker at international conferences and an experienced workshop conductor, he currently acts as credit rating expert to the World Bank as part of various large-scale projects involving government-owned entities of several African nations. Previously, he led the rapid risk solutions team at a major UK banking group. Prior to that he established and managed the firm's surveillance and performance analytics team, overseeing one of the world's largest portfolios of structured finance bonds. His latest book, *Securitization and Structured Finance Post Credit Crunch* (Wiley, 2011), has been hailed as a "rare feat," "encyclopedic," "unique," and "a model of clarity of exposition."

Jérôme L. Kreuser is executive director and founder of the RisKontrol Group in Bern, Switzerland. He holds a PhD in mathematical programming/numerical analysis and a master's in mathematics from the University of Wisconsin. He specializes in strategic asset–liability and risk management for sovereigns, (re) insurance, pension funds, and hedge funds. He develops and consults on risk management systems which apply dynamic stochastic optimization models integrated with stochastic processes that originated in a project he undertook at the World Bank, where he held various posts from 1974 to 1998. Kreuser has served as a reserves management adviser to the IMF and is an adjunct full professor of operations research at George Washington University. He is editor of a series on risk management for sovereign institutions for Henry Stewart Talks.

Steven V. Mann is professor and chair of the finance department at the Moore School of Business, University of South Carolina. He has coauthored and coedited several books on the bond market. He is also associate editor of *The Handbook of Fixed Income Securities*, the eighth edition of which was published in January 2012. Professor Mann is an accomplished teacher, having won more than 20 awards for excellence in teaching, including the two highest awards given by the University of South Carolina. He is an active consultant to clients that include some of the largest investment/commercial banks in the world, as well as a number of Fortune 500 companies. He also serves as an expert witness in court cases involving fixed-income-related matters.

Jyothi Manohar serves as a director for a CPA and consulting firm in the United States that has international affiliations. She is an accounting, audit, and consulting professional focusing on the community banking industry. Her experience covers US banking regulations, risk management, internal controls, accounting, financial, and regulatory reporting, and audit committee responsibilities. She also has experience writing articles and presenting relevant topics for community bankers at industry conferences and on webcasts. She has assisted in creating staff training material and providing training for staff and senior auditors serving the banking industry.

Krzysztof M. Ostaszewski holds a PhD in mathematics from the University of Washington in Seattle. He is a chartered financial analyst, a member of the American Academy of Actuaries, a fellow of the Society of Actuaries, a chartered enterprise risk analyst, and a fellow of the Singapore Actuarial Society. He is a professor of mathematics and the actuarial program director at Illinois State University, a center of actuarial excellence. Ostaszewski is also the research director for life insurance and pensions at the Geneva Association, International Association for the Study of Insurance Economics.

Corrado Pistarino is head of insurance, liability-driven investment, at Aviva Investors, which he joined in 2009. He has more than 15 years' experience in investment banking, including trading, structuring, and advising institutional clients. At Aviva he is responsible for developing and implementing a new range of investment frameworks for insurance clients, moving from traditional liability-driven investment to more advanced balance-sheet management solutions. Prior to Aviva, Corrado was at Deutsche Bank, advising institutional clients. He also worked at Dresdner

Kleinwort in a similar role, and at ABN AMRO, where he was part of the global structuring group. Before that he traded interest rate derivatives and worked as a structurer. He has a degree in theoretical physics from the University of Turin and a master's in finance from the London Business School.

Mario Schlener leads business strategy and product development at Navigant Capital Markets Advisers—Europe. Prior to that, for four years he headed the quantitative and analytics group at Deloitte Vienna, and before Deloitte he gained 10 years' banking experience at a major Austrian banking group in the corporate finance, fixed-income, and structured products sales department in Vienna and New York. He has extensive experience in advising banks, asset managers, and pension funds. Schlener holds BA and MA degrees in banking and finance from the University of Applied Sciences BFI Vienna and an MBA in economics from the University of Chicago's Booth School of Business. Currently a PhD in finance candidate at the EDHEC Risk Institute, he is also an external lecturer at Vienna University of Technology.

Amarendra Swarup is a respected commentator and expert on financial markets, alternative investments, asset–liability management, regulation, risk management, and pensions. He was formerly a partner at Pension Corporation, a leading UK-based pension buyout firm, and was at an AAA-rated hedge fund of funds in London before that. Swarup is a CAIA charter-holder and sits on the CAIA examinations council, the AllAboutAlpha.com editorial board, and the Adveq advisory board. He was a visiting fellow at the London School of Economics, setting up the Pensions Tomorrow research initiative, and a member of the CRO and Solvency II committees of the Association of British Insurers. Swarup holds a PhD (cosmology, Imperial College, London) and an MA (natural sciences, University of Cambridge). He has written extensively on diverse topics and is currently writing a book on financial crises throughout history and the common human factors underlying them, to be published by Bloomsbury in 2013.

Hovik Tumasyan is a director with PwC's risk advisory practice in Toronto. He has 15 years of experience in the areas of risk capital and liquidity management. He has managed financial risks for and advised a wide variety of financial institutions that range from broker/dealers and investment banks to regional and government-sponsored banks in North America, the United Kingdom, and Asia-Pacific. He regularly publishes and makes speaking engagements. Tumasyan holds a postgraduate diploma in mathematical finance from the University of Oxford and a PhD in Physics from the University of Miami.

Francesco Vallascas is a lecturer in banking and finance at the University of Leeds and is on leave from the University of Cagliari, where he is a lecturer in financial intermediation. His research examines banking risk in Europe and its implications for the reregulation of the financial industry. Recently, his research has appeared in the *Journal of Banking and Finance*, the *Journal of Corporate Finance*, and the *Journal of Financial Services Research*.

The Big Challenges

Stress-Testing in Asset and Liability Management: A Coherent Approach

by Alex Canavezes[a] and Mario Schlener[b]

[a] Quant Analytics, London, UK
[b] NCMA, Europe

This Chapter Covers

- How traditional stress tests are performed and why they are meaningless.
- How to assign a probability number to a given stress event.
- Exposition of the frequentist methodology.
- Exposition of the subjective methodology.
- Application of the frequentist methodology to a case study in asset management.

Introduction

In light of recent extreme events, such as the collapse of Lehman Brothers in 2008, both the financial services industry and its regulators have keenly felt the need to complement traditional percentile-based risk management tools (such as value-at-risk (VaR) or economic capital) with stress tests and scenario analyses.

Following the logic of Dermine (2003), asset and liability management (ALM) can be interpreted as the main management tool for controlling value creation and risks in a financial institution. Additionally, ALM should be the main management tool for discussions, in an integrated way, of fund transfer pricing, deposit pricing (for fixed and undefined maturities), loan pricing, the evaluation of credit risk provisions, the measurement of interest rate risk for fixed and undefined maturities, the diversification of risk, the marginal risk contribution, and also the allocation of economic capital.

Learning from the past misbehaviors of all market participants (especially the overreliance on quantitative measures with "statistical entropy," on diversification, and the assumption that capital is always available), risk management evolved from being just used as a risk-minimization, insurance, or diversification tool to an optimization tool for managing the risk–return profile. This implies that financial institutions have to develop forward-looking models (i.e. to cover tail/extreme events) and decision-making tools that cover the amount of available capital, leverage adjustment costs, and the duration mismatches of assets and liabilities.

The fundamental basis for every ALM model is to define future scenarios of risk parameters and value assets and liabilities. One of the main challenges in that process is to come up with scenarios. These scenarios are usually based on historical observations or forward-looking simulations (using Monte Carlo) and typically do not cover tail risks—the so-called extreme events.

It is clear that stress tests are much needed in order to complement the usual VaR measures as a foundation for risk-adjusted decision-making. However, the traditional stress-testing approaches used by market participants and/or requested by the regulators suffer from a fundamental problem: there is no attempt to assign probabilities to the scenarios considered.

A framework is needed to express the likelihood of the various stress scenarios. A specific probability can be given to a stress test in, usually, two ways:

- on a nonobjective or judgmental basis—for example, by an economist/expert who provides context-sensitive and conditional stress scenarios;
- on an objective basis using historical data—i.e. one requiring a long period of history in order to observe stressed situations.[1]

Stress-testing as a risk management tool has been in existence for more than a decade but was not really applied by the financial services industry as an enhancement of the daily decision-making process. The reasons for this reluctance are well explained by Aragones, Blanco, and Dowd (2001) (quoted by Rebonato, 2010):

"...the results of [traditional] stress tests are difficult to interpret because they give us no idea of the probabilities of the events concerned, and in the absence of such information we often don't know what to do with them. ...As Berkowitz [1999] nicely puts it, this absence of probabilities puts 'stress testing in a statistical purgatory. We have some loss numbers, but who is to say whether we should be concerned about them?' ...[we are left with] two sets of separate risk estimates—probabilistic estimates (e.g. such as VaR), and the loss estimates produced by stress tests—and no way of combining them. How can we combine a probabilistic risk estimate with an estimate that such-and-such a loss will occur if such-and-such happens? The answer, of course, is that we can't. We therefore have to work with these estimates more or less independently of each other, and the best we can do is use one set of estimates to check for prospective losses that the other might have underrated or missed..."

The main goal in this chapter is to explore ways in which a probability number can be assigned to stress tests in order to make sense of them and be able to integrate them within ALM in a meaningful manner.

Asset–Liability Management: Stress Testing

A financial institution will traditionally perform stress tests by stressing certain variables such as interest rates, default rates, etc., with a view to analyzing the impact of such movements on its balance sheet. No assessment of the likelihood of such scenarios is attempted. This state of affairs is clearly unsatisfactory. In order to price risk, we need the probabilities of outcomes. This includes both the probabilities of recurring events and the probabilities of extreme events.

There are two ways in which to approach this problem.

- We can make use of extreme value theory to fit an appropriate joint probability distribution of exceedances to the historical distribution of extreme events. We could call this the "frequentist" approach, where the data are left to speak for themselves.

- We can postulate a model of the world in which the causal links between extreme events are determined, leading to a more intuitive determination of the joint probability of extreme events. This is known as the "subjective" approach and makes use of Bayesian theory.

Important Results

Stress tests are performed by financial institutions as part of their asset–liability management to assess the impact of large movements of underlying economic variables on their balance sheet.

- Stress tests by themselves are meaningless. To make sense of stress tests, the probabilities associated with large movements need to be determined.
- There are two ways in which one can attempt to determine the joint distribution of extreme events: the *frequentist* approach and the *subjective* approach.

The Frequentist Approach

The first approach we will consider is the frequentist approach. Here one tries to fit a joint probability distribution function to the data that are available. The difficulty here arises from the different *shapes* of the distribution implied by the data for common or rare events. Although for usual events (relatively small movements in the underlying variables) the normal distribution can be a good fit, this is not the case for rare events.

To see why, let us remind ourselves of the central limit theorem (CLT). CLT states that the sum of a very large number of independent variables, each with finite variance, is normally distributed. Relatively small movements in the underlying variables tend to happen under normal market conditions, when the underlying risk factors are largely independent of each other. So it comes as no surprise that a normal distribution should be a good fit under normal market conditions. However, during times of market turbulence, "correlations among asset classes become more polarized, tending towards +100% or –100%" (Rebonato, 2010). This means that in times of market turbulence the CLT does not apply, and indeed we observe that the normal distribution is a very bad fit. The obvious example that comes to mind is the recent credit crisis. After the collapse of Lehman Brothers, it became very difficult for an investor to diversify his or her market position efficiently, because the correlations between the various asset classes converged to 100%.

To quote Greenspan (1995): "From the point of view of the risk manager, inappropriate use of the normal distribution can lead to an understatement of risk, which must be balanced against the significant advantage of simplification. ...Improving the characterization of the distribution of extreme values is of paramount concern."

A sophisticated ALM model must be able to include the right probability distribution for extreme events.[2] The problem comes down to finding the probability distribution that best fits the available data. A whole section of statistics, known as extreme value theory (EVT), is devoted to this task. Standard EVT techniques can be efficiently applied when the dimensionality is relatively low. Dimension reduction techniques can be employed, but even after a successful reduction "an effective dimensionality between five and ten, say, still poses considerable problems for the application of standard EVT techniques. By the nature of the problem extreme observations are rare. The curse of dimensionality very quickly further complicates the issue." (Balkema and Embrechts, 2007).

Balkema and Embrechts (2007) propose an enlightening geometric theory for EVT. From a mathematical perspective, a geometric theory is appealing as the theory applying to the *objects* (vectors representing portfolio positions) will be invariant under coordinate transformations.

In the univariate case, i.e. for one variable only, the condition that extreme scenarios can be described by a probability distribution leads to a one-parameter family of fat-tail shapes, the generalized Pareto distribution (GPD) (Balkema and Embrechts, 2007):

$$G\xi x(\upsilon)=1-(1+\xi\upsilon)^{-\frac{1}{\xi}}, \xi \geq 0$$

The shape parameter ξ determines how "fat" the tail is—i.e. how much more frequent extreme events are than in the normal distribution. A large value of ξ means a distribution close to the normal distribution, whereas a small value of ξ means a very fat tail. By continuity, G_0 is the standard exponential distribution function $G_0(\upsilon)=1-e^{-\upsilon}, \upsilon \geq 0$.

As an example, let us consider the history of the S&P 500 Index. The values and relative movements of the S&P 500 over the period 1968–2008 are shown in Figure 1 and Figure 2, respectively. A quick look at the daily movements in Figure 2 reveals a lot of relatively small movements, but also a significant number of very large movements. This suggests the existence of a normal "core" and a fat tail.

Figure 1. Values of S&P 500 Index, June 1968–January 2008. (*Source*: Bloomberg)

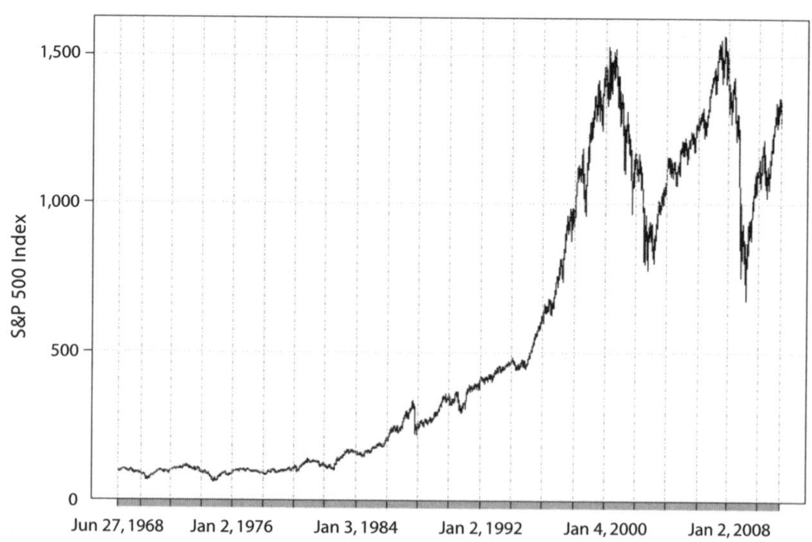

Figure 2. Relative movements of S&P 500 Index, June 1968–January 2008. (*Source*: Bloomberg)

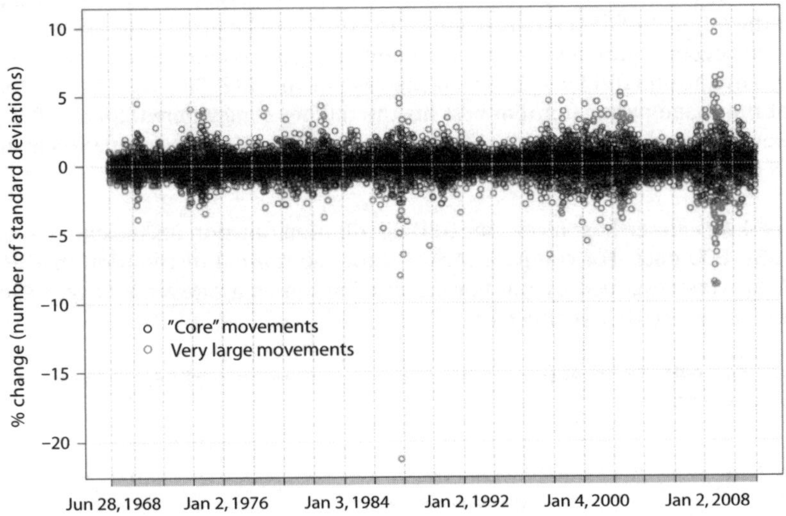

Indeed, we can fit a GPD to the daily log-differences with a varying number of exceedances[3] and analyze how the shape of the distribution varies as a function of the threshold[4] that determines the number of exceedances. Figure 3 shows how the shape of the tail x_i varies with this threshold.

Figure 3. The shape parameter xi as a function of exceedances for relative movements of S&P 500 Index, June 1968–January 2008

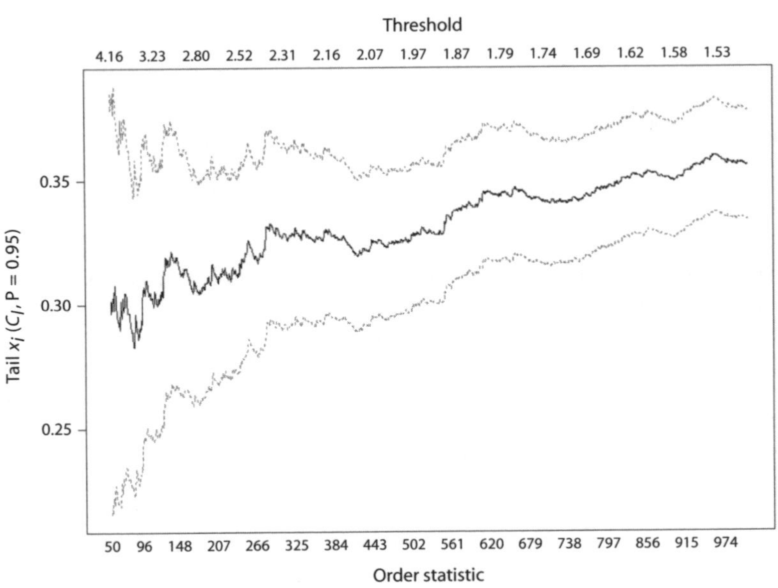

By varying the threshold that determines the number of movements larger than the threshold itself (the order statistics), we obtain a different value for the shape parameter. The further we are from the core—i.e. the larger the threshold and the smaller the number of data points to which the GPD is to be fitted—the better the fit to the fat tail becomes until, eventually, the number of data points becomes far too small to draw any meaningful conclusion. In the case of the S&P 500 we can see that the value of the shape parameter that best fits the tail lies somewhere 0.25 and 0.35. For a number of exceedances less than 50, the associated error in the calculation increases and it is no longer possible to draw any significant conclusion.

In Figure 4 we can see how nicely our GPD distribution function fits the extreme events in the S&P 500 data. For comparison, we show the normal distribution that fits the core. What was described by the normal distribution as a once-in-200-year event is seen now to be a once-a-year event!

Figure 4. The GPD fit to extremes in absolute movements of S&P 500 Index, June 1968–January 2008

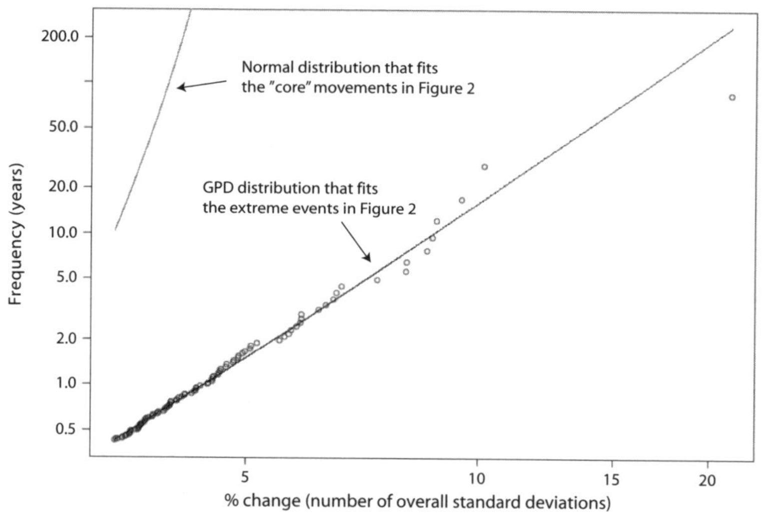

The corresponding multivariate theory is described in great detail by Balkema and Embrechts (2007). It is not trivial to expand to more than one dimension. However, one can in general define a metric in the multidimensional space such that the size and direction of the movements become well defined.

To illustrate this, let us consider the following two-dimensional example: a portfolio composed of only two hypothetical assets a and b. We shall define Δa and Δb as the number of standard deviations away from the mean for movements in the net asset value (NAV) of asset a and asset b, respectively. We then define the two-dimensional distance $r = \sqrt{\Delta a^2 + \Delta b^2}$ and the angle θ that determines the direction of the joint movement as $\theta = \tan^{-1}(\frac{\Delta b}{\Delta a})$. Figure 5 shows the result of plotting the points for which the joint relative movements are larger than three.

Figure 5. Hypothetical two-dimensional asset space showing percentage changes in NAV for assets *a* and *b*

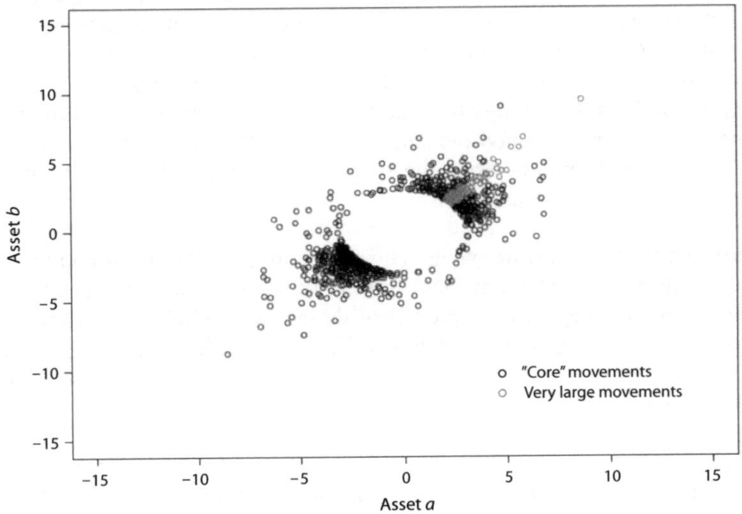

A quick look at Figure 5 suggests that tails can be measured for given directions, such as the tail shown in gray corresponding to an angle of 45°. In our hypothetical data set, extreme movements in the NAV of asset *a* are positively correlated with extreme movements in the NAV of asset *b*. This correlation can be viewed in Figure 6, which shows how the number of joint extreme events (e.g. r larger than 3) per 10° angle aperture changes with θ and reaches a maximum at $\theta = 45°$, indicating a positive correlation between extreme movements in the NAVs of our hypothetical assets *a* and *b*.

Figure 6. Number of extremes as a function of the "angle" defined by the movements in the hypothetical two-dimensional asset space

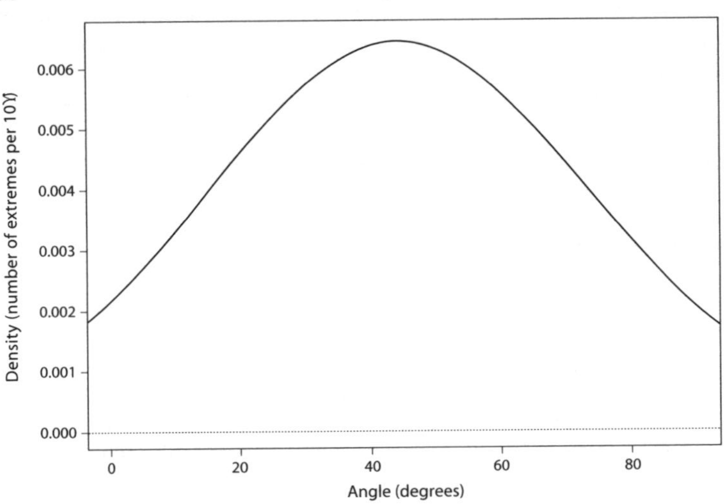

Now we can, for example, define the region between the angles θ_1 and θ_2 and look at the distribution of extremes within that area. By fitting a GPD to the data points located between θ_1 and θ_2 we could, in principle, extract the value of the shape parameter. Fitting a GPD to data points defined by another angle area would, in general, yield a different value of the shape parameter. This shape parameter could then be indexed with the angle for a given angle aperture. The issue here resides with the quality of the data available. To be able to index the shape with the angle requires a certain number of extreme events to be sampled per angle aperture. We can, if the number of data points is large enough, parameterize the shape of the tail distribution of returns with the angle defined by the two asset returns.

This is indeed a very interesting result. The direction is itself determined by a pair of numbers (in the two-dimensional case) representing the relative returns for the two assets. If we were to price, say, a simple out-of-the-money (OTM) hybrid determined by this pair of numbers, the shape parameter of its corresponding tail distribution would be the crucial quantity to calculate. The price would have a one-to-one relationship with the shape parameter ξ.

Now, imagine that prices for OTM hybrids are computed for each direction using this technique. It is not difficult to see how one can take advantage of an arbitrage situation: there will be an arbitrage situation whenever there are significant differences between the prices computed using the GPD fit and the market prices.

Important Results

- The central limit theorem (CLT) is appropriate during normal market conditions. CLT implies a normal (Gaussian) distribution of market movements.
- CLT is not appropriate for extreme market movements. The *tails* of the distributions of market movements are *fat*, i.e. extreme events are more probable than otherwise predicted by CLT.
- A generalized Pareto distribution (GPD) can be used to fit the tails of the distribution of market movements. Its shape parameter ξ determines how fat the tail is.
- A generalization to a multivariate theory is not trivial. However, one can, in general, define *directions* in the space of the market movements.
- When there are enough data, the shape of the tail can be parameterized as a function of an angle defining the direction.

The Subjective Approach

In his book, Riccardo Rebonato (2010) explains how one can draw conclusions about the joint probability of extreme events by making use of causality networks. We will explore this concept in some detail in this section.

In the previous section, where the frequentist approach was outlined, we placed all the emphasis on the level of *association* between variables. The subjective approach, on the contrary, places the emphasis on the *causal links* between variables. The main advantage of this approach is the fact that it is cognitively much easier and more natural.

To illustrate what we mean, consider the following example. Suppose that the variable we are interested in is whether a particular church in Lisbon is damaged or not. We know that in 1755 an earthquake and tsunami destroyed vast areas of the city. The other variables in this example could be, say, whether the church was damaged by the earthquake or not or whether there was a fire. One could take a purely associative approach and build all the relevant probability tables. To do this, we need some numbers such as the standalone probabilities (the marginals), which are relatively easy to calculate, and some singly conditioned probabilities (the probabilities of one event, conditional on another). These singly conditioned probabilities could be, in turn, either simple and natural, such as the probability that the church was damaged given that an earthquake had occurred, or they could be difficult and awkward, such as the probability that an earthquake had occurred given that the church was damaged. The first formulation is of a *causal* nature, which is why we find it cognitively easier to arrive at an answer (the probability would be close to one), whereas the second is *diagnostic* in nature, and because there are many possible causes for the same effect, the answer in the second case is hard to guess.

There is another reason why causal models are more powerful than associative models: the fact that small changes in the causal structure of the model can give rise to large changes in the joint probabilities. It is easy to encode changes in the causal links between variables. However, from a purely associative point of view, they may be very difficult to explain.

Let us outline the goals of the subjective approach: the final goal is—just as in the frequentist approach—to gain access to the joint distribution of extreme events. However, instead of attempting to fit a generalized Pareto distribution to the data directly, as we do in the frequentist approach, we inject more information about how we expect the world to behave. It then becomes possible to derive the full joint distribution from a small number of marginals, singly conditioned probabilities, and (at most) doubly conditioned probabilities. This is achieved by applying Bayes' theorem across the causality net and using the concept of conditional independence.

A simple example will help to explain how this is done. Consider the events A, B, C, and D, which are defined thus:

- A = Earthquake;
- B = Fire;
- C = Tsunami;
- D = Church on the hill is damaged.

And the very simple model of our world:

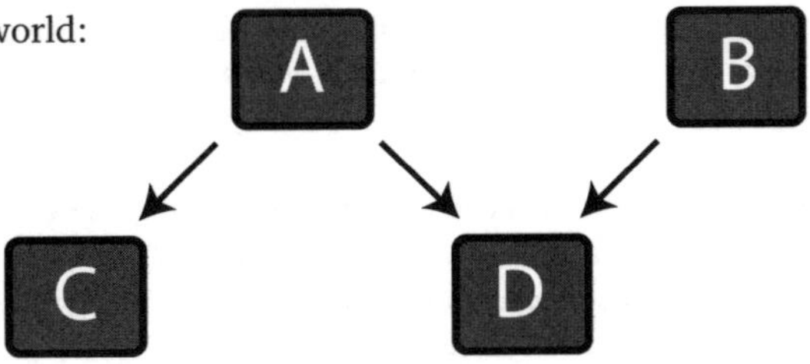

In this model, A causes C and D; and B causes D. A and B, the earthquake and the fire, are assumed to be independent (they are the roots of the causality net). Note that all the information affecting C originates from A. Hence, given A, C, and D are independent, C and D are said to be *independent, conditional* on A. This characteristic of Bayesian nets is crucial to the evaluation of the full joint distribution.

In this very simple model, the joint probability distribution is defined by $2^4 - 1 = 15$ numbers (all possible combinations of the four Boolean variables minus 1 from the condition that the total cumulative probability must equal unity). Utilizing the information provided by the causality net and making use of Bayes' theorem allows us to derive all 15 numbers from only $4 + 3 = 7$ numbers (four marginals plus three singly conditioned probabilities). In general, and as long as we keep the causality net simple, we are reducing a $2^n - 1$ problem to a $2n - 1$ problem. For a large n, this is a massive simplification.

Let us calculate the probability of one joint event in our mini-model to see how this is done in practice. Starting from the marginals P(A), P(B), P(C), and P(D), and the conditional probabilities P(C|A) and P(D|A), let us calculate the probability that there was a tsunami, that an earthquake has occurred, that there was a fire, but that the church is not damaged. We will define this as P(A, B, C, ~D):

$$P(A, B, C, \sim D) = P(C, A, \sim D, B)$$

$$= P(C|A, \sim D, B) \times P(A, \sim D, B)$$ [5]

$$= P(C|A) \times P(A, \sim D, B)$$ [6]

$$= P(C|A) \times P(A|\sim D, B) \times P(\sim D, B)$$ [7]

$$= P(C|A) \times P(A|\sim D) \times P(\sim D, B)$$ [8]

$$= P(C|A) \times [P(\sim D|A) \times P(A)/P(\sim D)] \times P(\sim D, B)$$ [9]

$$= P(C|A) \times [1 - P(D|A)] \times P(A) \times P(\sim D, B)/[1 - P(D)]$$ [10]

$$= P(C|A) \times P(A) \times [1 - P(D|A)] \times P(\sim D|B) \times P(B)/[1 - P(D)]$$ [11]

$$= P(C|A) \times P(A) \times [1 - P(D|A)] \times [1 - P(D|B)] \times P(B)/[1 - P(D)]$$ [12]

However convoluted this calculation might look, the important result is that we are able to obtain the joint probability only from the marginals and the singly conditioned probabilities, making use of Bayes' theorem and our specific model of the world, the causality net.

Note, however, that it is sometimes impossible to obtain a meaningful value for the joint probability (a number between zero and one), given a specific set of inputs. This imposes bounds on the initial marginals and singly conditioned probabilities defining the subset of feasible inputs.

A fully automated system can be built, given a particular causality net and set of feasible inputs. The topological structure of the causality net must be characterized in a way that can be understood by a computer algorithm. Linear programming can then be used for the joint distribution (Rebonato, 2010).

Important Results

- Some conditional probabilities seem more *natural* than others. This is explained by the causal links between variables.
- If we postulate that we understand the way the world works through a causality net, we add more information to the *natural* probabilities that are easy to compute.
- Using Bayes' theorem, and in the case when the inputs constitute a *feasible* solution, one can, in general, recover the full joint distribution of extreme events.

However, the choice of model remains subjective.

Case Study

Our case study is an EVT analysis of a global macro fund and a distressed fund. Our analysis focuses on the distribution of extreme events for both funds and their classification, and concludes with a comparison with other "traditional" risk measurement techniques, such as VaR. Although this could be considered pure asset management (rather than asset–liability management), we think that it illustrates the issues surrounding stress-testing that are discussed in this chapter.

We analyze the percentage changes in the net asset values over the last eight years. The results for the HFR Global Macro fund are shown in Figure 7, where the percentage changes are quoted as the number of total standard deviations for the period.

Figure 7. Global macro fund: changes in net asset value 2003–10

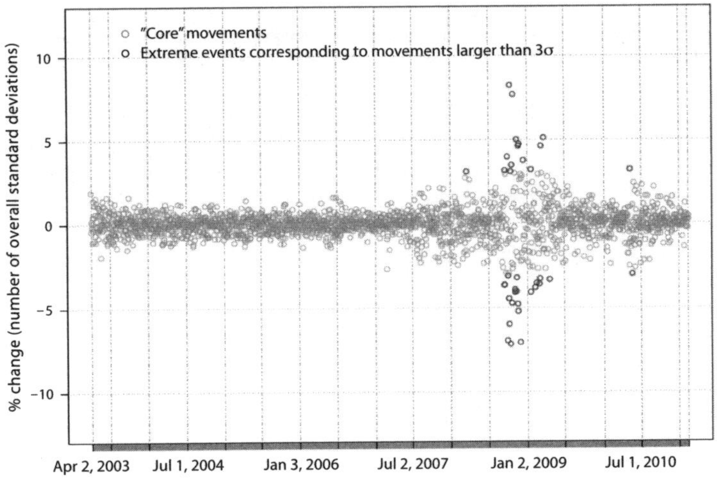

One might be tempted to identify extreme events as those corresponding to movements larger than three standard deviations (see Figure 7). However, we would like to differentiate between two very different types of extreme movement:

- type 1: the type of extreme that is driven by volatility;
- type 2: the type of extreme that is a genuine "black swan" (fat-tail) event.

The first type of extreme appears to be an extreme simply because the volatility has increased, whereas the second type is a genuine extreme because the volatility has not increased, yet the event still occurred. In order to correctly identify the genuine extremes (i.e. those of type 2), one must rescale the percentage changes to a moving average measure of the local volatility prior to performing the GPD fit. Figure 8 shows how the movements compare to this local definition of extreme in the case of the global macro fund. Here the dark lines correspond to the limits plus three standard deviations and minus three standard deviations that define an extreme event.

Figure 8. Global macro fund

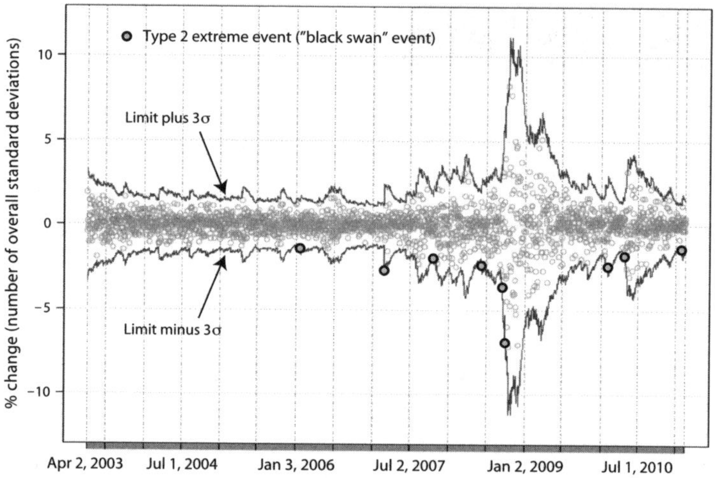

It now becomes apparent that all the large positive movements in the global macro fund occur *after* there is an increase in volatility, making them type 1 extremes. However, some negative extremes occur *before* the increase in volatility, making these type 2 extremes. The best-fit distribution for positive movements is indeed the normal distribution, as shown in Figure 9.

Figure 9. Global macro fund: best-fit distribution for positive movements

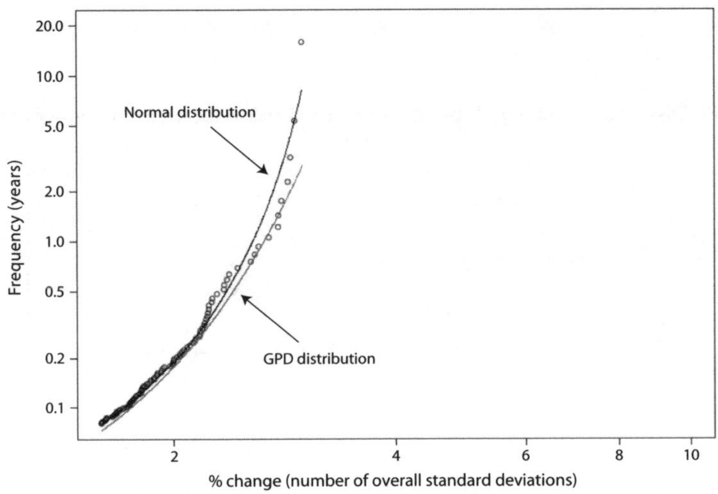

By contrast, the HFR Distressed-strategy fund shows genuine fat tails for positive movements, as we can see in Figure 10. Note that some extreme events occur *before* there is an increase in volatility—in fact it is they themselves that cause the spikes in volatility. This makes these events type 2 extremes.

Figure 10. Distressed-strategy fund: Changes in net asset value 2003–10

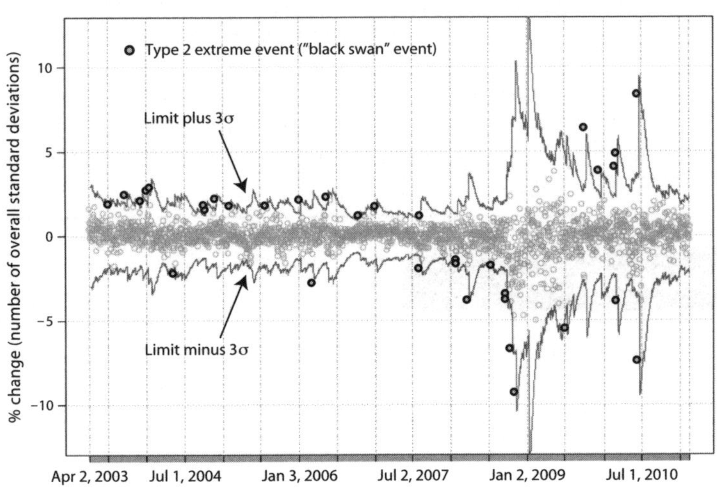

It is also interesting to note that there are large positive movements during normal times when the volatility of the market is relatively small and stable. This indicates that the distressed strategy is working for this fund.

A GPD fit for positive movements in the HFR Distressed-strategy fund shows, unlike the HFR Global Macro fund, a very fat tail, as shown in Figure 11.

Figure 11. Distressed-strategy fund: best-fit distribution for positive movements

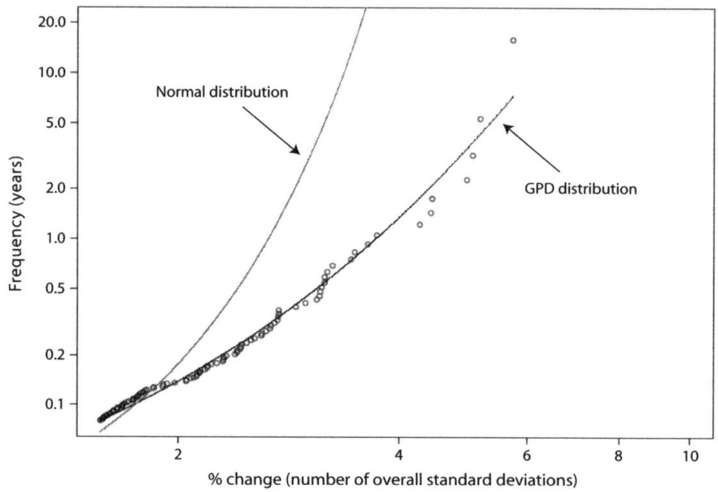

Let us consider an investor with a short position in either of these funds who is concerned with the measurement of his or her risk. In the case of the global macro fund, the *usual* way of calculating VaR—i.e. measuring the standard deviation and assuming a normal distribution—would produce a realistic assessment of risk because the normal distribution is a good fit for positive increments in the net asset value (negative movements in the investor's position). On the other hand, the same calculation for the distressed fund would produce a highly unrealistic assessment of risk as it would fail to capture the tail.

Summary and Further Steps

- "Traditional" stress-testing is done on a *standalone* basis. It is then not possible to combine probabilistic estimates of risk (such as VaR) with the loss estimates produced by the stress tests. This situation renders the (traditional) stress tests meaningless. To make sense of stress tests, the probabilities associated with extreme events need to be determined.
- There are two ways in which one can attempt to determine the joint distribution of extreme events: the *frequentist* approach and the *subjective* approach.
- In the frequentist approach (aka the "let the data speak" approach), one attempts to fit a probability distribution to extreme events directly, using whatever data are available.
- In the subjective approach, a model of the world is postulated in which the causal links between the various variables are established.

- Normal distributions are appropriate during normal market conditions, when underlying variables are largely independent of each other. During periods of market turbulence, however, correlations become more polarized, the central limit theorem no longer applies, and the normal distribution is no longer a good fit.
- The generalized Pareto distribution (GPD) is the appropriate fit to extreme events. Its shape parameter ξ determines the fatness of the tail. The smaller the value of ξ, the fatter the tail. The larger the value of ξ, the closer the distribution becomes to the normal distribution.
- If one follows the subjective approach, the addition of extra information in the form of a causality net (or model of the world) allows calculation of the full joint distribution of extreme events starting from a relatively small number of inputs. These inputs are the marginal distributions (the standalone distributions) and some natural conditional probabilities.
- We define two types of extreme event. A type 1 extreme is one that is driven by volatility, and, as such, it happens *after* there is an increase of volatility. A type 2 extreme is the genuine black swan that happens *before* there is an increase in the volatility—one could say that the volatility is driven by the type 2 extreme.
- Traditional calculations of VaR assume normal distributions.
- Whereas for assets that are prone to type 1 extremes the traditional calculation of VaR might produce a realistic assessment of risk, for assets prone to type 2 extremes the same calculation is wholly unrealistic, as it fails to capture the tail of the distribution.
- One further step that can be taken is to apply the multivariate EVT techniques outlined in the section on the frequentist approach to a space of investment classes, parameterize the tail shape parameter as a function of direction, and explore arbitrage opportunities between different directions.
- Another interesting line of research would be to try to combine the frequentist and subjective approaches, in effect testing the robustness of a given model of the world.

More Info

Books:

Balkema, Guus, and Paul Embrechts. *High Risk Scenarios and Extremes: A Geometric Approach*. Zürich: European Mathematical Society, 2007.

Bouchaud, Jean-Philippe and Marc Potters. *Theory of Financial Risk and Derivative Pricing*. Cambridge: Cambridge University Press, 2009.

Rebonato, Riccardo. *Coherent Stress Testing: A Bayesian Approach to the Analysis of Financial Stress*. Chichester, UK: Wiley, 2010.

Articles:

Aragones, Jose Ramon, Carlos Blanco, and Kevin Dowd. "Incorporating stress tests into market risk modelling." *Derivatives Quarterly* 7:3 (Spring 2001): 44–49.

Berkowitz, Jeremy. "A coherent framework for stress-testing." *Journal of Risk* 2:2 (1999): 5–15.

Dermine, Jean. "ALM in banking." Working paper. INSEAD, July 17, 2003. Online at: tinyurl.com/76tk8gm [PDF].

Greenspan, Alan. Presentation to Joint Central Bank Research Conference, Washington, DC, 1995.

Notes

1. Historical data are available to estimate probability—for example:
   - credit spreads: Baa and Aaa spreads back to the 1920s;
   - default frequency by rating: from rating agencies back to the 1920s;
   - equities: S&P 500 Index back to the 1920s;
   - interest rates: Treasury bond yields back to the 1920s;
   - crude oil prices: back to 1946;
   - foreign exchange: historic data may not be so meaningful because currencies change roles.
2. For the purposes of this chapter we define an "extreme event" as a market movement larger than three standard deviations away from the mean.
3. By exceedances we mean the number of extremes to which the GPD is to be fitted.
4. The threshold is the number of standard deviations above which data points are considered for the purpose of fitting a GPD.
5. From Bayes' theorem.
6. From conditional independence, C is independent of D and B, conditional on A.
7. From Bayes' theorem.
8. A and B are independent.
9. From Bayes' theorem.
10. From completeness.
11. From Bayes' theorem.
12. From completeness.

Modeling Market Risk

by Marius Bochniak

Lloyds TSB Bank, London, UK

This Chapter Covers

- The definition of market risk.
- General approaches to the measurement of market risk.
- Regulatory requirements concerning market risk.
- The definition of value-at-risk (VaR).
- Historical and Monte Carlo simulation of VaR.
- The scaling of VaR between different time horizons.
- A comparison of historical simulation and Monte Carlo methods.

Introduction

Every financial institution with a portfolio exposed to market risk should have a model in place which is designed to measure that risk. Such a model allows one to control and to limit the market risk taken by each desk or by the traders and to charge each portfolio position a cost of capital required to cover its market risk. Success in meeting these objectives serves the interests of the stakeholders in the firm.

The measures of market risk employed by financial institutions are usually based on the mathematical concept of value-at-risk (VaR). Roughly speaking, VaR is defined as the maximum loss of a portfolio over some target period that will be not exceeded with a specified probability, or confidence level. Various techniques have been developed to estimate the VaR of trading portfolios. Some, like the variance–covariance approach, are outdated and rarely used in practice as they are incompatible with regulatory requirements to capture the nonlinear behavior of derivative instruments and they ignore event risk. The two main approaches currently used in financial institutions are historical simulation and Monte Carlo methods.

In the present overview we briefly describe the main ideas of market risk modeling and present the two main approaches to such modeling in more detail. As the simple forms of both historical simulation and Monte Carlo have some undesirable properties, we show how both approaches can be improved. Finally, we compare the benefits and the drawbacks of the different approaches.

Market Risk

According to the Basel II framework, the banks must mark-to-market their trading books at least daily, which means that they must revalue all trading book positions at readily available close-out prices in orderly transactions that are sourced independently (Basel Committee on Banking Supervision (BCBS), 2006). Market risk is the risk that the market value of positions may change in the future. It is of little consequence to investors who purchase financial instruments with the intention of holding them until maturity or for long time periods.

The market value of trading book positions depends on:

- risk factors that are observable on the market, such as share and commodity prices, interest rates, credit spreads and foreign exchange rates;
- additional pricing parameters like volatilities and correlations that are not directly observable and which must be implied from the market prices of financial instruments.

All pricing parameters contribute to the market risk of positions, but the set of pricing parameters that must be captured in a particular market risk model depends on the regulatory requirements.

The same framework sets capital requirements to cover potential losses resulting from market risk in the trading book. These capital requirements are formulated in terms of several risk measures which capture different types of market risk.

How to Measure Market Risk

Due to the stochastic nature of financial markets, it is obviously not possible to predict exactly the future value of a portfolio. However, knowing the past behavior of the risk factors that drive the market value of the portfolio, it is possible to generate a stochastic set of possible scenarios for the future value of the portfolio. The idea is as follows:

- we describe the past behavior of underlying risk factors by means of probability distributions;
- we generate stochastic forecasts of the future behavior of the risk factors using their probability distributions;
- we revalue the portfolio for each forecast of the risk factors.

In this way we obtain a probability distribution of the possible future values of the portfolio. The risk measures can now be defined as special characteristics of this distribution.

The risk measure used in the Basel II capital requirements is the value-at-risk, or VaR, which is defined in the following way. Let us denote by P_t the value of the portfolio at time t and by P_{t+h} the value at the end of the forecast period $[t, t+h]$. Then the loss distribution at time t for the forecast horizon h is defined by

$$X_{t,h} = B_{t,h} P_{t+h} - P_t$$

Here we take the time value of money into account, i.e. $B_{t,h}$ is a discounting factor such that $B_{t,h}P_{t+h}$ is the value of P_{t+h} at time t.

VaR is defined as a threshold value such that the probability that loss on the portfolio over the given time horizon will exceed this value is the given probability level, $1-\alpha$, i.e. value-at-risk is the negative of the α-quantile of the loss distribution

$$P\left(X_{t,h} < -VaR_{t,h,\alpha}\right) = 1-\alpha$$

Note that in this notation losses correspond to negative values and profits correspond to positive values of $X_{t,h}$. Furthermore VaR is positive.

Regulatory Requirements

The Basel II framework defines several market risk measures based on the value-at-risk concept, which differ in:

- the set of risk factors to be simulated;
- the capital horizon, h;
- the confidence level, α.

The original Basel II framework from June 2004 required banks to capture by means of a VaR model the market risk due to changes of all pricing parameters that were deemed relevant. The confidence level for market risk VaR was set to 99% and the capital horizon was 10 days. In the case that a risk factor was incorporated in a pricing model but not in the VaR model, the bank had to justify the omission to the satisfaction of its supervisor.

As a consequence of the 2007–08 financial crisis, in July 2009 the Basel Committee revised the Basel II market risk framework and introduced several supplementary risk measures to capture market risks that were not properly taken into account by the market risk VaR: these are the so-called stressed VaR, the incremental risk charge, and the comprehensive risk measure.

The stressed VaR is intended to replicate a value-at-risk calculation that would be generated on the bank's current portfolio if the relevant market factors were experiencing a period of stress. It should be based on the 10-day, 99th percentile, one-tailed confidence interval value-at-risk measure of the current portfolio, with model inputs calibrated to historical data from a continuous 12-month period of significant financial stress relevant to the bank's portfolio (BCBS, 2009a). In this way, the stressed VaR addresses some shortcomings of traditional stress tests that do not assign probabilities to stress scenarios.

The incremental risk charge applies to all credit spread-sensitive financial instruments with the exception of securitizations and resecuritizations. It is defined as the 99.9% quantile of the loss distribution due to defaults and rating migrations over the capital horizon of one year. Thus, the incremental risk charge is a risk measure with credit risk and market risk components (BCBS, 2009b).

The comprehensive risk measure, which applies to the correlation trading portfolio only, combines the incremental risk charge with the market risk VaR. It captures not only incremental default and migration risks, but all price risks. The confidence level and capital horizon are the same as for the incremental risk charge (BCBS, 2009a).

In the following we describe modeling techniques for the market risk VaR.

Quality of Market Risk VaR Models

The quality of a market risk VaR model is usually investigated by looking at the VaR exceptions—i.e. days when portfolio losses exceed VaR estimates. The VaR exceptions should have the following two properties.

- The number of VaR exceptions should be consistent with the confidence level. A VaR model with too few exceptions overestimates the risk. If the number of exceptions is too large, the risk will be underestimated.
- The VaR exceptions should be independent and uniformly distributed in time.

In order to decide whether the number of exceptions is reasonable or not—i.e. whether the market risk VaR model is correct—some statistical analysis is required.

The most widely used statistical test for the consistency of the number of VaR exceptions with a given confidence level is the proportion of failures (POF) test suggested by Kupiec (1995). Under the null hypothesis of Kupiec's test that the VaR model is correct, the number of exceptions follows the binomial distribution. Hence, the only information required to implement a POF test is the number of observations, the number of exceptions, and the confidence level, as shown in Table 1.

Table 1. 95% confidence regions for the POF test. (*Source*: Nieppola, 2009)

VaR confidence level	Nonrejection region for number, N, of VaR exceptions		
	255 days	510 days	1,000 days
99%	N < 7	1 < N < 11	4 < N < 17
97.5%	2 < N < 12	6 < N < 21	15 < N < 36
95%	6 < N < 21	16 < N < 36	37 < N < 65
92.5%	11 < N < 28	27 < N < 51	59 < N < 92
90%	16 < N < 36	38 < N < 65	81 < N < 120

Historical Simulation

Historical simulation is a nonparametric approach to the estimation of VaR that does not require any assumption about the probability distribution of changes of risk factors. Instead, the future values of risk factors are obtained by applying the observed historical changes of risk factors to their current values. This can be formalized in the following way. We assume that for each risk factor its current value and the value on M previous days is available (here 0 denotes the current day):

$X_{-Mh}, X_{-(M-1)h}, \cdots, X_{-h}, X_0$

Then we can define M scenarios, $\widetilde{X}_h^i, i = 1, \cdots, M$, for the value X_h of the risk factor after time h by applying the historical changes (returns), $R_h^i = X_{-(i-1)h} / X_{-ih}, i = 1, \cdots, M$, to the current value, X_0, of the risk factor:

$$\widetilde{X}_h^i = X_0 R_h^i = X_0 \frac{X_{-(i-1)h}}{X_{-ih}} \qquad (1)$$

The historical simulation consists of the following steps.

1. For each risk factor, convert the time series of its $M + 1$ values into a series of M daily returns.

2. For each risk factor, compute M possible future values (scenarios) by applying the daily historical returns to the current values of the risk factors.
3. For each of the M scenarios, reprice the portfolio and determine the corresponding profit-and-loss (the difference between the value of the portfolio under the new scenario and the current value of the portfolio). This results in M possible profit-and-loss values for the portfolio.
4. Order the profit-and-loss scenarios in ascending order and determine the required risk measure. For example, if the risk measure is the standard 99% VaR and M = 300, then VaR is the negative of the third smallest value; if M = 500, then VaR is the negative of the fifth smallest value. For M = 200, some interpolation between the second and the third smallest values will be required.

Sometimes, instead of historical returns, the VaR model employs historical differences, $X_{-(i-1)h} - X_{-ih}, i = 1, \cdots, M,$ between the values of a risk factor. This leads to historical simulation with additive scenarios:

$$\widetilde{X}_h^i = X_0 + \left(X_{-(i-1)h} - X_{-ih}\right), i = 1, \cdots M \qquad (2)$$

Historical simulation is probably the most widely used VaR method. Finger (2006) remarks that this popularity is due to the following views of many risk managers about historical simulation:

- it is easy to explain;
- it gives insight into what could go wrong;
- it is "assumption-free;"
- it is conservative;
- it captures fat tails.

As the data for several banks about the number of VaR exceptions in 2008 show (see, for example, Lazaregue-Bazard (2010)), the last two views are clearly wrong. Banks that employed historical simulation with equally weighted input data reported up to 50 VaR exceptions in 2008. One of the reasons for the failure of these VaR models is that the historical simulation is not really assumption-free. For example, it implicitly assumes that the historical scenarios (historical returns in Equation (1) or historical differences in Equation (2)) are stationary, i.e. that their volatility does not vary with time.

Furthermore, VaR models based on historical simulation encounter different practical difficulties.

- The time series used for the generation of historical scenarios must not have any gaps. If there are gaps, they must be filled or appropriate proxies must be used. However, the introduction of proxies leads to artificially high correlations that are not present in the historical data.
- Historical simulation based on additive scenarios may result in negative values for the risk factors which are nonsensical for credit default swap (CDS) spreads, equity prices, etc. Flooring such scenarios at zero changes the distribution of the historical scenarios and the correlation structure between the risk factors.

Historical Simulation with Volatility Adjustment (Filtered Historical Simulation)

The problem of time-varying volatility in the historical simulation can be dealt with by adapting the volatility of the historical returns. However, this requires some parameterization of the volatility evolution, resulting in a semiparametric model.

The basic idea is to remove the volatility from the observed sample in such a way that the resulting adjusted historical returns have time-independent volatility and then to scale the volatility of the adjusted returns to the current volatility of the risk factor.

If we denote by σ_i the volatility of the returns $R_h^i = \frac{X_{-(i-1)h}}{X_{-ih}}$ at time $t = -(i-1)h$, then the volatility-adjusted returns are defined by R_h^i / σ_i. The resulting scenarios are

$$\widetilde{X}_h^i = X_0 \frac{\sigma_0}{\sigma_i} \frac{X_{-(i-1)h}}{X_{-ih}} \quad (3)$$

The volatility adjustment solves the problem of nonstationary input data and improves significantly the performance of VaR models based on historical simulation. In fact, both of the bank VaR models that performed best in 2008 (Lehman Brothers and Goldman Sachs) were based on historical simulation with four years of input data and volatility updating (Lazaregue-Bazard, 2010).

Monte Carlo as an Extension of Historical Simulation

Equation (1) for the scenarios of a risk factor can be written in the following equivalent way:

$$\widetilde{X}_h^i = X_0 \exp^{\ln\left(\frac{X_{-(i-1)h}}{X_{-ih}}\right)}$$

The idea of Monte Carlo VaR simulation is to fit the log-returns $\ln\left(\frac{X_{-(i-1)h}}{X_{-ih}}\right), i = 1, \cdots, M,$ to some parametric distribution and to replace the historical log-returns in the above equation by samples for the probability distribution. The choice of the probability distribution has a big impact on the properties and performance of the VaR model. Most banks model the log-returns of the risk factors by a multivariate Gaussian distribution, which has the disadvantage that scenarios larger than three times the standard deviation will be very unlikely, excluding from the simulation large, rare events which occur in the market more frequently than predicted by the Gaussian distribution. Therefore some banks use multivariate heavy-tailed distributions like the Student's *t* or the normal inverse Gaussian distribution.

The Monte Carlo simulation consists of the following steps.

1. For each risk factor, convert the time series of its $M + 1$ values into a series of M daily log-returns.
2. For each risk factor, fit the log-returns to the normal distribution $N(0, \sigma^2)$.
3. Generate for each risk factor N samples, ξ_i, $i = 1, \dots, N$, from the corresponding probability distribution $N(0, \sigma^2)$.
4. For each risk factor, compute N possible future values (scenarios) by

$$\widetilde{X}_h^i = X_0 \exp^{\xi_i} \quad (4)$$

5. For each of the N scenarios, reprice the portfolio and determine the corresponding profit-and-loss (difference between the value of the portfolio under the new scenario and the current value of the portfolio). This results in N possible profit-and-loss values for the portfolio.
6. Order the profit-and-loss scenarios in ascending order and determine the required risk measure.

If the market value of the portfolio depends on more than one risk factor, the market risk model must capture the dependence of the risk factors, which is usually described by means of linear correlations. We assume that the generated scenarios should have the same correlation (covariance) structure as the input data.

Let us suppose that the value of the portfolio depends on K different risk factors, and let us denote by $X^k = (X^k_{-Mh}, X^k_{-(M-1)h}, \cdots, X^k_{-h}, X^k_0), k = 1, \cdots, K,$ the historical values of the kth risk factor, by R^k the corresponding vector of historical log-returns, and by Σ the corresponding covariance matrix, i.e.:

$$\Sigma_{ij} = \text{cov}\left(R^i, R^j\right)$$

If we generate for each risk factor N normally distributed random numbers

$$\xi_i^k \sim N\left(0, \sigma_k\right), i = 1, \cdots, N$$

then the covariance of the random vectors $\xi^k = \left(\xi_1^k, \cdots \xi_N^k\right), k = 1, \cdots, K,$ should coincide with Σ.

The generation of normally distributed random numbers with a given covariance matrix is usually based on the Cholesky decomposition of the covariance matrix.

Let $\zeta = \left(\zeta^1, \cdots \zeta^K\right)$ be a vector of pairwise independent $N(0, 1)$ normally distributed random numbers and let Σ be a given semipositive definite covariance matrix with Cholesky decomposition $\Sigma = QQ^T$. Then the random numbers $\xi = \left(\xi^1, \ldots, \xi^K\right)$ defined by $\xi = Q\zeta$ are normally distributed with covariance matrix Σ.

Monte Carlo with Linear Regression

The Monte Carlo approach presented in the previous section has two large drawbacks. If the number of risk factors is very large, the Cholesky decomposition of the covariance matrix may be very time-consuming. Moreover, the rank of the covariance matrix is $\min\{K, M\}$. Thus, if the number of risk factors is larger than the length of the historical time series, i.e. $K > M$, the covariance matrix will have rank M and will be singular. Consequently, there can be at most M risk factors which can have pairwise linearly independent scenarios. The same is true for historical simulation: the number of linearly independent risk factors is limited by the length of the historical time series.

Both drawbacks can be resolved by regressing all risk factors against a smaller set of suitable risk factors (regression factors). In practice, risk factors used as regression factors are commonly used industry sector and region indices: equity indices, CDS spread indices, etc.

Let us denote by $R_h^i = \ln\left(\frac{X_{-(i-1)h}}{X_{-ih}}\right)$ the log-return of a risk factor and by $R_h = (R_h^1, R_h^2, \cdots, R_h^M)$ the corresponding time series of historical log-returns. Suppose that R_h is regressed linearly against a regression factor $I_h = (I_h^1, I_h^2, \cdots, I_h^M)$, i.e. that there exist a parameter β and an error term $\varepsilon \sim N(0, \sigma^2)$ independent of I_h such that

$$R_h = \beta I_h + \varepsilon \quad (5)$$

This leads to a new Monte Carlo scheme with steps 3 and 4 of the sequence given in the previous section replaced by the following.

3a. For each regression factor I_h, generate N samples $\xi_i, i = 1, \cdots, N,$ from the corresponding probability distribution $N(0, \sigma^2(I_h))$.

3b. For each risk factor, generate N samples $\varepsilon_i, i = 1, \cdots, N$, from the probability distribution $N(0, \sigma^2(\varepsilon))$ of the corresponding error term.

4. For each risk factor, compute N possible future values (scenarios) by $\tilde{X}_h^i = X_0 \exp^{\beta\xi_i + \varepsilon_i}$.

Regressing the log-returns of risk factors against a smaller set of industry sector and region factors has the following two benefits.

- Instead of generating correlated random numbers directly for all risk factors, we generate only correlated random numbers for the much smaller set of regression factors. Thus the covariance matrix will have a much smaller size.
- Since the error terms of all risk factors are by definition pairwise-independent, the number of risk factors which receive linearly independent scenarios is limited only by the number of scenarios and not by the length of the time series.

General Monte Carlo

The Monte Carlo scheme presented in the previous section but one (as an extension of historical simulation) was formulated in a way which makes it clear that historical simulation is in fact a Monte Carlo method with scenarios generated in a particular way. However, both historical simulation and the Monte Carlo approach presented in the previous sections are applicable in practice only to short time horizons as they require historical market data for the past *Mh* days. For example, in order to estimate 10-day VaR with historical simulation based on 250 scenarios, the model would require historical market data for the past 2,500 days—i.e. 10 years.

Furthermore, both VaR approaches presented above have the following serious drawbacks.

- They lead to implausible scenarios for risk factors over longer time horizons.
- They are not applicable to all types of risk factors. For example, the values of implied correlations are limited to the (0, 1) interval, but the approaches described above cannot guarantee that the simulated values for the risk factors will be less than one.

Luckily, it is possible to easily get rid of these restrictions and to widen the applicability of Monte Carlo VaR methods. The starting-point is the observation that the simulation

Equation (4) written as

$$\widetilde{X}_h^i = X_0 \exp^{\sigma_i \xi}$$

where $\xi \sim N(0, 1)$ is the exact solution of the stochastic differential equation

$$dX_t = \sigma X_t dW_t$$

Thus, the idea is to choose for each risk factor a stochastic differential equation

$$dX_t = \mu(t, X_t)dt + \sigma(t, X_t)dW_t \quad (6)$$

with appropriately chosen coefficients μ and σ, which describe its time evolution, and to replace Equation (4) for this risk factor by the exact solution of Equation (6) or by the Euler discretization of (6):

$$X_h^i = X_0 + \mu(0, X_0)h + \sigma(0, X_0)\sqrt{h}\xi_i \quad (7)$$

where $\xi_i \sim N(0, 1)$.

The coefficients of Equation (6) can be determined from the time series of daily values of the risk factor, even in the case that the time horizon is longer than one day. Consequently, longer time horizons do not require longer historical time series.

Simulation of Base Correlations

Base correlations are of fundamental importance in pricing models for collateralized debt obligations (CDOs). As their values are limited to the (0, 1) interval and they exhibit strong mean-reverting behavior, their time evolution may be modeled by means of so-called Jacobi processes, which have the form:

$$dX_t = k(\theta - X_t)dt + \sigma\sqrt{X_t(1 - X_t)}dW_t$$

Under some weak conditions, the $\sqrt{X_t(1 - X_t)}$ term in the stochastic differential equation prevents the base correlations from becoming negative or larger than one.

Monte Carlo simulation of risk factors based on special stochastic differential equations should be used with great care. The model may be misspecified due to a bad choice of the form of the stochastic differential equation and the assumption of a Gaussian Brownian motion, W_t, may be inappropriate in some applications.

The parameter estimation for a stochastic differential equation may pose considerable practical difficulties. A good example is Jacobi processes, where there is no closed-form expression for the log-likelihood function and one has to resort to approximate maximum-likelihood techniques. Moreover, the lack of long enough time series may prevent stable parameter estimation.

Another difficult point with general Monte Carlo methods is the modeling of the dependence structure between different risk factors. If the scenarios of each risk factor are driven by a Brownian motion W_t, the dependence structure between the risk factors is captured by the correlation structure between the Brownian motions of the risk factors. This implies a Gaussian copula, which contradicts the empirical finding that large market movements are usually more strongly correlated than "ordinary" ones. However, banks refrain from using more realistic dependence models due to the heavy estimation problems that are encountered in the case of copulas with tail dependence.

Scaling of VaR Between Different Risk Horizons

As we have seen before, the calculation of one-day market risk VaR by historical simulation with 250 scenarios would require one year of historical data, but the calculation of 10-day VaR—which is required by Basel II—would require 10 years of historical data, much more than is available in most banks. Therefore the banks usually prefer to calculate the one-day market risk VaR and then scale it up to the horizon of 10 days.

Under the assumption that log-returns of the portfolio are i.i.d. and that $N(0, \sigma^2)$ is normally distributed, we have $VaR_{h,\alpha} = \Phi^{-1}(\alpha)\sigma\sqrt{h}$, where Φ denotes the standard normal distribution function. In particular, for $\alpha = 0.99$ one has $VaR_{h,0.99} = 2.32635\sigma\sqrt{h}$. Thus, for two different capital horizons h_1 and h_2:

$$\frac{VaR_{h_1,\alpha}}{VaR_{h_2,\alpha}} = \Phi^{-1}(\alpha)\sigma\sqrt{\frac{h_1}{h_2}}$$

Consequently

$$VaR_{10days,\alpha} = \sqrt{10}VaR_{1day,\alpha}.$$

Unfortunately, the portfolio log-returns are rarely i.i.d. and normally distributed, so applying the square root rule to obtain the 10-day market risk VaR may lead to a serious misstatement of the risk. For this reason, in July 2009 the Basel Committee included in its "Revisions to the Basel II market risk framework" the requirement that banks must demonstrate that the use of the square root of time to scale from a one-day holding period to a 10-day holding period is appropriate and does not underestimate risk (BCBS, 2009a).

See Provinzionatou, Markose, and Menkens (2005) and Degen and Embrechts (2011) for some theoretical and empirical studies of scaling rules for non-Gaussian distributions.

Which Method Is the Best?

Monte Carlo is the only VaR methodology that is applicable to long time horizons or to high confidence levels like 99.9%. The question as to which method for measuring one-day 99% VaR is the best—Monte Carlo or historical simulation—has been a topic of discussion for a long time, but opinion is still divided. This is somewhat surprising as the performance of banks' market risk VaR models during the 2007–08 financial crisis shows a clear failure of VaR models based on historical simulation without volatility adjustment. The VaR models that performed best were, according to Lazaregue-Bazard (2010), models based on historical simulation with long observation horizons (four years) and volatility adjustment. This is not surprising as the filtered historical simulation seems to be very popular in academia due to the mathematical properties of this method. Unfortunately, most banks do not have sufficient quality-assured historical market data to be able to implement it.

The overview of VaR model performance presented by Lazaregue-Bazard (2010) contains only a limited amount of information about banks that employ Monte Carlo methods, but the few data that are available give an indication of performance between historical simulation with and without volatility adjustment.

The bad performance of VaR models based on historical simulation without volatility updating is due to some serious drawbacks of this approach.

- The VaR estimates react very slowly to changes in the market regime, especially if longer observation periods (in excess of one year) are used.
- The number of scenarios is limited by the length of the historical time series used in the simulation, leading to inaccurate VaR estimates.
- The number of linearly independent risk factors is limited by the number of scenarios.
- With short observation horizons (one to two years), rare events are not properly captured. For example, if the observation period contains events that happen once in *N* years, their frequency will be overestimated. If no such events are present in the history, they will be not be simulated at all.

All these issues can be solved to a large extent by choosing a longer observation period and updating the volatility of the scenarios (filtered historical simulation).

VaR models based on Monte Carlo have no limitations caused by the length of the historical time series and the number of Monte Carlo scenarios can be chosen to be arbitrarily large. Rare events can be captured by replacing the normal distribution by an appropriate probability distribution with heavy tails, such as Student's *t* or the normal inverse Gaussian.

The main difficulty of Monte Carlo-based VaR models is the modeling of the dependence structure of the risk factors. In the case of historical simulation, the scenarios have by definition the same dependence structure as the historical market data. This is an issue for models with short observation horizons as the historical data may capture only a very limited set of correlated market movements. VaR models based on Monte Carlo must make some assumption about the dependence structure of risk factors. Most such models describe the dependence by means of linear correlations (Gaussian copula). This assumption contradicts empirical findings as the market data for most risk factors exhibit tail dependence that cannot be captured by simple correlation models.

Summary and Further Steps

Two main approaches are currently used to estimate market risk VaR: historical simulation and Monte Carlo. Although VaR models based on simple historical simulation performed very badly during the recent financial crisis, they continue to be widely used by most banks. This shows that the properties of VaR models are not well understood by many market risk quants and market risk managers. This is partly due to the lack of appropriate literature describing advanced market risk modeling techniques. The books available on the market, such as McNeil, Frey, and Embrechts (2005), Jorion (2007), and Alexander (2008), are somewhat academic and are useful to people who want to learn about the main modeling techniques, but they mainly consider elementary methods that are rarely used in practice, or modeling techniques that are too difficult to calibrate. In particular, none of them is devoted to the new risk measures introduced in 2009 that combine credit and market risk—the incremental risk charge and the comprehensive risk measure. Therefore, for advanced modeling techniques applicable to those risk measures we refer readers to the very few available original technical papers, in particular Grundke (2005) and Wilkens, Brunac, and Chorniy (2011).

More Info

Books:

Alexander, Carol. *Market Risk Analysis: Value-at-Risk Models* (Vol. 4). Chichester, UK: Wiley, 2008.

Jorion, Philippe. *Value at Risk: The New Benchmark for Managing Financial Risk*. 3rd ed. New York: McGraw-Hill, 2007.

McNeil, Alexander J., Rüdiger Frey, and Paul Embrechts. *Quantitative Risk Management: Concepts, Techniques, and Tools*. Princeton, NJ: Princeton University Press, 2005.

Articles:

Basel Committee on Banking Supervision. "International convergence of capital measurement and capital standards." Revised framework, comprehensive version. Bank for International Settlements, June 2006.
Online at: www.bis.org/publ/bcbs128.htm

Basel Committee on Banking Supervision. "Revisions to the Basel II market risk framework." Bank for International Settlements, July 2009a.
Online at: www.bis.org/publ/bcbs158.htm

Basel Committee on Banking Supervision. "Guidelines for computing capital for incremental risk in the trading book—Final version." Bank for International Settlements, July 2009b. Online at: www.bis.org/publ/bcbs159.htm

Degen, Matthias, and Paul Embrechts. "Scaling of high-quantile estimators." *Journal of Applied Probability* 48:4 (December 2011): 968–983.
Online at: www.math.ethz.ch/%7Edegen/DE_scaling_2009.pdf

Finger, Christopher C. "How historical simulation made me lazy." *RiskMetrics Research Monthly* (April 2006). Online at: tinyurl.com/74r4tab [PDF].

Grundke, Peter. "Risk measurement with integrated market and credit portfolio models." *Journal of Risk* 7:3 (Spring 2005): 63–94.

Kupiec, Paul H. "Techniques for verifying the accuracy of risk measurement models." *Journal of Derivatives* 3:2 (Winter 1995): 73–84. Online at: dx.doi.org/10.3905/jod.1995.407942

Lazaregue-Bazard, Céline. "Exceptions to the rule." *Risk* 23:1 (2010): 106–108.
Online at: tinyurl.com/7skytmh

Nieppola, Olli. "Backtesting value-at-risk models." Master's thesis. Helsinki School of Economics, 2009. Online at: tinyurl.com/brjnbfw [PDF].

Provinzionatou, Vikentia, Sheri Markose, and Olaf Menkens. "Empirical scaling rules for value-at-risk (VaR)." Preprint, Department of Economics, University of Essex, April 2005. Online at: tinyurl.com/6n7umy3 [PDF].

Wilkens, Sascha, Jean-Baptiste Brunac, and Vladimir Chorniy. "IRC and CRM: Modelling approaches for new market risk measures." *SSRN* (April 2011). Online at: dx.doi.org/10.2139/ssrn.1818042

ALM in Financial Intermediation: The Derivatives Business

by Krzysztof M. Ostaszewski

Illinois State University, USA

This Chapter Covers

- Asset–liability management (ALM) is often viewed as a methodology for hedging risks—or even of eliminating them—to lock in the spread earned by the business.
- But ALM is not that. Risks in financial intermediation cannot be eliminated; they are an intrinsic part of the business of banks and insurance companies.
- The worlds of traditional banking and insurance and derivatives markets seem very different but they are merely different expressions of the same business process.
- In reality, financial intermediation is conceptually equivalent to dealing in derivatives.
- The bar for ALM must be raised to that of managing a complex portfolio of derivative securities, as that is the underlying nature of the business.

Introduction

The headlines about the credit crisis of 2008 and the subsequent downturn in the global economy often name the exploding trade in derivative securities as the villain in this economic calamity. This attribution of the cause of the crisis is related to the perception that derivatives are somehow new, mysterious, and incomprehensible to the clients of banks, insurance firms, and other financial intermediaries. I consider this perception not only incorrect, I view it as distorting. By association, major dealers in derivatives are also viewed as villains, and are subject to increased scrutiny. In this chapter I propose that this view is misguided, as the growth of derivative instruments represents merely a new form of traditional financial intermediation. Although the investment bankers might be villains in their own right, they earned that distinction the old-fashioned way, not through the use of new financial technologies.

Derivative securities are not villains, they are tools.

In other words, I claim here that the wave of financial innovation we have experienced over the last three decades—with the vast expansion of new derivative instruments, such as futures, options, and swaps—is essentially *not* a new reality, but rather that this new technology is just a new expression of the same reality that has always existed.

When I want to challenge my students to have a more general perspective on financial issues, I ask them: "How was this done in the year 1000?" I propose that it is quite helpful to pose that challenge when facing a decision on financial matters. For example: How was executive compensation handled in the year 1000? Obviously, we have developed a more sophisticated theoretical base than that existing a millennium ago. With the contribution to understanding of the agency problem by Becker and Stigler (1974) and Shapiro and Stiglitz (1984), and see also Myerson (2011), we have understood that dynamic moral-hazard problems with limited liability, of which the executive compensation problem is the most significant manifestation, are efficiently solved by promising large end-of-career rewards for agents who prove good performance. For example, an efficient solution to moral hazard in banking involves long-term promises of large rewards at career-end for successful bankers. Interestingly enough, the medieval system of transferring the business from master to apprentice was very similar. The reward came in the form of ownership of the business, and it came only after many years of service proving good long-term performance. We now have new ways of expressing this idea, and new technologies, but the idea remains basically the same.

What Are Derivative Securities?

A derivative security is defined as a financial instrument whose cash flows are *derived* (hence the name) from some other financial instrument (Hull, 2012; also Ostaszewski, 2002, 2003). They are, completely unnecessarily, often presented as mysterious and mathematically complex. The three core types of derivatives are described below.

> The core types of derivatives—forwards, futures, options, and swaps—are building blocks for more complex portfolios.

Forward Contracts

Forward contracts are agreements to buy (for the party long forward) and sell (for the party short forward) an asset or financial instrument (called the *underlying*) at a future date but at a price specified today. A forward contract is a private agreement between two parties about the transaction just described. Thus it involves substantial risk of nonperformance by the other party. That risk is remedied in *futures contracts*, which are standardized, written by a clearing house that operates an exchange where the contract can be bought and sold. Notably, the clearing house imposes the requirement that parties involved in the transaction post a security deposit, i.e. a *margin deposit*, which serves as collateral for performance of the contract obligation. Let us also observe that when the transaction is consummated in the future, the market price may be different than the one named in the contract, and because the two parties to the contract trade between themselves, the benefit of one party is the cost of the other party.

Options

Options are contracts that give the owner (party long the option contract) the right, but not the obligation, to buy (in this case the option is called a *call option*) or the right to sell (known as a *put option*) an asset (called the *underlying*). The transaction takes place at a specific time, or in a specified time period, at a price also specified in the contract (known as the *strike price* or *exercise price*). The right acquired by the owner of an option does not appear miraculously out of nowhere, it is actually created by the other party to the contract, the party that assumes the obligation to deliver the promise embedded in the option contract. Thus, the right to buy gold at a price of $1,500 per ounce embedded in a call option on gold is also an obligation to sell gold at $1,500 for the party on the other side of the transaction. That party on the other side is said to *write* the option, is short the option contract, and actually creates it out of nowhere.

For that service, the short party is paid the *premium*, which is a certain amount of money representing the market price of the option, by the long party (the party that owns the option). Whereas the long party has the right, but not an obligation, the short party does have an obligation when the right of the long party is exercised.

This situation is not unusual, and not just mathematical: a right of one person is always an obligation of other people. For example, when a person arrested by authorities has the right to remain silent, this is just another way of saying that the authorities have an obligation to respect that silence and not to try to break it by force. Because the short party in an option contract assumes an obligation to either sell (in the case of a call option) or buy (in the case of a put option), that party has substantial risk. Because of that high risk, most option contracts are traded on exchanges, and the short party is required to post a margin deposit, with the exchange also guaranteeing performance. The only cost to the long party is the premium paid for the option, but the long party enjoys all benefits in the case of a price increase of the underlying (in the case of a call option) or price decline (in the case of a put option). The only benefit to the short party is the premium received for the option, with the entire risk of a price increase of the underlying (in the case of a call option) or decline in the price of the underlying (in the case of a put option) borne by that party. Note again the phenomenon of the benefit of one party being the cost of the other party; this is an important principle, which I will discuss further later in this chapter.

Swaps

Swaps are contracts to exchange cash flows between two parties on or before a specified future date based on the underlying value of currencies/exchange rates, bonds/interest rates, commodities, stocks, or other assets. The cash flows exchanged may be in different currencies, or may even be cash payments by one side and physical commodity payments by the other side. Until the 2008 credit crisis debacle these transactions were largely unregulated and treated as private transactions between two parties. But such private transactions are subject to the risk of nonperformance by the other party to the contract, and without any regulation or exchange where swaps are traded no mechanism exists to protect against the credit risk of such nonperformance. As in the case of forwards/futures and options, the gain of one party to the transaction is a loss to the other party in the transaction.

Other Derivatives

While forward contracts, options, and swaps are the three main types of derivative securities, over time market participants have been active in creating a variety of other derivatives. The credit crisis of 2008 made *mortgage derivatives* famous—or, to be more precise, infamous. Mortgage derivative securities have their cash flows derived from payments made by a specified pool of mortgage loans. When borrowers make payments of principal and interest, such payments are received by a processing agent and then distributed to investors according to formulas specified in the documents describing the derivative structure (formulated and distributed on its creation and, in the United States, also filed with the Securities Exchange Commission).

The simplest mortgage-backed securities were basically pro-rata shares of payments. Subsequently, more complex securities, called *collateralized mortgage obligations*

(CMOs), were subsequently created. In the United States the Tax Reform Act of 1986 allowed the creation of tax-free real estate mortgage investment conduits (REMICs), which are special-purpose vehicles created for the express purpose of issuing mortgage derivatives (Fabozzi and Modigliani, 1992; also Haubrich, 1995). Let us note that, in a manner similar to swaps, these were not traded on an exchange and no margin requirement exists for them, although dealers in these securities have been subject to regulatory capital requirements.

A representative of a dealer in those derivatives who spoke at a meeting of a local society of financial analysts which I attended in the 1990s provided an interesting comment on the marketing of these securities. CMOs have been generally structured as a series of *tranches* of differing levels of security. Conservative investors buy the most secure of those tranches. A person present at the meeting asked the representative of a dealer who in that case bought the riskiest tranches. The representative responded that many purchases were made by speculative investors, but that sales people had also created what was known as the "slow deer theory" about the sales of the risky tranches. What was the slow deer theory? When one drives on country roads in upstate New York, Michigan, or rural Pennsylvania one occasionally encounters deer crossing the roads. Some deer are fast and run away when they see a car approaching. Others become fascinated by the headlights, carefully observing them while slowly crossing the road. Those slow deer have significantly lower chances of survival.

Mr Filip's Principle

> A derivative security is basically a bet on the underlying. By itself, a bet does not affect the outcome of the underlying economic process.

I attended high school in Poland during the Soviet occupation of the country (an occupation that lasted from 1945 until 1989). We did not hear much about derivative securities or financial markets. We did know, from experience, a great deal about the permanent economic crisis under communism, and we heard a lot about the permanent economic crisis in the capitalist countries of the decadent West. Our physics teacher, Mr Filip, was very demanding, quite strict, and not very popular among students, even though he did offer us a substantial knowledge of his field. The boys in the class were far more interested in the better parts of life, such as soccer and the European Champion Clubs' Cup, in which professional soccer teams competed for the title of the best team in Europe.

We had an extensive betting scheme on those games. One day, Mr Filip caught the bookie with all the incriminating details written in his books, which the outraged and principled educator confiscated. Subsequently, Mr Filip gave us a stern speech in our next physics class. He said: "I am shocked. I can't believe that you are making bets on soccer games. Don't you know that when two people make a bet, one of them is a pig and the other one is stupid?" I still remember thinking (but not saying): "Mr Filip, but that's precisely the point!" Mr Filip's outrage and indignation were caused by the fact that, in a bet like this, the amount gained by the winning party is exactly the amount lost by the losing party (with adjustments for any compensation of the bookies). No actual value is created.

Recall our discussion of derivative securities from the previous section. In every case, we pointed out that any gains from the transaction to one party were balanced by the losses to the other party. A derivative security is in fact a bet on the underlying—nothing more, nothing less. Politicians, activists, and the like argue that this makes derivatives markets into one big gambling house that contributes nothing, and which in fact extracts value in the process because bookies need to be paid, the house needs its profits, and excessive betting may develop that causes addictions and personal financial tragedies.

But do we really know whether the process of gambling in the derivatives markets affects the real economy? Mr Filip probably did not assume that our betting would affect the outcomes of soccer games. He was, however, worried about our character. After all, there are two ways to think about the ways we obtain money. The first is that money comes from work and the second is that money comes from other people. If we believe the first, we are inclined to work. If we believe the second, we are inclined to seek ways to squeeze money from other people. Of course, both perceptions are correct on the microeconomic scale, but Mr Filip was right to be indignant, because on the macroeconomic scale only the first way is true. The mere receipt of money does not mean that one has created value in return for the funds, but in order for the money to have value, the good or service received for it later on must be produced.

There are typically three perspectives on the relationship between the derivatives markets and the real economy. I propose that they be called:

- the Wall Street value creation theory;
- the Main Street irrelevance theory;
- the Washington greed theory.

The Wall Street value creation theory proposes that by creating derivative securities—and in fact by all of its functions—Wall Street, and financial intermediaries in general, add value because they allocate capital efficiently. The Main Street irrelevance theory proposes that the only true value added to the economy is that created by work, in the real business world, and that what Wall Street, bankers, insurance firms, and investment gurus do is just shuffle paper (or, to be more precise, shuffle electronic entries) with no relevance to the real world. The Washington greed theory takes it one step further by claiming that the shuffling of paper (or electronic entries) is, at best, costly beyond any reasonable level and, at worst, outright fraud, where the finance gurus use the access they have to other people's money to enrich themselves immensely, without any consideration for the economic pain they inflict on the unsuspecting public. Of course, the supreme irony of this third theory lies in the fact that when the greedy finance gurus were caught with their pants down in 2008, they were saved by the political system and offered bailouts, often by the same political agents that once were quick to condemn them.

The Modigliani–Miller theorem implies that a method of financing affects an economic process if it affects tax costs, bankruptcy costs, or agency costs.

The issue raised by these three theories had been addressed by financial theory. Modigliani and Miller (1958), in a secular work of modern finance, showed that, under specific conditions, the value of the firm does not depend on its leverage policy, or the method of financing of the firm in general. The answer provided by them was that, in the absence of taxes, bankruptcy costs, or agency costs, the value of the firm is fundamentally determined by its earnings, and not by the way the firm is financed. Subsequent research (for example, Miller and Modigliani, 1961; and Stiglitz, 1969, 1974) has pointed out that taxes, bankruptcy costs, and agency costs do affect the value of the firm; and if the method of financing influences the tax costs, bankruptcy costs, or agency costs (especially the incentives of all the stakeholders of the firm, or the structure of distribution of information among those stakeholders, given information asymmetries among them), then the leverage policy or dividend policy becomes relevant. Over time, more specific research on how these factors affect the value of the firm developed.

What Do Financial Intermediaries Do?

The old adage about the work of a banker is: "Borrow at 3%, lend at 5%, be on the golf course at 4." This concept of financial intermediation presents it basically as a *spread business*, i.e. a business of living off the difference between the cost of funds and investment returns. While this adage is very old indeed, it evolved in the modern financial world into the idea that financial intermediation is basically an *arbitrage business*. Arbitrage (Delbaen and Schachermayer, 2006) is defined as the creation of a short/long portfolio without an outlay of capital and without any risk of loss, yet earning income with positive probability. We tend to expect markets to be arbitrage-free, because arbitrage opportunities would be exploited until they disappeared. In the case of the banker, we do not expect the bank's customers to ignore the existence of the investment opportunities that would allow them to earn the full 5%, instead of the 3% offered by the bank.

But if financial intermediaries do not do arbitrage, what do they do? In a world without financial intermediaries, the economy's flow of funds would be between the household sector, which contains net savers, or equivalently, net purchasers of securities, and the production (i.e. business) sector, which contains net borrowers, or net providers of securities, and users of funds. However, because of price risk, monitoring costs, liquidity costs, etc., the typical household saver may view investment in the securities provided by the business sector as unattractive. Financial intermediaries step in between and "grease the wheels of commerce." They provide products (financial assets, even though typically not traded) that are accepted by the household sector (thus financial intermediaries assume a short position in those financial assets), which uses the funds to purchase securities supplied by the corporate sector (therefore assuming a long position in those securities) and other net issuers of securities (governments, government-sponsored enterprises, and even consumers themselves when they borrow). I submit that the creation of such a short/long portfolio is the essence of the intermediation business and, therefore, the essence of asset–liability management (ALM).

It is now generally acknowledged that financial intermediaries write options that are included in their products and in their portfolios in general. For example, the minimum interest rate guarantee, so common in long-term savings products, is a form of a put on the interest rate and a call on a fixed-coupon bond paying that interest rate. What I would like to point out is that the products of banks, insurance companies, and investment companies in general are in fact conceptually equivalent to derivative securities. For example, banks and insurance companies invest in a portfolio of certain assets and pay their customers cash flows derived from those created by that asset portfolio. The resulting short/long portfolio payments are not substantially different from the payments of a swap. In fact, an interest rate swap in which a swap dealer pays a variable interest rate and receives a fixed interest rate on a specified notional amount is exactly equivalent to borrowing the notional at a fixed interest rate (the one named in the swap) and investing it in a bond paying a floating interest rate named in the swap contract. An insurance company that issues a guaranteed investment contract at a fixed interest rate paid at regular intervals and invests in an asset paying a variable rate is in an exactly equivalent position. Ostaszewski (2003) also points out that the life insurance business can be viewed as a form of a derivative security based on human capital.

> ALM is about restructuring asset cash flows into liability cash flows. That's basically the same business as that of writing derivative securities.

Thus, financial intermediaries effectively restructure cash flows provided by securities of the business sector into the cash flows demanded by the household sector. The derivative created by a financial intermediary, however, must be understood in a much broader sense than is commonly used—i.e. not one restricted to just options, or futures, or swaps. In the popular perception it is often assumed that derivatives increase risk. One of the most common features of the derivatives issued by financial intermediaries is that they actually reduce the risk faced by their customers. But the risk does not disappear—in fact it is retained by the financial intermediary. This perspective implies that financial intermediaries *always face financial risks*, i.e. risks caused by changing values of market variables, such as interest rates, credit risk, share prices, liquidity, etc.

Credit Default Swaps (the *Villain Extraordinaire*), and Mr Anszperger's Strawberry Principle

The ideas presented here are illustrated very well by the credit default swaps market and its role in the credit crisis of 2008, as well as in the subsequent sovereign debt crisis seen in Europe. A credit default swap (CDS) is a transaction between a buyer of a CDS and a seller of a CDS. Of course, as you should realize by now, it is a bet. The buyer of a CDS makes a series of payments (each of which is called a *fee*, or a *spread*) to the seller. The seller, in return, is required to make a full payoff of the loan, or other credit instrument named in the contract, when that loan goes through a specified *credit event* (which could be a default, but could also be a ratings downgrade, or any event specified in the contract). In the case study below I show that a CDS is, in fact, identical to a package of transactions carried out in traditional banking.

Case Study

Writing CDSs on Risky Bonds, or Buying Risky Bonds with Borrowed Money

Let us illustrate the functioning of the CDS market with a simple case. Imagine that you are an investment actuary in a hypothetical Swiss life insurance company. You notice that the country of Freedonia issues 10-year bonds denominated in Swiss francs and which currently pay a 3% annual coupon. The Swiss franc is not the currency of Freedonia. In fact, Freedonia uses its own currency, the *freebie*. The government of Freedonia plans to pay the interest and principal by collecting tax revenues in freebies and converting them at the market rate into Swiss francs to make payments. Since the interest rate offered is quite attractive (in the second half of 2011, the Swiss National Bank kept its interest rate target band at 0.00– 0.25%, an extremely low level), you consider this an attractive investment and purchase SFr 1 million worth of those bonds. Subsequently, you are approached by a CDS dealer, Really Smart Investment Bank, Inc., (RSIB). RSIB offers you insurance against a default by Freedonia. In return for an annual fee, RSIB will pay you the full principal amount of the loan in case of default by the government of Freedonia, if such a default happens. This transaction is of course a standard credit default swap, written by the RSIB and purchased by you.

At the same time another company—let us call it the Swiss Medieval Bank (SMB)—accepts a deposit from a customer in the amount of SFr 1 million and buys the same amount of Freedonia's bonds with the funds. SMB pays its customer a rate of 0.25% annually. The conditions of the customer's deposit contract state that the customer will withdraw funds immediately if Freedonia's bond purchased by SMB defaults (a simple model to represent the risk of a run on a bank). Every year, SMB has a net profit of 2.75%, but if Freedonia defaults on its bond SMB must collect the market value of the now defaulted bond and then top it off with its own capital to repay SFr 1 million to its depositor.

The key point of this story is that, all other factors being equal, the situations that the RSIB and the SMB find themselves in are identical. The RSIB operates in the new sophisticated derivatives markets with fancy mathematical models, while the SMB might as well be doing its business in the year 1000. But their payoffs, and hence spreads collected, must be identical. Specifically, in the case of the RSIB transaction:

- before bond default, the RSIB is paid 3% – 0.25% = 2.75% (the CDS spread) on the principal of SFr 1 million;
- upon default, the RSIB pays SFr 1 million less the market value of the defaulted bond.

In the case of the SMB:

- before bond default, the SMB is paid 3% – 0.25% = 2.75% (the spread between the bond yield and the deposit rate) on the principal of SFr 1 million;
- upon default, the SMB pays SFr 1 million less the market value of the defaulted bond.

The price of a derivative security is determined from the price of a *replicating portfolio* of cash and the underlying.

The idea of equivalence illustrated in the case study lies behind the use of the concept of arbitrage (or, more precisely, the lack of it) for the pricing of derivative securities (Delbaen and Schachermayer, 2006). To put it simply: two financial instruments that make identical payments, no matter what the circumstances, must have the same price. In fact, if they make identical payments no matter what the circumstances, they are the same thing, regardless of what we choose to call them. I call this the "strawberry principle." I learned it from my elementary school mathematics teacher, Mr Anszperger. As you already know, I attended elementary school in Poland under communist Soviet occupation. Mr Anszperger was not only an excellent mathematics teacher in my school, he was an amateur stand-up comedian, and he usually started every class with an anticommunist joke. We pupils were very worried about his safety, but apparently nobody in the school was a rat because he was not arrested during my years there. A very important part of our education was learning about the great achievements of the Soviet Union and of Russia in the pre-Soviet period. We were taught (by other teachers more dedicated to the cause than Mr Anszperger) that all great inventions and scientific discoveries (the light bulb, radio, electricity, etc.) had been made by Soviet and Russian scientists. We did not treat this propaganda too seriously, and I still remember how astonished I was when I learned that Dmitri Mendeleev actually did invent the periodic table. One day, Mr Anszperger came to class and very seriously announced that Soviet scientists had just invented a new and revolutionary type of raspberry. It was revolutionary because it was as big as a strawberry. It also smelt like a strawberry, looked like a strawberry, tasted like a strawberry, and had the same consistency as a strawberry. Thus, Mr Anszperger had independently discovered the fundamental theorem of asset pricing (Delbaen and Schachermayer, 2006), though I much prefer to refer to his discovery as the Strawberry Principle.

Implications of ALM

In the story of Freedonia's bond purchase told in the case study, the key insight is that the cash flows of the transactions of the RSIB and SMB are identical—thus must have the same price, and are in fact the same transactions. Why then do we have a CDS market when the same transaction can be created by a standard short/long portfolio of a financial intermediary? The answer is obvious: regulatory requirements for those two transactions are different. This represents a stern warning for regulators, who somehow believe that they can control financial markets through accounting entries and not by paying attention to real economics, especially to risk-taking, of financial institutions.

But this observation also provides important advice for the management of financial institutions. Asset–liability management cannot be viewed as a process of eliminating risks in order to earn a riskless spread. Such a perspective, while often exhibited by ALM, contradicts the very nature of financial intermediation. Financial intermediaries are not in a spread business; they are, and always have been, in a derivatives business. We have developed new technologies for creating derivatives. But our sophisticated mathematical models for pricing derivatives rely on one underlying (strawberry) principle: in order to price a derivative we seek to replicate it (often dynamically, in continuous time) with cash and the underlying. Although the derivative may not have existed in the year 1000, cash and the underlying (maybe in somewhat different form) did. Thus, risk management and pricing issues in banking, insurance, and finance in general must be viewed in the same light and with the same frame of mind—as risk management and pricing in derivatives markets, and vice versa. Granted, it was actually the derivatives dealers who gave us the worst examples of "spread business mentality" in the recent crisis. But their debacle also gave us examples of how this spread business mentality (which is really an arbitrage-seeking mentality) ALM has failed. We must become much more serious about the representation of the risk of extreme events in our models, pay attention to how that risk is priced by the markets, and not fall prey to simplistic models that avoid deeper mathematical questions, the way investment bankers did.

When in doubt, let us ask ourselves again: How was this done in the year 1000? The central issue of the recent crisis was credit risk. How was credit risk addressed in the year 1000? Let us note that derivatives traded on the exchanges—where credit risks are mitigated by design—came through the credit crisis smoothly. The blowup happened in privately traded derivatives and in the short/long derivatives portfolios of financial institutions. The mechanisms used to mitigate credit risk on the exchanges are actually the same as those used in the year 1000. There are only two such mechanisms. If a young entrepreneur with no established credit or reputation in the year 1000 wanted to borrow some money from a wealthy merchant in his/her town, two credit enhancement procedures existed. The entrepreneur could offer collateral—for example a cow, or a piece of land—or the entrepreneur could have the loan cosigned by his/her wealthy uncle. Nowadays, everybody wants theirs cosigned by Uncle Sam, who may not turn out to be as wealthy as expected, but the principle remains the same.

■ Say goodbye to the "spread business" mentality. Say hello to derivatives.

The most stunning phenomenon to be brought into daylight by the credit crisis was, as I see it, the hubris of investment bankers, satisfied by simplistic models that avoid any humbling mathematics. If the perspective of this chapter is correct, then all financial intermediation is a complex process, with many risks of extreme events, and where mathematical models must be used extensively, with extreme humility, and updated continuously to fit with the changing world. If we are serious about risk, this is how we must price derivatives, and this is how we must approach ALM in financial institutions.

Summary and Further Steps

The modern financial world has brought about intense competition and financial innovation. But the essence of the business has not changed. Derivative securities allow simpler and more direct risk and financing transfers, but they are still financial products and work well or badly because the underlying business model or finance structure works well or badly, respectively.

Thus, in asset–liability management, we should remember that:

- ALM is not about hedging risks, or arbitrage, it is about managing risks.
- A financial intermediary who does not take risks should not earn any profits.
- Risks of ALM are functionally equivalent to risks of derivatives market maker.
- Derivative securities are equivalent to packages of simpler, underlying securities, and do not create value by their mere existence.
- Derivatives may even destroy value, especially when their complexity is not appreciated and not studied with appropriate mathematical models.
- ALM is not an esoteric speculative endeavor where money is made through miracles of smart arbitrage.
- ALM serves the underlying real business, and it should be structured to increase its value.

More Info

Books:

Delbaen, Freddy, and Walter Schachermayer. *The Mathematics of Arbitrage*. Berlin, Heidleberg: Springer, 2006.

Fabozzi, Frank J., and Franco Modigliani. *Mortgage and Mortgage-Backed Securities Markets*. Boston, MA: Harvard Business School Press, 1992.

Hull, John C. *Options, Futures, and Other Derivatives*. 8th ed. Boston, MA: Prentice Hall, 2012.

Ostaszewski, Krzysztof M. *Asset–Liability Integration*. Society of Actuaries (SOA) monograph M-FI02-1. Schaumberg, IL: SOA, 2002. Online at: tinyurl.com/7lfz89k

Ostaszewski, Krzysztof M. "Modigliani, Miller, and Mortgages." In *Housing in Retirement*, Society of Actuaries (SOA) monograph M-FI09. Schaumberg, IL: SOA, 2009. Online at: tinyurl.com/7ebt5ww [PDF].

Articles:

Becker, Gary S., and George J. Stigler. "Law enforcement, malfeasance, and compensation of enforcers." *Journal of Legal Studies* 3:1 (1974): 1–18. Online at: tinyurl.com/77q37zu

Haubrich, Joseph G. "Derivative mechanics: The CMO." *Economic Commentary*, Federal Reserve Bank of Cleveland, Issue Q1 (September 1995): 13–19. Online at: tinyurl.com/7pv68ot [PDF].

Miller, Merton H., and Franco Modigliani. "Dividend policy, growth, and the valuation of shares." *Journal of Business* 34:4 (1961): 411–433. Online at: www.jstor.org/pss/2351143

Modigliani, Franco, and Merton. H. Miller. "The cost of capital, corporation finance and the theory of investment." *American Economic Review* 48:3 (1958): 261–297.

Myerson, Roger B. "A model of moral-hazard credit cycles." Working paper, March 2010, revised February 2011. Online at: tinyurl.com/7t43lw2 [PDF].

Ostaszewski, Krzysztof. "Is life insurance a human capital derivatives business?" *Journal of Insurance Issues* 26:1 (2003): 1–14.

Shapiro, Carl, and Joseph E. Stiglitz. "Equilibrium unemployment as a worker disciplinary device." *American Economic Review* 74:3 (1984): 433–444.

Stiglitz, Joseph E. "A re-examination of the Modigliani–Miller theorem." *American Economic Review* 59:5 (1969): 784–793.

Stiglitz, Joseph E. "On the irrelevance of corporate financial policy." *American Economic Review* 64:6 (1974): 851–866.

Optimal Long-Term Property and Casualty ALM with Risk Capital Control

by Giorgio Consigli[a] and Massimo di Tria[b, 1]

[a] University of Bergamo, Italy
[b] Allianz Investment Management Milano SpA and Bocconi University, Milan, Italy

This Chapter Covers

- Property and casualty (P&C) portfolio management under liability constraints: the economics of the traditional P&C business are linked together with modern ALM theory to clarify the implications of recent development in insurance enterprise-wide risk management.
- Short-term profitability and long-term sustainability concepts are defined with respect to a long-term decision problem, emphasizing their trade-off properties within an integrated view of ALM practice.
- The definition of economic risk capital measures as a result of the Solvency II agreement is introduced in relation with a generic risk-control problem, shown to be endogenous to the definition of optimal risk-adjusted performance measures.
- An optimization framework for long-term P&C ALM is introduced and its methodological implications described with respect to a test-problem for a large insurance company.
- The fundamentals of the complex interaction between the risk management, investment, and technical divisions induced by a competitive insurance sector with capital constraints are clarified.

Introduction

Increasing competition and record property and casualty (P&C) insurance claims reported by global players in recent years (Comité Européen des Assurances, 2010) have generated remarkable pressure on the financial stability of P&C divisions within insurance companies, leading to increased technical reserves and higher capital requirements. At the same time investment management divisions have expanded, reinforcing the role of insurers as institutional investors competing in fixed-income and equity markets with other players, such as pension and mutual funds. Furthermore, the Solvency II regulatory agreement (see European Parliament, 2009) is currently forcing a historic change toward risk-based capital allocation measures for insurance companies as a whole.

In this context, a strong operational incentive has facilitated the integration of the historical insurance business with the investment management business. Such integration is also motivated by the perceived role of the P&C division as a liquidity buffer generated by fixed-income portfolios that are typically held by risk-averse investment divisions.

In this chapter we clarify the complex interaction between the operational constraints of the investment and insurance functions, which motivates a strategy based on short-term profit targets and longer-term risk-adjusted return goals. From a mathematical viewpoint, the problem finds a natural formulation as a dynamic stochastic program (DSP) (Ziemba and Mulvey, 1998; Zenios and Ziemba, 2007a; Bertocchi, Consigli, and Dempster, 2011) that integrates a realistic representation of the asset–liability management (ALM) problem with an uncertainty model which captures insurance and investment risks. Contrary to current standards in insurance-based investment divisions, which rely largely on one-period static approaches, the adoption of a dynamic approach allows both the extension of the decision horizon and a more accurate short-term modeling of P&C variables.

One-period, static decision models are typically based on a one-year horizon, with estimates of premiums, claim reserves, and all relevant P&C liabilities, as well as financial market scenarios, all projected at the year horizon. The markets' dynamics generate the risk that the investment manager is required to monitor over time. In a static model, end-of-year goals typically focus on the achievement of an operating profit that captures both the company's technical activity and its investment policy.

The neglect of the time beyond the end of the current accounting year may, however, severely affect the likelihood of achieving investment goals at the three-year industrial plan horizon. At a longer 10-year horizon, an additional decision criterion may be considered to take into account the company's overall risk exposure and its long-term business sustainability.

In this chapter we summarize the key elements of an asset–liability management problem, integrating the definition of an optimal asset allocation policy over a 10-year horizon with the inclusion of liability constraints generated by an ongoing P&C business (Consigli *et al.*, 2011; Mulvey and Erkan, 2005). The investment universe includes fixed-income and equity asset classes as well as real estate and alternative investments. The results come from a representative, real-world case problem, developed for a global P&C insurance company. As for many other global players in the market, the insurance company for which the model has been developed has a historic record of liability-driven strategic asset allocation that largely relies on sophisticated statistical models and simulation tools, as well as one-period optimization techniques.

Dynamic stochastic programming techniques have only occasionally been applied to ALM problems for the insurance sector since the seminal work by Cariño *et al.* (1994; see also Zenios and Ziemba, 2007) for the Japanese Yasuda Kasai Insurance Company. A notable example, which specifically addresses a strategic management problem for P&C insurance through stochastic programming approaches, is given by Mulvey and Erkan (2005) for the US market in particular. Far more extensive is the related literature on institutional ALM problems, which have similar features to the analysis presented here (Ziemba and Mulvey, 1998; Bertocchi, Consigli, and Dempster, 2011).

P&C Strategic Planning Under Liability Constraints

We consider, for illustrative purposes, an insurance company that regularly issues P&C policies along several protection lines, including motor, property, accident, and health, and collects the associated cash flows over an accounting year. Premium levels are left exogenous, and we will not go into pricing issues in this chapter. We may assume that premiums are exogenous and determined by strong market competition. Each year the company seeks to expand its market through new and more convenient protection schemes, but it also faces possible market contractions due to increasing competition. In extreme summary, the annual net profit generation depends on a limited number of key variables, as indicated in Table 1.

Table 1. Stylized P&C income generation for example company

Income statement	
+	Insurance premiums
–	P&C insurance claims
–	Salary and staff costs
–	Administration and other costs
=	**Technical income A**
+	Realized capital gains
+	Equity dividends
+	Margin of interest
=	**Investment income B**
A + B = Profit before taxes	
–	Taxes
=	**Net profit**

For a given level of insurance premiums, the annual technical income will depend on the insurance premiums and claims, human resource costs, and administrative efficiency.

The investment income, on the other hand, will depend on the asset portfolio strategy adopted, which, for given P&C reserves, is expected to adjust to periods of decreasing premium flows and/or increasing insurance liabilities. Thus, the issuance of P&C premiums leads to a complex financial management problem that involves both the technical business of the company (related to the claims arising from P&C activity) and the investment business (associated with the insurance company's institutional role as a portfolio manager). This is shown in Figure 1, which clarifies the interdependence of technical and investment profits from the collection of premiums and the core P&C insurance activity.

Figure 1. Simplified dependence structure of P&C divisions in example company

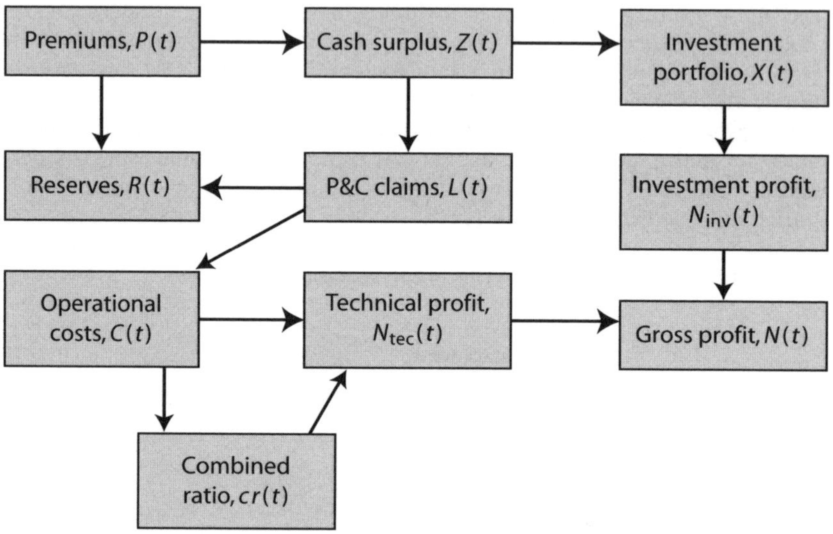

Cash surpluses generated by contract renewals and new business will partially fund insurance claims (due to pending liabilities from the different insurance lines) and partially fund the investment portfolio. As the amount of P&C policies varies, the insurer will modify its insurance reserves, possibly above the minimum compulsory levels. In normal times technical and financial profits may be regarded as relatively independent of each other. As competition in the P&C industry increases and/or insurance liabilities increase and/or financial markets take a negative route, such independence disappears and an integrated approach becomes necessary.

Focusing on the technical activity only, a quantity known as the "combined ratio" provides a comprehensive indicator of the business. This is defined as the sum of two coefficients: the loss ratio, which is the ratio of liability claims to earned premiums, and the expense ratio, which is the ratio of expenses to earned premiums. The P&C company will do its best to keep the combined ratio below 100%. Unprecedented property claims in the United States have recently heavily affected the combined ratios of large US P&C companies, which reached values well above one. This can be referred to as a stressed liability scenario, such as that described by Consigli *et al.* (2011).

Depending on annual premium renewals and the evolution of the combined ratio, the P&C actuarial divisions will determine the appropriate evolution of insurance reserves from the current time up to a specified future horizon. Such time span may be referred to as a liability term structure, which is relevant to assess the company's exposure to interest rate risk. Figure 2 shows a representative insurance liabilities maturity profile typically adopted by insurance companies.

Figure 2. An illustrative insurance liability maturity profile

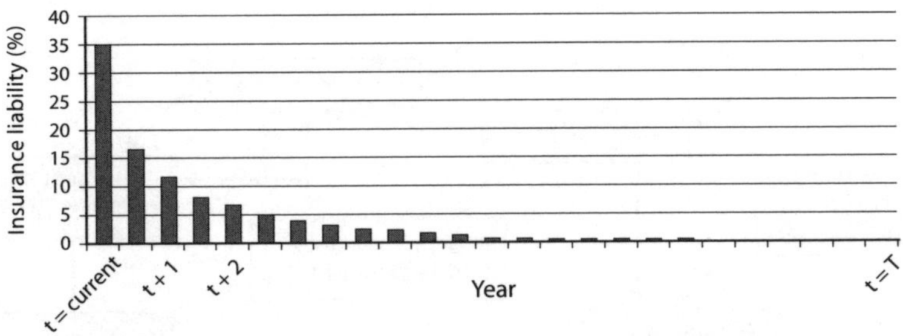

From the standpoint of the investment division, insurance liabilities can be treated as exogenous constraints in the definition of the optimal portfolio strategy. However, what will determine the performance of the investment division is the ability to follow the markets and protect the value of the institution's portfolio from excessive volatility and downturns. The definition of foreseeable insurance and market scenarios, relevant to the P&C strategy, is key to the derivation of an optimal policy. As is canonical in dynamic financial analysis, an optimal ALM policy explicitly defined under liability and market uncertainty is essential in this context. Multistage stochastic programming (MSP) formulations (Ziemba and Mulvey, 1998; Zenios and Ziemba, 2007; Bertocchi, Consigli, and Dempster, 2011) allow the derivation of optimal contingency plans for given objective function and scenario-dependent constraints. Quite often institutional investors, to define their strategies, have relied to date on external economic and financial scenario generators without necessarily solving an optimization problem. We claim, however, that a mathematical formulation will frame the ALM problem in a far more effective way, without imposing any sort of normative "do this" solution. The dynamic P&C ALM model integrates forward asset and liability scenarios with optimal investment strategies, taking fully into consideration all the insurance constraints imposed either by regulatory agreements or by internal decisions.

Quite realistically, given what happened in the years 2009–11 in both the US and European markets, today we can still regard as current a scenario of increasing combined ratios and extremely volatile financial markets almost everywhere in the developed economies. In that case, two relevant concepts—effectively captured by the Solvency II regulatory framework—come about: namely, the *actuarial*, or *technical, risk capital* and the *investment risk capital*. Beyond regular annual provisioning due to average insurance and investment portfolio losses, those two risk measures take only unexpected losses into account. We show that the introduction of company risk capital as a reference risk concept in the insurance world has far-reaching implications for the definition of optimal P&C strategies in the long run as well.

Consider two *independent* worst-case scenarios for insurance claims and the financial markets. The risk management division of the P&C company will accordingly determine the overall risk exposure of its investment portfolio. This is sketched in Figure 3, which clarifies the long-term implications of the insurance activity. The extension to the insurance world of a risk-based capital allocation policy leads to a relevant concept of business sustainability in the long run.

Figure 3. Risk exposure and scenarios

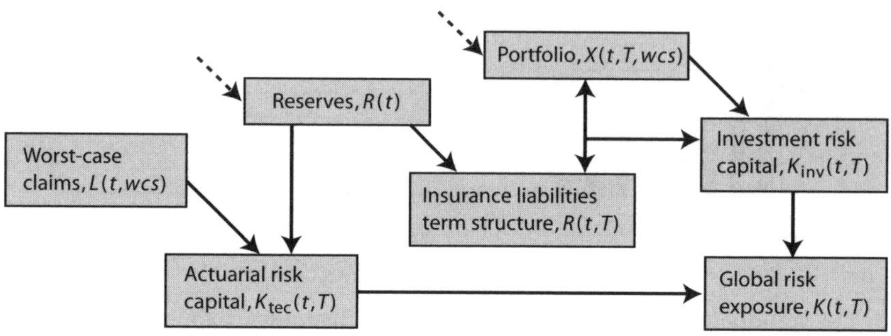

The actuarial risk capital may depend on catastrophic events, whose likelihood appears to be increasing over the years and which are outside management control. The investment risk exposure, instead, depends on the portfolio strategy.

In Figure 3 we denote by *X(t, T, wcs)* the portfolio value at time *t* with duration *T* under a worst-case financial scenario *wcs*. Such a portfolio will carry two types of risk exposure. The first is exposure to interest rate risk, due to the possible difference between the durations of assets and liabilities (*R(t, T)* in Figure 3). The second, and far more relevant exposure, is that of the asset portfolio to heavy market losses. As market turbulence increases, the exposure to large portfolio losses also increases and we are in the realm of fat tails and extreme risk measures. In the presence of historically low interest rates for several years, the attractiveness of fixed-income markets has dropped dramatically, and increasingly P&C managers are extending their investment universe to include alternative investments such as private equity funds, renewable energies, and infrastructures.

Short-Term Profitability and Long-Term Sustainability

The P&C operating profit[2] can be taken as a relevant first-year target variable for the management, while control of the company's long-term risk exposure will determine the business sustainability. Between year one (short-term strategy drivers) and year 10 (long-term business sustainability), a canonical three-year industry goal must be considered an essential part of any strategic plan.

Two concepts will now be introduced to analyze investment policies beyond the first year: the investment value created (IVC) and the return on risk-adjusted capital (RORAC). The first quantity can be regarded as an extension to the insurance world of a classical surplus return measure. It is defined as the difference between (realized and unrealized) investment profit (net of the cost of funding and of any fiscal liability) and the cost of capital (Table 2).

Table 2. Investment value created

	Item
+	Investment profit
+	Unrealized gains and losses
–	Cost of funding
=	**Realized and unrealized investment profit**
x	(1 – Tax rate)
–	Investment risk capital × Capital remuneration rate
=	**Investment value created**

The cost of funding is strictly related to the estimated risk exposure, as indicated in Figure 3: it is determined by market interest rates and the company's liabilities. As the corporate tax rate increases this will directly affect the ability of the insurance company to create investment value, which is key to its medium-term profitability. Similarly, the riskier the investment portfolio, the higher, *ceteris paribus*, the capital that needs to be allocated to hedge unexpected losses and, for a given shareholder remuneration rate, the lower the investment value created.

Both the capital remuneration rate and the portfolio risk exposure are factors that impact the company's medium- to long-term sustainability.

In the longer term, we assume that the P&C management will be focusing on risk–reward indicators at the company level. This is captured by the RORAC, which is defined at a long-term horizon as the sum of investment and technical profit per unit company risk capital—as shown in Table 3.

Table 3. Company RORAC

	Item
+	Investment profit
+	Unrealized gains and losses
+	Technical profit
=	**Realized and unrealized profit**
x	(1 – Tax rate)
=	**Return proxy**
÷	Company risk capital
=	**Return on risk-adjusted capital**

This return measure has deep implications for the internal organization of the P&C company. In particular, it closely involves the actuarial and investment divisions as profit centers and the risk management division as the risk-control center. The latter carries the responsibility of making an accurate assessment of the long-term risk exposure of the company. Such a trade-off is captured by the relationships summarized in Figure 4.

Figure 4. Long-term risk–reward relationships

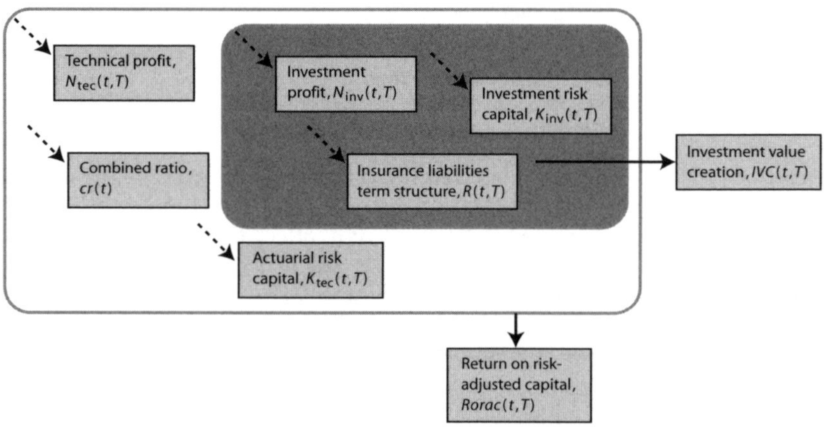

Interestingly, a relevant effort by the profit centers to generate increasing income may be jeopardized in the presence of increasing risk capital allocation. The focus in the long term is on the ability of the management to generate profit per unit risk exposure.

Economic Risk Capital Control

The company risk capital reflects the overall economic resources available to hedge unexpected losses from a balance-sheet perspective. In a competitive insurance sector in volatile financial markets, decision-makers will be looking for a profitable strategy that is under strict risk control. By reinsuring its P&C policies and/or by introducing derivatives for hedging purposes in its investment portfolio, the company will reduce the risk capital requirements but at the same time lose part of its profit potential. In the long term this policy will reduce the return on capital to minimal levels.

The denominator of the RORAC is nothing other than the total (technical and investment) long-term exposures to tail risks. Unlike the actuarial risk capital, however, the investment risk capital estimated at time t on the risk horizon $T - K_{inv}(t, T)$ in Figure 4 does depend on the optimal strategy employed by the portfolio manager. Moving from a static one-year definition of P&C strategy to a dynamic setting based on revisions of the strategy is possibly the most relevant recent innovation in the economics of P&C corporations.

Two elements contribute to the interaction between risk assessment and optimal portfolio strategy. On the one hand, individual asset positions are exposed to market fluctuations (Figures 3 and 4), and a classical value-at-risk measure can be introduced to capture the impact of exogenous risk factors on the portfolio (see Pflug and Romisch, 2007, and chapters in Bertocchi, Consigli, and Dempster, 2011).

On the other hand, a positive mismatch between the dollar duration of the asset portfolio and the liability reserves will expose the activity to exogenous interest rate fluctuations; the impact of this will be positive in periods of decreasing interest rates and negative in the opposite case. Due to well-established prudential rules in the insurance world, P&C portfolios are largely dominated by fixed-income allocations: these include short- and long-term government bonds, as well as corporate securities—primarily investment-grade, but also speculative-grade bonds. The so-called ALM interest risk exposure (ALM IR risk) can thus play an important role in the evolution of the overall P&C company risk exposure (Figure 5).

Figure 5. Investment risk control

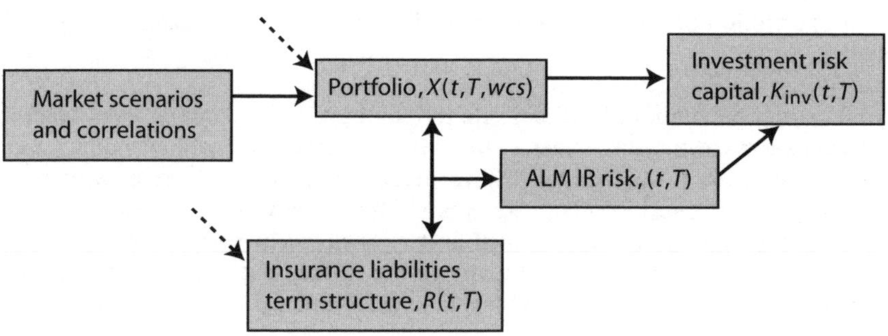

Due to the unprecedented market turmoil that began in 2007 in the corporate market, and which is now also involving sovereign debt in OECD countries, even strongly risk-averse investors are finding it extremely difficult to generate investment profit. A prolonged low interest rate scenario is adding to this to modify deeply the underlying market correlations. In this context a dynamic risk-control approach can become a key element to regaining a positive medium- and long-term outlook.

From an operational standpoint, as already emphasized, such policy requires a strong interface between the P&C investment division and the risk management division, whose risk models must be taken into account in defining the risk-adjusted performance indicators for the investments. Negative correlation between risky positions will mitigate the overall risk exposure despite high risk coefficients on individual asset classes. In contrast, if individual positions carry low risk coefficients, the overall risk exposure may increase because of highly correlated markets.

The introduction of risk-adjusted return measures based either on the difference (see Table 2 for IVC) or on the ratio (see Table 3 for RORAC) between positive returns and financial costs incorporates the key element of any modern ALM objective: the decision-maker will determine his or her optimal strategy considering not only the positive contributions generated by the investment and insurance portfolios, but also the associated risk exposure whose evolution over time needs to be monitored carefully.

These concepts are now increasingly penetrating the insurance industry, inducing a remarkable improvement of an otherwise very traditional managerial philosophy, and they are key elements of a general ALM model for the strategic P&C optimal planning problem.

An Optimization Framework for Long-Term P&C ALM

As the end of the current balance-sheet year approaches, the management of the P&C corporation evaluates the last-year company performance and defines the capital allocation for the forthcoming year. Both the year-one budget and the year-three industrial plan targets require definition of the liability and asset scenarios that the optimal strategy will depend on. The long-term nature of the insurance business and the limitations of static decision approaches have motivated the proposal of a dynamic, multiperiod optimization framework. We have emphasized that in the presence of a very competitive P&C market, the management has a strong incentive to solve a dynamic portfolio optimization problem while internally maximizing its operational efficiency.

A dynamic approach not only allows one to look beyond the coming year, facilitating convergence toward the three-year industrial plan target, but will also allow a closer monitoring of cash flows and operating income over the first year with possible strategy adjustments at the end of each quarter. As we move from the short to the long term, additional decision criteria—including unrealized investment gains, insurance reserves for unexpected losses, cumulative investment, and technical profits (net of the cost of capital)—will come into play, leading to more robust and stable strategies (Figure 6).

Figure 6. Short-, medium-, and long-term objective function criteria

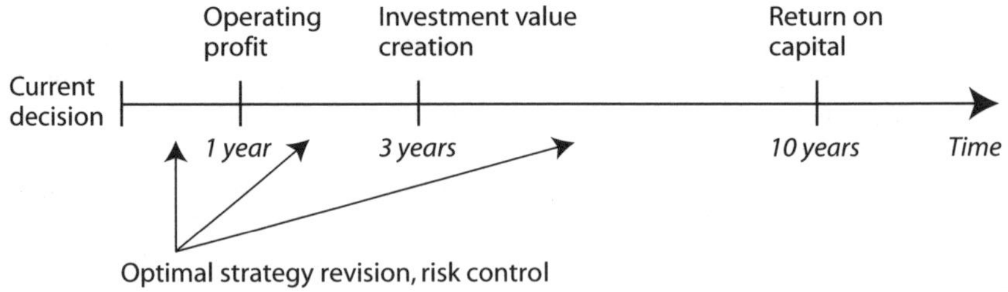

We show in Consigli *et al.* (2011) that the inclusion of longer-term goals, while introducing a long-term view, will not jeopardize the achievement of ambitious first-year targets. In the long run, optimal portfolio bounds and liquidity and solvency bounds, plus possible combined ratio constraints, will determine the definition of the optimal strategy. Limiting risk capital constraints are also considered, particularly under negative insurance and/or financial scenarios.

As was briefly explained in the previous section, the definition of a return on risk-adjusted capital requires estimation of the portfolio exposure to extreme market losses. This in turn calls for definition of the portfolio profit and loss distribution and, crucially, derivation of the losses to be left unhedged: the lower that percentage, the higher will be the company's rating. In turbulent financial times the management will sacrifice part of current profit generation to preserve long-term sustainability, while in normal times reduced weights will be given to longer-term business sustainability criteria.

In summary, an accurate formulation of the asset–liability management problem for a P&C insurance company can be regarded as a complex managerial problem whose solution is based on the optimization of short-, medium-, and long-term targets, and it must consider the interactions between:

- insurance claims, premium renewals, and statutory reserves in the short term, and the reserves time structure and technical risk capital in the long term;
- short- and long-term investment return drivers and the maximization of risk-adjusted returns;
- combined ratio scenarios and portfolio policy: in the presence of increasing overall operational costs and a highly competitive insurance market, a relatively independent management of traditional actuarial and investment divisions in large insurance companies can no longer be accepted.

This evidence leads naturally to the definition of computer-based decision support systems (DSS), which are increasingly penetrating the financial and insurance world. DSSs enable decision-makers to achieve their institutional objectives within a user-oriented and flexible environment: the decision process is framed taking the specific aspects of the business into account.

We present in Figure 7 an overview of the building blocks supporting the realization of a decision tool for long-term institutional asset–liability management. We refer to Bertocchi, Consigli, and Dempster (2011) and Mulvey and Ziemba (1998) as early references for an extended set of real-world applications based on such a framework.

Figure 7. Modular structure of advanced institutional ALM decision systems

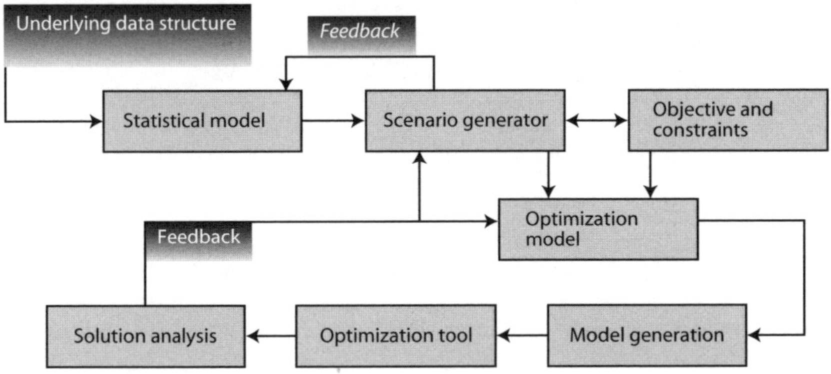

The statistical model includes the financial and insurance models that are needed to specify the uncertainty faced by the decision-maker. As inputs, we have a historical data series of asset returns and liabilities along specific P&C lines, and, as outputs, asset and liability scenarios over possibly long-term horizons. These scenarios are interfaced to the mathematical outline of the optimization problem to yield a mathematical program whose solution will provide optimal allocation strategies to management.

We complete our summary of modern P&C insurance economic analysis with a case study that was developed based on a decision support system for a large insurer.

Case Study

We present a set of results from a case study developed for a primary international insurance company (with figures disguised for reasons of confidentiality). Liabilities are generated by the group's actuarial division, and the investment manager faces a multiobjective optimization problem based on the criteria introduced above.

Consider for illustrative purposes a €10 billion portfolio that includes fixed-income, equity, and real-estate assets and an objective function giving a weight of 0.5 to a first-year operating profit target, a weight of 0.2 to a third-year IVC target, and a weight of 0.3 to a long-term return target on risk-adjusted capital. Then projected asset scenarios and insurance claims will lead to an optimal portfolio policy captured by the initial allocation and a subsequent scenario-dependent risk control policy.

In the figure, *A* to *F* define some of the methodological steps in the definition of an optimal strategy over a 10-year horizon. We consider an initial asset–liability structure based on a €10 billion portfolio with Treasury and corporate bonds, equities, and direct and indirect real estate investments, €6.5 billion of reserves, an estimated €2.2 billion of insurance claims in the coming first year, and an average €4 billion of P&C annual premiums. The management targets include an operating profit of €400 million, an investment value created over three years of €100 million, and an 8% return on risk-adjusted capital at the 10-year horizon.

The definition, achieved through common Monte Carlo simulation methods, of future liability and market scenarios anticipates the solution of the ALM problem *C* and derivation of the optimal policy, as shown in *D* and *E*. The optimal portfolio in *D* is the only one under complete uncertainty over future scenario evolution to be taken at the current time. For this reason this is also referred to as the optimal *here-and-now* solution or implementable decision. In step *E* we indicate an optimal portfolio evolution along an average asset and liability scenario. The strategy shown in *E* is expected to yield the achievement of all introduced targets. At the end of the 10-year period the portfolio value is estimated on average to be worth €14 billion.

When input asset or liability scenarios are modified, the resulting strategy will also change. Sensitivity and what-if analysis can in this setting be easily performed as out-of-sample market back-testing, which is commonly required by large corporations. The adopted simulation framework will also allow estimation of the likelihood that the targets will be achieved.

Summary and Further Steps

We summarize key learning points to be considered by P&C managers and professionals in the definition of their strategies, together with few ideas for the future.

- Optimal decision processes need to take into account the interaction between short-term profit objectives and longer-term risk concepts, leading to an optimal wealth allocation.
- Risk assessment at an aggregate P&C level will include not only traditional risk measures for the insurance and financial business—such as loss, risk and combined ratios, market volatility, and price dispersions—but also risk capital measures that capture the overall long-term exposure of the risk of the company.
- Reward measures are not limited to premiums per unit liability or financial returns, but include concepts such as value creation and return per unit risk exposure.
- Premium inflows are increasingly dependent on the diversification of protection vehicles on several business lines by P&C insurers, which are witnessing a growing market competition and the need to define accurate pricing methods, here left exogenous in the treatment of the ALM problem.
- Modern insurance and financial markets require a careful integration and strong synergies between actuarial, investment, and risk management divisions, whose role is increasing as a consequence of recent regulatory reforms in OECD countries (e.g. the Solvency II framework) and due to the unprecedented losses experienced during the 2008–10 period.
- Scientific and computational advances allow today the definition of user-friendly systems that are able to capture all the key complexities underlying the asset–liability management of large P&C conglomerates. These systems are expected to replace current portfolio optimization tools (which are primarily based on static approaches) over the years, leading to more robust and stable strategies by key institutional investors and inducing in the long run a reduction of premiums in the market.

In the future we expect the following substantial developments for the insurance industry.

- Increasing product diversification on the liability side and an increasing importance of alternative investments on the asset side.
- An internal transformation leading to the integration of technical P&C divisions—which historically have been attached to actuarial mathematical methods—with the investment and risk management divisions. The result will be a greater openness to modern results in financial and insurance mathematics, with a positive impact on the pricing and risk measurement techniques adopted, as well as on the definition of strategic asset allocation policies.
- Increasing competition in personal financial services, with the insurance professional increasingly able to handle in an optimal way complex individual portfolios with financial and insurance products that rely on definitions of the overall risk profile; such processes will also require the adoption of long-term dynamic methods such as those considered in this chapter.

More Info

Books:

Bertocchi, Maria Ida, Giorgio Consigli, and Michael A. H. Dempster (eds). *Stochastic Optimization Methods in Finance and Energy: New Financial Products and Energy Market Strategies*. New York: Springer, 2011.

Consigli, Giorgio, Massimo di Tria, Michele Gaffo, Gaetano Iaquinta, Vittorio Moriggia, and Angelo Uristani. "Dynamic portfolio management for property and casualty insurance." In Bertocchi, Consigli, and Dempster (eds). *Stochastic Optimization Methods in Finance and Energy: New Financial Products and Energy Market Strategies*. New York: Springer, 2011; pp. 99–124.

Mulvey, John M., and Hafize Gaye Erkan. "Decentralized risk management for global property and casualty insurance companies." In Stein W. Wallace and William T. Ziemba (eds). *Applications of Stochastic Programming*. Philadelphia, PA: Society for Industrial and Applied Mathematics and the Mathematical Programming Society, 2005; pp. 503–530.

Pflug, Georg Ch., and Werner Romisch. *Modeling, Measuring and Managing Risk*. Singapore: World Scientific Publishing, 2007.

Zenios, Stavros A., and William T. Ziemba (eds). *Handbook of Asset and Liability Management. Volume 1: Theory and Methodology*. Amsterdam: Elsevier, 2007a.

Zenios, Stavros A., and William T. Ziemba (eds). *Handbook of Asset and Liability Management. Volume 2: Applications and Case Studies*. Amsterdam: Elsevier, 2007b.

Ziemba, William T., and John M. Mulvey (eds). *Worldwide Asset and Liability Modeling*. Cambridge, UK: Cambridge University Press, 1998.

Articles:

Cariño, David R., Terry Kent, David H. Myers, Celine Stacy, Mike Sylvanus, Andrew L. Turner, Kouji Watanabe, and William T. Ziemba. "The Russell–Yasuda Kasai model: An asset/liability model for a Japanese insurance company using multistage stochastic programming." *Interfaces* 24:1 (1994): 29–49. Online at: dx.doi.org/10.1287/inte.24.1.29

Comité Européen des Assurances (CEA). "CEA statistics no. 42: European insurance in figures." November 2010. Online at: tinyurl.com/79phvho [PDF].

Europe Economics. "Retail insurance market study MARKT/2008/18/H. Final report by Europe Economics." November 2009.

European Parliament. "Directive 2009/138/EC of the European Parliament and of the Council of 25 November 2009 on the taking-up and pursuit of the business of insurance and reinsurance (Solvency II) (recast)." *Official Journal of the European Union* L335/1, December 17, 2009. Online at: tinyurl.com/74jwwjh [PDF].

Notes

1. We acknowledge the support given by the research project PRIN2007 "Optimization of stochastic dynamic systems with applications to finance" no. 20073BZ5A5, and by an ongoing R&D project sponsored by Allianz Investment Management. We are obliged and extremely grateful to Michele Gaffo and Davide Musitelli of Allianz Investment Management for their continuous support and critical views on the topics discussed here and to Vittorio Moriggia, Gaetano Iaquinta, and Angelo Uristani of the University of Bergamo for their commitment and remarkable skills in handling theory and implementation. The views expressed in this article do not necessarily reflect Allianz's policy, nor do the results presented here represent actual figures or operational approaches currently adopted by the Allianz Group.
2. In extreme summary, the operating profit of a P&C company can be decomposed into the investment operating profit and the actuarial operating profit. The former includes all portfolio interest earnings, operational gain and losses, insurance fees and commissions net of borrowing costs, portfolio expenses, and provisions. The latter includes P&C premiums net of liability claims, operational costs, and expenses.

A Practitioner's Perspective on Investment Management for Shareholder Funds of European Insurers

by Kambiz Deljouie and Corrado Pistarino

Aviva Investors[1]

This Chapter Covers

- The push toward Solvency II will lead to a detachment of assets and liabilities and an increase in mark-to-market volatility as liquidity premium is squeezed out.
- This creates a focus on the sustainability of return on (economic) capital over time.
- Simple buy-to-hold strategies are unable to withstand adverse market scenarios over a multiperiod horizon, when the cost of capital is nonlinear.
- This is demonstrated by applying a simple algorithm to a portfolio of equity and credit.
- Thus, there is a conflict between long-term assumptions and the leveraged nature of an insurer's balance sheet. Additionally, there is a need to implement tactical investment views.
- A new practitioner's approach to managing shareholders' funds is proposed, while stressing the key role of integrated investment governance.

Introduction

The leveraged insurer's balance sheet is the key structural element to consider when designing an investment framework for managing shareholders' funds. Capital is a scarce (and costly) resource to replenish. With the exception of unit-linked products, all other books of business contain payment obligations, which are ultimately guaranteed by the company's shareholders and are met by the performance of the investment portfolios. To ensure that those expectations are realized and the solvency position of the company is preserved, a robust investment discipline is needed.

Although gaining recognition across the industry, the emphasis on capital preservation and on maximization of return on capital over a multiperiod horizon is not yet fully established.

The in-force regulations (e.g. premium matching for the annuity book, which shelters capital from mark-to-market volatility of assets), overemphasis on liquidity (e.g. the perceived need of property and casualty insurers to hold extremely liquid portfolios with small market risk), and the complexity of the business (e.g. the embedded optionality in with-profit funds) all conjure to favor simplified investment frameworks such as buy-to-hold investing, long-term investment return (LTIR), etc. Therefore, the interaction between capital preservation and portfolio management is largely ignored.

The aim of this chapter is to illustrate that, despite the introduction of a risk-based solvency regime for capital calculation, the impact of mark-to-market on the insurer's balance sheet can severely strain its solvency position, making the interaction between capital and investment activity paramount. By focusing on the shortcomings of traditional (and still very popular) buy-to-hold investing, including the rather unshakable faith in the power of diversification, and by highlighting the alarming weakness in the insurer's balance sheet, we hope to convince the reader that a change to more dynamic investment approaches is needed.

Regulatory Challenges

In the United Kingdom, where a risk-based framework for computing regulatory capital has been in existence for a number of years, the transition to Solvency II is expected to be smoother than in other European jurisdictions. The notion of the survival of capital over a given time horizon, based on the aggregate risks of an insurer's balance sheet, is already part of the existing regulatory framework.

However, a large portion of the insurance business is still managed under a legacy solvency regime which allows discounting of the insurer's liabilities using part of the expected future returns on assets. The net effect of using this approach is the "capitalization of the liquidity premium," which, essentially, is the creation of a buffer of capital by recognizing an intrinsic net positive value in the asset portfolio. This approach is particularly prevalent in UK annuity management and is sometimes referred to as "matching premium."

Matching premium is done using fixed-income assets, and capitalization of the liquidity premium is justified by observing that cash bond credit spreads are *often* higher than historical defaults. This implies that the liquidity premium is related to the *type* of assets that an insurer holds, and therefore that the discounting basis for liabilities is *endogenous* (i.e. derived from the actual portfolio of assets held by the insurer). This creates a direct link between assets and liabilities, which effectively immunizes the insurance capital from the mark-to-market volatility in the asset portfolio.

The recognition of a liquidity premium has practical consequences on the investment framework: it disincentivizes asset reinvestment strategies and creates a strong preference for a cash flow matching approach to portfolio construction. Besides, there is little motivation for active management of the investment portfolio, despite the obvious fact that optimality in portfolio construction changes with time.

Solvency II is set to implement significant changes to the valuation of the liabilities by moving from a *real-world* (using asset yield) to a *market-consistent* discounting curve. Because the discounting basis is *exogenous* (it is not linked to the particular type of investment), it should lead to a detachment between assets and liabilities and exposure of capital to mark-to-market volatilities. If the liquidity premium is squeezed out or deemphasized, the following outcomes are likely.

- The traditional, static cash flow matching approach fails to achieve portfolio optimality; besides, with no recognition of a liquidity premium, it would attract a significant amount of solvency capital.

- Capital preservation will instigate a fresh appetite for reinvestment risk as the simplest risk-reduction strategy.
- The modular approach to capital calculation will force an explicit deconstruction of the various sources of market risk and will enhance clarity of purpose. The distinction between risk-taking decisions and hedging strategies will become clearer.[2]
- Although not explicitly stated, the alignment of solvency and economic capital (and market reality!) should imply the inclusion of government bond risk within the larger spectrum of credit risk. There is no longer a risk-free instrument available for perfect cash flow matching.

This new regulatory regime, in its purest form, seats capital in the midst of mark-to-market moves. To protect the *new* and fragile capital the insurer has to give attention to dynamic investment and think about downside protection. A more dynamic approach to investment should inevitably improve investment governance as well as give greater focus to the investment and risk management issues in the context of asset–liability management.

A number of objections have been raised by the insurance industry regarding the impact of the new solvency regime on the day-to-day conduct of its business. Among the industry's concerns—especially in the United Kingdom—are the capital strain on the annuity business, the cost of continuing to hold large portfolios of long-term credit assets post the implementation of Solvency II (or the cost of disposal of the long credit book), and a potential increase in the cost of retirement products. In response to those concerns, the latest version of the regulatory framework, the Fifth Quantitative Impact Study, or QIS 5, allows for a long transition phase in which an element of liquidity premium[3] will continue to be recognized. However, this new form of liquidity premium will continue to be exogenous, with no connection with the running yield of the asset portfolio. As a result, the principle of detachment of assets and liabilities would remain unscathed, and so would the need for a change in the insurers' investment perspective.

The Shortcomings of the Traditional Investment Framework

At the core of the traditional thinking for managing insurance funds is the central belief that the institutional investor, and in particular the insurance book, is a long-term, buy-to-hold investor capable of withstanding market upheavals. Although, by and large, this has been the case during the current market turmoil, one can argue that the regulatory regime played a role in shielding the insurer's balance sheet from the effects of extreme mark-to-market volatility.

Given the forthcoming regulatory changes, and the emphasis on an economic approach to the structure of the balance sheet, the old paradigm is now questionable. We have already indicated that, in the new world of Solvency II and risk capital, a levered balance sheet would be more fragile as it will be exposed to mark-to-market volatility. In this section, an attempt at a more concrete rationale for this assertion is provided.

The Impact of Leverage

The first step is the recognition that an insurer's balance sheet is leveraged: if the insurer's solvency position is, for example, 10% of the value of the asset portfolio, a

10% fall in the value of the asset portfolio is enough to wipe out the insurer's capital. That loss may be sustainable for a nonleveraged investor; for an insurer, such an event would lead to insolvency.

One can imagine a utility function for an insurer where risk aversion increases as capital gets exhausted. Since capital is expensive to replenish, investment profits should be significantly outweighed by the damage caused by potential losses in the portfolio: downside protection, i.e. capital preservation, is critical.

Asset allocation designed to provide an investment framework for insurance funds should be set up after taking into account this core principle. The expected performance of the portfolio cannot be simply measured in terms of expected returns per unit of risk, but the insurer needs to take into account the negative impact of losses which lead to injections of capital at higher levels of cost.

Technically, the insurer's risk-aversion can be modeled as a penalty function, which describes the increasing cost of raising capital in adverse market conditions as a result of losses in the investment portfolio.

A simple functional form, $K(\cdot)$, that penalizes the raising of new capital on a cumulative basis is shown in Figure 1. EC_t denotes the total amount of economic capital engaged up to a particular time. The investment begins with an initial amount of capital, EC_0, and as losses occur more capital is injected to sustain the buy-to-hold investment positions. But the new capital is raised at a higher cost—hence the shape of the graph in Figure 1. This simple framework enables us to examine a multiperiod buy-to-hold investment for different asset classes as well as for a multiasset portfolio.

Figure 1. A functional form for cost of capital is introduced to model the increase in cost of capital when capital is exhausted by investment losses

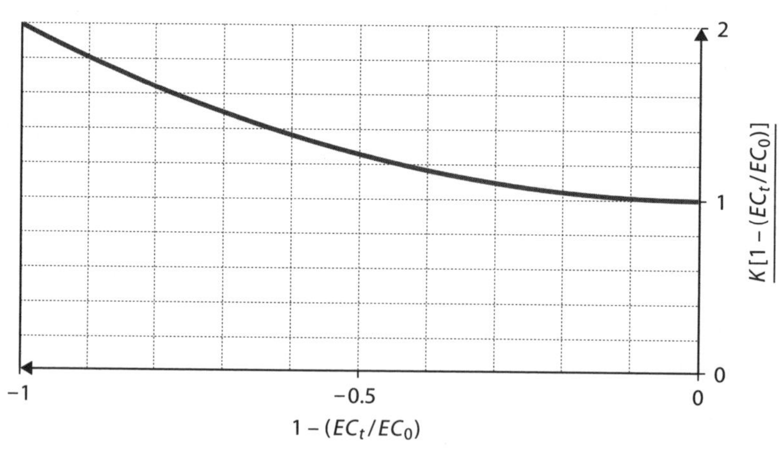

Single-Period vs Multiperiod Investment Framework

The current regulatory framework uses a one-year economic capital which targets a survival rate of 99.5% (1 in 200 events over one year). Regulators have taken the view that setting a tight confidence level for one year is sufficient to manage an insurance book over time. Solvency II and internal capital models also focus on managing the risk with the same one-year confidence level.

Surprisingly, a multiperiod framework for capital setting is not part of the ongoing discussion between the industry and regulators concerning the principles of the new solvency regime. Let us counter this approach. Consider, for example, an insurance book with an investment strategy that begins with $1 of capital. Assume that the market falls and 50% of the capital is exhausted. The regulatory framework assumes that in the second year the insurance company may take three possible actions.

- Reduce the investment risk by one half to match the 50¢ of capital. This would reduce return on capital, making the business unprofitable, or, depending on the cost of funding, making the business unsustainable.
- Continue with the same investment strategy by injecting a further 50¢ of capital. This option is likely to be expensive, as the new capital is raised when share prices are low, thus increasing the cost of capital. This strategy is likely to fail unless one assumes significantly higher returns (i.e. higher risk premia) to meet the increased cost of capital.
- Reduce the size of the book. Given the long-dated, illiquid nature of the liabilities, this option is likely to be the least economic.

All three options will have a substantial impact on the long-term profitability (and survival) of the firm. A single-period approach fails to capture the dynamics between portfolio decisions and the solvency position of the insurer.

Measuring Economic Gain

For an investment strategy, terminal economic gain for a particular time horizon is defined as the net gain over the cost of capital and after the repayment of any capital borrowed. Additionally, in this setting, any profit is paid back to investors as a bonus or dividends and losses are replenished by raising new capital at an increasing cost. Future profits are retained in part or in full to repay the capital borrowed and the associated costs. This simplified framework to a large extent captures the market reality: companies have little incentive to retain profits when they are doing well, whereas after periods of upheaval they are seen to be strengthening their capital position. Since the cost of capital is nonlinear, one would expect to observe a fat tail in the distribution of economic gain.

From a purely technical perspective, it may be more appropriate to consider a dynamic asset allocation within the context of multiperiod stochastic optimization (Hibiki, 2006). However, the simple multiperiod approach set out above can provide a deep insight into the interaction of investment and capital management. We will now examine the findings for equity and credit investing.

Economic Gain for Investing in Equity

We simulate an investment strategy where a long equity index position is held for 10 years. At inception, 30% economic capital is posted, guided by the regulatory regime (e.g. Solvency II), and each year the economic capital is replenished when losses occur. For the simulations the funding cost is set at 60 bp (this is the spread over risk-free which is used for discounting liabilities), the equity risk premium at 3.5%, and set the cost of capital at 8% (10-year gilts plus 5%).

Equity returns were simulated using both a lognormal model and Heston's stochastic volatility model (Heston, 1993) to demonstrate that our key findings are largely model-independent.

With both models the one-year distribution of economic gain exhibits a fat tail, as shown in Figure 2. We observe that the economic gain is small and positive after compensating economic capital for an 8% return. This is expected, as the equity risk premium net of cost of funds is sufficient to pay for the cost of capital.

Figure 2. Distribution of one-year economic gain. The distribution mean for both models is approximately 0.5%

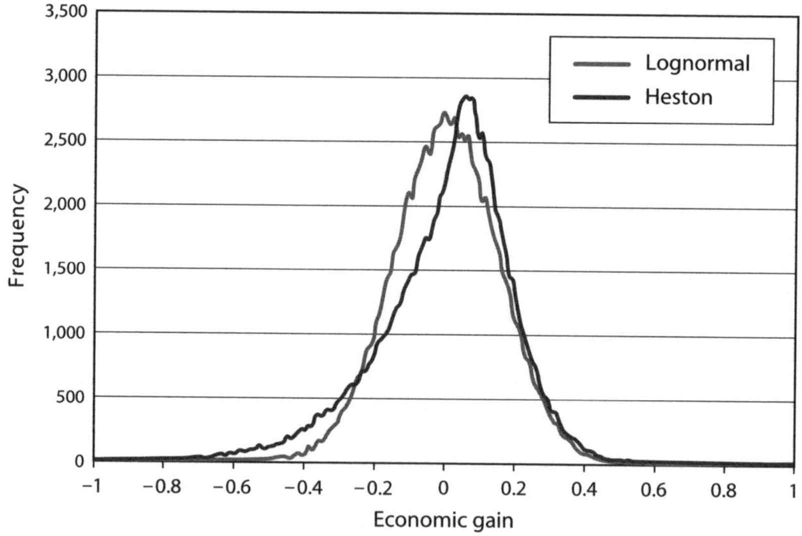

The investment strategy, however, deteriorates over a longer time period as capital needs to be raised at a higher cost to cover the losses in the portfolio (Figure 3). The increased cost of capital during the loss years introduces a pronounced fat tail to both distributions, and it impacts the expected economic gains, which in both cases are negative. This is consistent with the management of any levered positions, unless excess returns in the good years (deleveraging) are reserved to avoid raising capital in the bad years—a strategy that is difficult to implement in a competitive market, where short-term shareholder return is a key consideration.

Figure 3. Distribution of 10-year economic gain. The expected economic gain is approximately –57% for the Heston model and –36% for the lognormal model

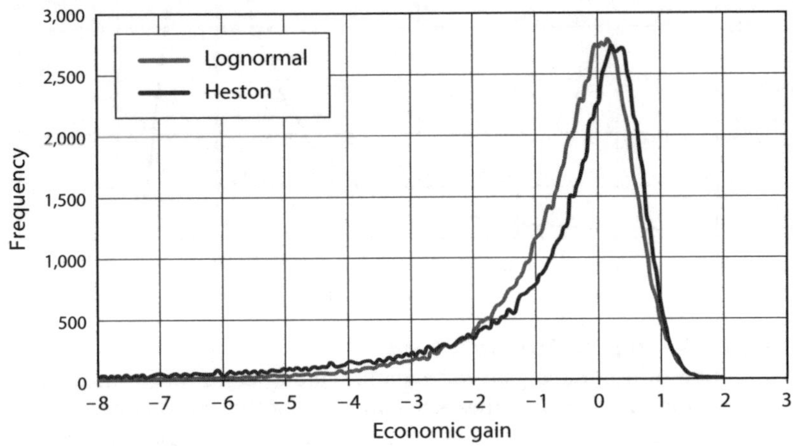

Economic Gain for Investing in Credit

To explore the effect of nonlinear cost of capital on credit investing, a 10-year buy-to-hold investment strategy was examined. The portfolio was invested 70% in A-rated and 30% in BBB-rated credit, with weighted average spread of 165 bp over gilts.

The logarithm of the spreads follows a mean-reverting process after Longstaff and Schwartz (1995), and the same methodology based on the penalty function was applied in order to examine the distribution properties of economic gain.

Since the objective is to test the robustness of buy-to-hold strategies, we also assumed that the probability of default varies in time as a fixed percentage (30%) of credit spreads. This was done to mimic the actuarial assumptions that are commonly used for the life books.

The distribution of economic gain outcomes is shown in Figure 4. Despite the relatively high levels of credit spread observed in the current market and the mean-reversion assumption, which benefits a buy-to-hold investor, the expectation of 10-year economic gain is negative, although significantly better than investing in equities.

Figure 4. Distribution of 10-year economic gain for credit investing. The expected economic gain is approximately –6%

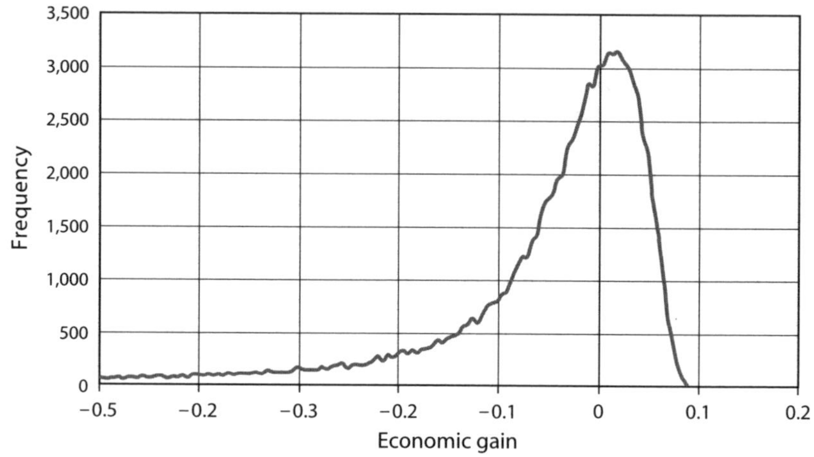

Summary of Findings on Economic Gain

The distribution of economic gain for a simple, multiperiod buy-to-hold investment strategy in equities or in credit appears to confirm that the one-year economic capital is insufficient to support a buy-to-hold strategy in a solvency regime where the mark-to-market losses are not shielded by a simultaneous repricing of the insurer's liabilities. This is the obvious result if a penalty function is introduced with cumulative effects over a multiperiod horizon, unless asset risk premia are set uncommonly high with respect to the company's cost of capital (a fact that would raise the question whether one should invest in the company at all).

If capital is larger, then investors need to accept a lower return on capital, or the management needs to pass the extra cost in terms of additional charges on to the client base (e.g. insurance products would become more expensive).

On average, one wouldn't expect much of a difference if the company were to raise the additional buffer of capital in its entirety at inception, at a known cost of capital, or incrementally, at an increased cost as losses materialize. The net result would be a substantial reduction in the expected return on capital for the business.

These findings probably reflect the common knowledge across the industry regarding derisking activities in the insurance sector in periods of severe market falls, thus leading to the crystallization of losses as well as an inability to raise capital economically.

Suitability of Long-Term Assumptions for Insurance Money Management

The estimation of risk premia, long-term volatilities, and long-term correlations lie at the core of traditional asset allocation techniques. However, we observe that the insurer's levered balance sheet is not strong enough to withstand mark-to-market volatilities and benefit from the long-run behavior of the assets. Therefore, the following observations can be made.

- Long-run return assumptions are only applicable to an investor who can hold an investment position over the long-term horizon. Parameters used for optimization-based asset allocations are unstable over a short-and medium-term horizon. Correlation, in particular, significantly increases among risky assets when markets fall, but also changes sign when one considers risky assets and bonds (see Figure 5). The state-dependent nature of correlation creates volatility skew in an asset and liability portfolio and exhausts the economic capital set against an insurance book.

Figure 5. The correlation between the Gilt 4.75% 12/07/2038 and the FTSE100 index. (*Source*: Bloomberg data)

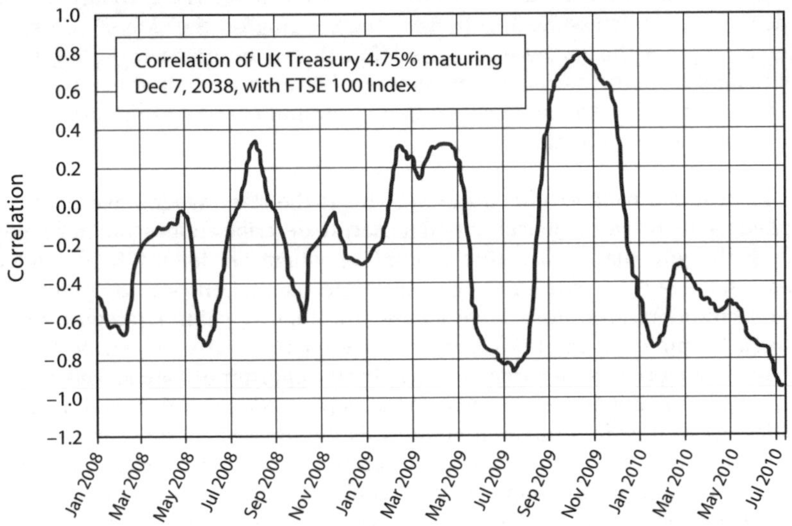

The chart in Figure 5 also calls into question the common belief that diversification helps to manage the insurance book. The simplistic belief in the efficacy of diversification has already been put to the test through the recent market upheavals: the comovement of risky assets during the market fall and the derisking of insurers' balance sheets at the bottom of the market, as well as the large and negative correlation experienced between bonds and equities, have been a contributing factor to the increase in funding deficits.

Some Proposed Improvements

The limitations outlined in the previous sections call for new thinking and a new framework for insurers' shareholder funds. Any new framework needs to benefit from an analytical backbone as well as an effective governance structure that can respond to market changes and opportunities. Detailed discussion of these issues is outside the scope of this chapter. Here the focus is on the key features of an investment framework—which we call CAR, short for constrained absolute return.

We argue that insurance money management is about maximizing multiperiod return on capital (capital being the constraint) while targeting an absolute level of return (or operating profit). This chapter focuses on a multiasset portfolio, which is largely invested in fixed income plus a small allocation to other return-seeking assets whose distribution profile can be managed using derivatives (equities, commodities, etc.). We see three distinct implementation steps: market-neutral asset allocation; tactical and relative-value investing; and security selection.

Step 1: Market-neutral asset allocation. For fixed-income instruments, our return assumptions are informed by traded market levels. We use market yields, or, specifically for credit, credit spreads above the overnight indexed swap (OIS) curve. Adjusting the traded spreads, as outlined in previous sections, is helpful, but it does not critically affect the asset allocation for a highly rated credit portfolio. The correlation between fixed-income sectors is assumed to be very high, erring on the side of conservatism in order to capture the increase in correlation that is observed in falling markets. The same applies to the correlation parameters between credit and equity. This step provides us with an investment portfolio that is optimum in terms of return on capital, with a neutral view on the market.

Step 2: Tactical and relative-value investing. This is the stage where investment views are applied. Here the word tactical is used loosely to describe an investment framework (including the governance structure around it) where we identify and implement multiasset relative-value strategies that are either capital-efficient or purely driven by capital considerations. To a large extent, the relative-value strategies are intra-asset class. Examples in the fixed-income space include trades where portfolios are repositioned along the credit curve, negative basis opportunities are locked into in the credit market, or anomalies in the swap/bond/repo market are exploited. Investment in equities, as well as in structured equities, is determined by the short-term views on those markets and the shape of the volatility skew, as outlined in the previous section. Those strategies are implemented within the limits of a risk budget, defined in units of economic capital. Because economic capital is simply a metric and the same quantity can be arrived at using different investment strategies, invariance of capital would not be sufficient to ensure that the fundamental construct of Step 1 is preserved. The portfolio manager would be able to significantly depart from the asset allocation, essentially taking ownership of the entirety of capital. We believe this would be incorrect and inappropriate.

Step 3: Security selection. Security selection, in particular, in the credit portfolio, needs to be used to both enhance capital-constrained returns and implement defensive strategies. Similar to Step 2, security selection needs to be performed under a tightly managed risk budget.

A brief remark on the governance related to investment may also be helpful. Most of the economic capital is engaged at Step 1 in the process. Although this step is rich in investment content, the principal ownership and decision on risk rests with the asset–liability management team of the insurer: their input and/or oversight is needed. Steps 2 and 3 are principally conducted by the portfolio manager and characterize the search for a new form of capital-efficient alpha.

Summary and Further Steps

We have used a simple framework to look at investment management under capital constraints, applicable to an insurer's balance sheet. Although the mathematical modeling was outside the scope of this chapter, an attempt was made to highlight the shortcomings of traditional asset allocation and to suggest an alternative way of approaching the problem of managing insurance funds. In summary, the following conclusions can be set out.

- Despite the uncertainties surrounding the final formulation of Solvency II—and in particular the treatment of the liquidity premium—assets and liabilities will be detached.
- Our findings suggest that under the Solvency II framework an insurance balance sheet would not be able to withstand the volatility of mark-to-market over a multiperiod horizon if the investment strategy is buy-to-hold. By removing the regulatory safeguard of Solvency I, the insurer's balance sheet becomes more fragile.
- Measuring the survival of an insurer over a one-year horizon does not capture the complex interaction between investment performance and capital preservation. If the measurement is applied to a multiperiod horizon and a penalty function is introduced to model the increased cost of raising capital in adverse market conditions, a different world is disclosed.
- A multiperiod buy-to-hold investment strategy in equities with a nonlinear cost of capital would lead to significant economic losses. The perception that holding equities under a Solvency-II regime is "costly" is correct. In reality, the cost is even higher.
- Credit is a more benign asset class. It behaves better because of the pull-to-par mechanism, as well as the hypothesis that historical defaults are less than implied market projections and the strong mean-reversion which is central to our modeling framework. However, a multiperiod buy-to-hold investment strategy in credit still would lead to terminal economic losses.

The above results seem to indicate that a move from a traditional buy-to-hold strategy to a more dynamic investment framework is needed. We believe it should be constructed around three key steps:

- Step 1: A market-neutral asset allocation for fixed-income instruments;
- Step 2: Tactical (including equity risk) and relative-value investing;
- Step 3: Security selection.

We call this framework CAR. While investment input is needed for construction of the asset allocation (Step 1), ownership rests with the asset–liability management team of the insurer. A risk budget, measured in units of capital, is assigned to the portfolio manager in order to implement Step 2 and Step 3, with the aim of creating additional value (capital-efficient alpha) or promptly reacting to adverse market conditions by implementing derisking strategies.

More Info

Articles:

Heston, S. L. "A closed-form solution for options with stochastic volatility with application to bond and currency options." *Review of Financial Studies* 6:2 (Summer 1993): 327–343. Online at: dx.doi.org/10.1093/rfs/6.2.327

Hibiki, Norio. "Multi-period stochastic optimization models for dynamic asset allocation." *Journal of Banking and Finance* 30:2 (2006): 365–390. Online at: dx.doi.org/10.1016/j.jbankfin.2005.04.027

Longstaff, Francis A., and Eduardo S. Schwartz. "Valuing credit derivatives." *Journal of Fixed Income* 5:1 (June 1995): 6–12. Online at: tinyurl.com/756n53r

Manning, Mark J. "Exploring the relationship between credit spreads and default probabilities." Working paper 225. Market Infrastructure Division, Financial Stability, Bank of England, 2004.

Zhang, Benjamin Yibin, Hao Zhou, and Haibin Zhu. "Explaining credit default swap spreads with equity volatility and jump risks of individual firms." Working paper 181. Monetary and Economic Department, Bank of International Settlements, September 2005.

Notes

1. The views expressed in this chapter are those of the authors and do not necessarily reflect the views of Aviva Investors.
2. As an example, when hedging a series of cash flows with a credit bond it should be understood that the decision combines two entirely separate considerations: hedging the interest rate risk of the liabilities by using a cash instrument; and taking a market view over a given credit duration and reserving capital against it.
3. Calculated as 50% of (iBoxx spread – 40 bp), but amortizing over a variable number of years. Cutoff for sterling-denominated liabilities is at the 30-year term.

The Impact of Financial Crisis

Capital Regulation After the Financial Crisis

by Jens Hagendorff[a] and Francesco Vallascas[b]

[a] University of Edinburgh, UK
[b] University of Leeds, UK

This Chapter Covers

- The scale and scope of the Basel III revisions of capital adequacy standards.
- The benefits and costs of the higher capital requirements that will apply to banks under Basel III. We distinguish between benefits and costs realized by banks and the financial system as a whole.
- The argument that the effect of Basel III on the costs of bank funding is likely to be less than is frequently suggested, because the reductions in bank leverage mandated under Basel III should lead to a reduction in the costs of bank equity compared with present levels.
- How the lower bank leverage that will result from Basel III will alter the influence that shareholders and debt-holders have on risk-taking by banks. Although equity-holders under Basel III will be forced to have more "skin in the game" than previously and should be less prone to risk-taking than the shareholders of less-capitalized banks, it will be interesting to observe how the riskiness of banks changes as debt-holders, who are more risk-averse than equity-holders, play a diminished role in the capital structure of banks.

Introduction

The capital structure of banks differs in important aspects from that of nonfinancial firms. One such aspect is that bank managements need to comply with capital adequacy rules that impose minimum capital requirements. To justify regulatory interference in the capital structure of banks, financial economists point to an important moral hazard problem. The argument goes that, in the absence of regulatory capital requirements, bank shareholders will minimize capital holdings and increase risk-taking.

Such risk-taking behavior will be advantageous for bank shareholders as they seek to maximize the value of deposit insurance and other implicit or explicit government guarantees. At the heart of the problem of risk-taking by banks, therefore, lies the financial safety net (for instance, in the form of deposit insurance and "too-big-to-fail" guarantees) and the protection it affords to shareholders and other creditor groups.

Given this moral hazard problem, regulatory capital requirements are designed to force banks to maintain more capital and thus to absorb more losses linked to higher-risk portfolios (e.g. Sharpe, 1978; Furlong and Keeley, 1989; Calem and Rob, 1999). However, if capital regulation is to prevent banks from holding insufficient capital against their asset portfolios, it is essential that regulatory capital requirements are highly calibrated to the riskiness of a bank's assets.

The financial crisis of 2007–09 has dented confidence in the effectiveness of international capital regulation. In particular, the sensitivity of capital requirements to bank risk has attracted criticism. It is now a widely accepted view that many banks entered the crisis with insufficient capital holdings, leading to widespread concerns over bank solvency and signs of panic in interbank funding markets during the crisis (Basel Committee, 2009 and 2010a; Hellwig, 2010). The widespread distress and numerous bank defaults which resulted from these solvency concerns illustrate the wholesale failure of capital regulation to ensure that capital requirements are linked to the riskiness of bank assets.

A case in point is provided by the International Monetary Fund (IMF). In a recent financial stability report, the IMF (2009) shows that banks in Europe and the United States that were in need of government assistance during the crisis were better capitalized (in terms of regulatory capital) than banks which were not in need of such help. The fact that better-capitalized banks were more (not less) likely to receive government support is hardly consistent with the view that capital regulations are "risk-based" in any meaningful way.

Doubts over the adequacy of capital regulations came after the Basel Committee on Banking Supervision (which has been charged with designing international capital rules) repeatedly revised the capital adequacy framework over the last two decades. However, despite numerous refinements and revisions of the Basel rules, the recent financial crisis has called for additional revisions to the regulatory framework. Although the latest Basel revisions, proposed by the Basel Committee at the end of 2010 and referred to as "Basel III," maintain many of the key elements of the previous capital framework, they introduce stricter requirements that affect both the quality and quantity of bank capital.

In this chapter, we summarize the evolution of capital regulation in the banking industry before the eruption of the financial crisis of 2007–09. We then discuss the expected benefits and costs of Basel III. In our discussion we distinguish between the costs and benefits as realized by banks, the financial system, and likely changes in the ability of debt-holders and shareholders to affect bank risk-taking as a result of changes in the capital structure of banks which will result from Basel III.

The Evolution of Capital Regulation in the Banking Industry

Capital Regulation Before the Financial Crisis

The first attempt to establish risk-based capital standards in the banking industry dates back to 1988 when the Basel Committee on Banking Supervision proposed a set of rules that linked bank capital holdings to credit risk. The Basel Accord—subsequently labeled Basel I to distinguish the original from its subsequent revisions—was adopted by participating countries from 1993 and boasted a simple framework to assess credit risk. At its core, Basel I mandated that banks hold, at minimum, an amount of capital that equals 8% of their risk exposure. Risk exposure was calculated as the risk-weighted sum of various on- and off-balance sheet exposures. Essentially, as detailed in Appendix 1, Basel I assigned risk weights to different types of assets based on credit risk. Off-balance sheet assets were converted into credit risk equivalents and then into risk-weighted assets to determine bank capital requirements.

Criticisms were raised against Basel I immediately following its introduction. First, the initial capital adequacy rules did not require capital holdings that were in line with market risk. Second, the weighting scheme proposed by the Basel Committee was simplistic. For instance, all loans to the corporate sector had to be converted with the same risk weighting irrespective of differences in the borrowers' creditworthiness. The simplistic nature of the risk weights made it advantageous for banks to engage in capital arbitrage by investing in assets that might be risky but attracted low capital requirements (Jones, 2000).

Although additions to the Basel Accord in 1996 introduced capital requirements for market risk, the previous system of risk weights that underpins the capital adequacy rules remained essentially unchanged until 2006, when the Basel Committee proposed a revised capital adequacy framework. The revised framework, known as Basel II, was an attempt to make the regulatory risk weights more risk-sensitive by introducing some important changes to the algorithm used to determine capital requirements as well as by broadening the range of risks against which banks need to hold capital (see Basel Committee, 2006).

Further, Basel II marked a move from a "one size fits all," where all banks apply the same weighting scheme, to a system where banks are given a choice over the approach they wish to employ to compute capital requirements. Under Basel II, banks could choose between two main regulatory risk assessment methods. The first, the *standardized approach*, is essentially a more refined version of Basel I with a more granular regulatory definition of the risk weights linked to different types of credit risk exposure. The second, *the internal ratings-based (IRB) approach*, forms the relatively more risk-sensitive approach. The IRB approach relies on a bank's internal risk measures to compute regulatory capital requirements. The key elements of the two approaches are summarized in Appendix 2.

However, giving banks the right to choose between alternative risk-weighting methods is controversial, because it may generate some unexpected effects. In particular, by creating an asymmetry in the treatment of identical portfolio risks across banks, the presence of a dual approach to risk assessment may impact on the types of risk a bank chooses. For instance, banks eligible for the IRB approach are likely to be tempted to focus on low-risk lending. Given the higher risk sensitivity of capital requirements under the IRB approach, banks that adopt IRB and reduce their portfolio risk will benefit from lower capital requirements. By contrast, it will be advantageous for banks which adopt the standardized approach to focus on high-risk lending to take advantage of the less risk-sensitive weighting system (Repullo and Suarez, 2004; Hakenes and Schnabel, 2011). Therefore, while there are clear advantages associated with a more risk-sensitive capital regime in general, giving banks a choice between approaches that vary in terms of their risk sensitivity may have some unintended consequences in terms of a bank's propensity to take on additional risk.

The Basel II Accord has also broadened the types of risk covered by the capital adequacy regulations. Next to capital requirements for credit and market risk, Basel II also mandated capital requirements against operational risk exposures. Thus, banks need to be able to absorb losses linked to inadequate or failed internal processes caused by people or systems or other adverse external events. As with credit and market risk, Basel II gives banks some choice over the methodologies they wish to employ to assess their operational risk exposure. These methodologies differ in terms of complexity and level of sophistication.

In spite of having only been fully adopted in 2008 (and only in some countries), the Basel II framework attracted strong criticisms during the financial crisis of 2007–09. Critics point to the general inability of the framework to ensure that banks were adequately capitalized as they entered the financial crisis. Specifically, many commentators believe that the recent crisis has demonstrated that the increased risk sensitivity of capital requirements under Basel II rules was insufficient to ensure that banks hold capital commensurate with the riskiness of their asset portfolios (Hellwig, 2010; Admati *et al.*, 2010).

The Financial Crisis and Basel III

Numerous bank defaults during the financial crisis of 2007–09 have been linked to banks being inadequately capitalized. Essentially, the losses that banks experienced on their banking and trading books quickly eroded the small capital base which many banks held going into the crisis, raising concerns over bank solvency and leading to numerous bailouts of institutions by regulatory authorities.

This view is also echoed by the Basel Committee in a document published in December 2010:

"One of the main reasons the economic and financial crisis, which began in 2007, became so severe was that the banking sectors of many countries had built up excessive on and off-balance sheet leverage. This was accompanied by a gradual erosion of the level and quality of the capital base." (Basel Committee, 2010a: p. 1.)

In response to the perceived failings of previous Basel accords, the Basel Committee (2010a: p. 3) proposed further revisions ("Basel III") in December 2010 that aimed to "raise both the quality and quantity of the regulatory capital base and enhance the risk coverage of the capital framework." Hence, the new rules—despite sticking to some key elements of the Basel II Accord (such as the choice between the standardized and IRB approaches and the important role of internally developed risk models)—introduce several regulatory changes with the aim of increasing the level and quality of bank capital.

The likely improvements in capital adequacy are the result of three important modifications of the Basel II Accord. First, as summarized in Figure 1, the minimum regulatory capital ratio may *potentially* be as high as 13%. This increase is due to the fact that Basel III introduces additional requirements in the form of a "conservation buffer" and a "countercyclical buffer" on top of the conventional 8% capital ratio. The conservative buffer equals up to 2.5% of the value of risk-weighted assets and can be used to absorb losses during periods of financial and economic distress. The countercyclical buffer will range from 0% to 2.5% of common equity (or other loss-absorbing capital) and will be implemented where national regulators see fit.

Its purpose is to protect the banking sector from periods of excess aggregate credit growth. For any given country, this buffer will only be in effect when there is excess credit growth and a system wide build-up of "excessive" risk.

Figure 1. Capital requirements under Basel III. (Source: Basel Committee on Banking Supervision, 2010a)

Calibration of the capital framework Capital requirements and buffers (all numbers in %)			
	Common equity (after deductions)	**Tier 1 capital**	**Total capital**
Minimum	4.5	6.0	8.0
Conservation buffer	2.5		
Minimum plus conservation buffer	7.0	8.5	10.5
*Countercyclical buffer range**	0–2.5		

*Common equity or other fully loss-absorbing capital.

On top of these two buffers, systemically important financial institutions may also be subject to additional capital requirements to reflect their too-big-to-fail status. In a recent consultative document, the Basel Committee (2011) raises the prospect of additional requirements for banks that are deemed to be systemically relevant because of their size, complexity, and interconnectedness with the rest of the financial system. For these institutions, the minimum regulatory capital ratio could increase to at least 16.5% (depending on the degree of systemic importance). Appendix 3 describes the rationale for these additional requirements and provides more details on how the additional requirements are designed for what the Basel Committee calls "global systemically important banks" (G-SIBs).

A second change that could play an important part in increasing bank capital holdings under Basel III is a stricter definition of equity for the purpose of capital regulation. The new accord places greater focus on common equity as the highest-quality component of bank capital and more strictly defines what qualifies as equity (the definition is now largely restricted to common shares and retained income).

The third change that should lead to an increase in bank capital is a stricter risk assessment (as evidenced by higher regulatory risk weights linked to certain activities compared with the previous rules). In particular, Basel III raises capital requirements for complex securitization exposures and the trading book, as both were regarded as major loss drivers for banks during the recent financial crisis. Furthermore, stricter capital requirements have also been introduced for counterparty credit exposures arising from derivatives, repo, and securities financing activities. All in all, the proposed changes in the risk-weighting methodology underlying capital adequacy rules are expected to produce an average increase of 23% in risk-weighted assets. Consequently, there will be a decline in capital ratios and a resulting need for banks to raise additional capital to remain in compliance with capital adequacy rules.

A comprehensive overview on how Basel III might impact capital requirements in the banking industry is provided in a recent quantitative impact assessment study by the Basel Committee (2010b). The study concludes that due to the combined effects of the three changes discussed above, internationally active banks show a present common equity shortfall of $577 billion. As a result, banks would see their average capital ratios decline from 14% to 8.4% once Basel III comes into effect.

Overall, the introduction of Basel III means that banks will have to raise their capital base considerably, mainly via large injections of common equity. The enormous funding needs of banks raise the question of whether the benefits associated with a stricter capital adequacy regime are indeed outweighed by the various costs. The next sections discuss the various benefits and costs to banks and the financial system, as well as how Basel III will alter the influence shareholders and debt-holders have on risks taken by a bank.

Benefits and Costs of Higher Capital Requirements

Benefits and Costs for Banks

Higher capital requirements (and the changes in bank capital structure that follow from higher capital requirements) may bring various benefits and costs to banks. This subsection focuses on two aspects that are likely to be affected by increased capital requirements: bank solvency and the funding costs of banks.

The expected impact of higher capital requirements on bank solvency is largely due to the fact that a larger capital base should improve the resilience of banks to shocks and reduce the likelihood of bank failures. This straightforward view of the role of increased capital requirements on bank solvency, however, has come under scrutiny by theoretical models. Santomero and Kim (1988) were among the first to suggest that increases in capital requirements might generate more (and not less) risky investments by bank managers. This is because managers will attempt to compensate for any losses in their expected returns which result from higher capital requirements by investing in more risky portfolios. It is, therefore, not surprising that the empirical literature provides conflicting evidence on the link between bank failures and capital strength (Berger, Herring, and Szego, 1995).

The expected impact of higher capital requirements on the funding costs of banks is a somewhat thorny issue. On the one hand, banks see raising equity as expensive in relation to other forms of bank funding, and any regulation that requires an increase in the share of equity is likely to see an increase in the overall costs of bank funding. Hence, there are concerns that as banks substitute debt with equity, increases in the weighted average cost of funding may well be passed on to borrowers in the form of higher loan costs.

On the other hand, the assumption that increases in the amount of equity in a bank's capital structure will inevitably increase the cost of bank funding is not obvious. In particular, this view does not consider the link between banking risk and funding costs. Specifically, the view that more equity means higher funding costs ignores the fact that the costs of both equity and debt are functions of the riskiness of banks (Hellwig, 2010; Admati *et al.*, 2010; Marcheggiano, Miles, and Yang, 2011). As more stringent capital regulation reduces bank risk (mainly via a reduction in bank leverage), the expected return required by both shareholders and debt-holders will be reduced. This is the spirit of Modigliani and Miller's (1958) famous proposition that (absent privileged tax treatment or government guarantees of debt) capital structure is irrelevant for the overall cost of funding.

The theoretical predictions of the Modigliani–Miller theorem are sometimes brushed aside on the grounds that, once the restrictive assumptions of the model are relaxed, it is unlikely that changes in the costs of equity and debt offset each other exactly. However, it is still the case that the costs of equity will change as decreasing leverage lowers the risk premium and, therefore, the costs of bank equity.

The overall effect of increases in bank equity on the costs that banks charge borrowers will then depend on the impact that Basel III has on the costs of different sources of bank funding. In this respect, several recent empirical analyses suggest that the long-run effect of Basel III on loan spreads is likely to be modest. Kashyap, Stein, and Hanson (2010) predict for US banks that, even under an extreme scenario of a 10% increase in capital requirements, banks' cost of lending will increase by between 25 and 45 basis points. Similarly, Marcheggiano, Miles, and Yang (2011) predict an increase in lending costs of 18 basis points if UK banks were to halve their leverage (in terms of Tier 1 capital). For the global banking industry, a recent assessment by the Basel Committee (2010c) indicates that a 1% increase in the ratio between common equity and risk-weighted assets would increase lending spreads by 13 basis points. However the Basel Committee recognizes that this is likely to represent an upper bound as the simulation did not consider the risk sensitivity of the cost of bank capital.

In sum, it appears that the type of reductions in bank leverage mandated under Basel III are likely to increase the costs of bank funds and, ultimately, the costs of borrowing. However, this ignores the risk-reducing benefits of lower leverage, which should reduce the costs of bank equity. Therefore, the effect of Basel III on the costs of bank borrowing is likely to be lower, as is frequently projected.

Benefits and Costs for the Financial System and the Real Economy

Arguably, the positive effects of increased capital requirements go well beyond those on individual banks and possibly extend to improved financial (systemic) stability and greater economic growth.

In particular, the ability of bank equity to absorb losses should play a key role in safeguarding the stability of the financial system. This is because a system that is characterized by more highly capitalized financial institutions should exhibit a lower risk of bank failures and banking crises. This argument is strongly supported by the Basel Committee on Banking Supervision (2010c), which estimates that a 2% increase in bank capital ratios should reduce the probability of a systemic crisis by about 2.9%.

Next to reducing the probability of a systemic crisis, increased capital requirements should also lower the expected costs of dealing with a banking crisis (Marcheggiano, Miles, and Yang, 2011; Berger, Herring, and Szego, 1995). These costs include losses in economic output when firms are unable to obtain financing for their borrowing needs, as well as the costs linked to bank rescues and government-sponsored bank recapitalizations. Further, increases in bank equity will make it less advantageous for bank shareholders to shift risk to regulators and taxpayers. This is because shareholders, having more equity at stake than previously, could play an important part in containing incentives to shift risk and will, thus, reduce the need for a bailout (Admati *et al.*, 2010).

However, the critics of tougher capital requirements point out that these potential systemic benefits do not come without costs. The most frequently cited example of such costs is the negative impact of higher capital holding on economic growth caused by a contraction in bank lending. According to this view, the increasing cost of financial intermediation that will result from stricter capital requirements will cause a contraction in the level of debt-financed investment and consumption. However, there are good reasons to believe that this effect will be of a relatively small magnitude. Recent analyses do not find a strong link between the lending choices made by large bank holding companies in the United States and their capital ratios (Berrospide and Edge, 2008).

Benefits and Costs Related to the Incentives Structure of Equity and Debt

It is likely that the benefits and costs of higher capital requirements also extend to the incentives they give to shareholders for risk-taking. This view is based on the notion that when banks operate with a high leverage ratio, shareholders will be tempted to favor risky investment decisions which (though optimal for them) are suboptimal from the point of view of other stakeholders and for society as a whole. The payoffs from equity for shareholders resemble those of a call option on the assets of a bank. On the one hand, shareholders benefit from high equity returns if risky investment strategies lead to success. On the other hand, the downside risk for shareholders is limited to the value of their equity. While this incentive problem is present in any organizational form that is characterized by limited liability, it is particularly pressing in banking, because the small amount of equity on the balance sheet of a bank relative to nonfinancial firms exacerbates the problem.

In contrast to shareholders, debt-holders do not benefit from the sort of increases in expected returns which shareholders may expect as they increase risk. Therefore, when leverage is high, shareholders may be tempted to make excessively risky investments to maximize the returns to equity at the expense of debt-holders (and taxpayers who will have to provide the funds to bail out failing institutions).

Next to affecting the risk preferences of shareholders and debt-holders, the capital structure of a bank will also have an effect on the risk preferences of bank managers. More debt (especially short-term, unsecured, and subordinated debt) may be employed as a tool to discipline bank managers (Admati *et al.*, 2010). The disciplining effect of debt is due to the fact that debt-holders will demand increases in yields—or will refuse to roll over or will even withdraw existing debt if they view a bank's activities as overly risky. Therefore, debt-holders will put pressure on managers to generate steady and positive cash flows and to avoid bankruptcy.

Jointly, the overall effect that Basel III, with its emphasis on additional equity and less leverage, has on bank risk-taking will depend on the extent to which decreases in leverage lower the conflict of interest over the riskiness of a bank between shareholders and debt-holders as well as between debt-holders and managers. The proposed changes will increase the importance of risk-neutral equity-holders, and because the proposals would force them to absorb a larger share of any losses that result from increased risk-taking, the influence of equity-holders on bank risk-taking may be somewhat tamed. This will mean that the overall result will be a strengthening of the influence of equity-holders over debt-holders. What exactly this means in terms of risk-taking by banks remains to be seen over the next years.

Summary and Further Steps

This chapter provides an overview of various changes that have been made to the Basel Accord for capital adequacy over the last 20 years. The benefits and costs of Basel III were examined as they pertain to banks, the financial system, and to incentive conflicts between the various stakeholder groups of a bank. Re-regulation of capital adequacy after the recent financial crisis has yet to be tested by time. This article is therefore able only to draw some initial conclusions and inferences and to paint a modestly positive picture of the various costs and benefits associated with Basel III.

Nonetheless, debates over the costs of bank funding that result from raising additional equity frequently ignore the effect that higher equity has on lowering the risk premium which bank creditors demand. Therefore, substantial increases in bank equity do not need to lead to anything like the sort of increases in bank lending costs that some commentators fear.

Further, because the capital structure of banks will change over the next years, the importance of equity-holders will increase relative to debt-holders. While equity-holders under Basel III will be forced to have more "skin in the game" than previously and should be less prone to risk-taking than the shareholders of less capitalized banks, it will be interesting to observe how the riskiness of banks changes as debt-holders become somewhat less important on a bank's balance sheet. Debt-holders who are risk-averse have been shown in the past to exert a risk-reducing effect on bank managers.

More Info

Articles:

Admati, Anat. R., Peter M. DeMarzo, Martin F. Hellwig, and Paul Pfleiderer. "Fallacies, irrelevant facts, and myths in the discussion of capital regulation: Why bank equity is not expensive." Research paper 2065. Stanford Graduate School of Business, August 27, 2010. Updated March 23, 2011. Online at: tinyurl.com/6dcoutl [PDF].

Basel Committee on Banking Supervision. "International convergence of capital measurement and capital standards: A revised framework." Bank for International Settlements, June 2006. Online at: www.bis.org/publ/bcbs128.htm

Basel Committee on Banking Supervision. "Strengthening the resilience of the banking sector." Consultative document. Bank for International Settlements, December 2009. Online at: www.bis.org/publ/bcbs164.htm

Basel Committee on Banking Supervision. "Basel III: A global regulatory framework for more resilient banks and banking systems." December 2010a. Online at: www.bis.org/publ/bcbs189.htm

Basel Committee on Banking Supervision. "Results of the comprehensive quantitative impact study." Consultative document. Bank for International Settlements, December 2010b. Online at: www.bis.org/publ/bcbs186.htm

Basel Committee on Banking Supervision. "An assessment of the long-term economic impact of stronger capital and liquidity requirements." Consultative document. Bank for International Settlements, August 2010c. Online at: www.bis.org/publ/bcbs173.htm

Basel Committee on Banking Supervision. "Global systemically important banks: Assessment methodology and the additional loss absorbency requirement." Consultative document. Bank for International Settlements, July 2011. Online at: www.bis.org/publ/bcbs201.htm

Berger, Allen N., Richard J. Herring, and Giorgia P. Szego. "The role of capital in financial institutions." *Journal of Banking and Finance* 19:3–4 (June 1995): 393–430. Online at: dx.doi.org/10.1016/0378-4266(95)00002-X

Berrospide, J. M., and R. M. Edge. "Linkages between the financial and real sectors: Some lessons from the subprime crisis." Working paper. Federal Reserve Board, 2008.

Calem, Paul, and Rafael Rob. "The impact of capital-based regulation on bank risk-taking." *Journal of Financial Intermediation* 8:4 (October 1999): 317–352. Online at: dx.doi.org/10.1006/jfin.1999.0276

Furlong, Frederick T., and Michael C. Keeley. "Capital regulation and bank risk-taking: A note." *Journal of Banking and Finance* 13:6 (December 1989): 883–891. Online at: dx.doi.org/10.1016/0378-4266(89)90008-3

Hakenes, Hendrik, and Isabel Schnabel. "Bank size and risk-taking under Basel II." *Journal of Banking and Finance* 35:6 (June 2011): 1436–1449. Online at: dx.doi.org/10.1016/j.jbankfin.2010.10.031

Hellwig, Martin. "Capital regulation after the crisis: Business as usual?" Working paper 2010/31. Max Planck Institute for Research on Collective Goods, 2010. Online at: www.coll.mpg.de/pdf_dat/2010_31online.pdf

International Monetary Fund. *Global Financial Stability Report*. April 2009. Online at: tinyurl.com/crs6d7 [PDF].

Jones, David. "Emerging problems with the Basel Capital Accord: Regulatory capital arbitrage and related issues." *Journal of Banking and Finance* 24:1–2 (2000): 35–58. Online at: dx.doi.org/10.1016/S0378-4266(99)00052-7 [PDF].

Kashyap, K., J. Stein, and S. Hanson. "An analysis of the impact of 'substantially heightened' capital requirements on large financial institutions." Unpublished working paper, 2010.

Marcheggiano, Gilberto, David Miles, and Jing Yang. "Optimal bank capital." Discussion paper 8333. Centre for Economic Policy Research, 2011. Online at: ssrn.com/abstract=1810296

Modigliani, Franco, and Merton H. Miller. "The cost of capital, corporation finance, and the theory of investment." *American Economic Review* 48:3 (1958): 261–297. Online at: tinyurl.com/7b5wwf6

Repullo, Rafael, and Javier Suarez. "Loan pricing under Basel capital requirements." *Journal of Financial Intermediation* 13:4 (October 2004): 496–521. Online at: dx.doi.org/10.1016/j.jfi.2004.07.001

Santomero, Anthony, and Daesik Kim. "Risk in banking and capital regulation." *Journal of Finance* 43:5 (1988): 1219–1233.

Santomero, Anthony M., and Michael Koehn. "Regulation of bank capital and portfolio risk." *Journal of Finance* 35:5 (1980): 1235–1244.

Sharpe, William F. "Bank capital adequacy, deposit insurance and security values." *Journal of Financial and Quantitative Analysis* 13:4 (November 1978): 701–718. Online at: dx.doi.org/10.2307/2330475

Website:
Basel Committee on Banking Supervision: www.bis.org/bcbs

Appendix 1: Credit Risk Assessment and Capital Adequacy under the Basel I Capital Accord

In the initial version of Basel I, bank assets had to be assigned to four categories with risk weights equal to 0%, 20%, 50%, and 100%, respectively. The highest risk weights were assigned to commercial, industrial, and credit card loans. The regulatory risk assessment extended, with some refinements, to off-balance sheet assets. These assets had to be transformed into an equivalent amount of on-balance sheet activities and then into risk-weighted assets (RWA) through the application of credit risk weights.

For instance, unused bank loan commitments over more than one year had to be converted into the equivalent on-balance sheet assets via the application of a conversion factor of 0.50 and, then, into RWA with the application of a weight equal to 100%. Thus, a bank's unused loan commitments for €1,000,000 had a corresponding value in terms of RWA of €500,000.

The regulatory capital ratio (CR), with a minimum requirement fixed at 8%, was defined as follows:

$$\text{CR} = \frac{\text{Regulatory capital}}{\text{Risk-weighted on-balance sheet total} + \text{Risk-weighted off-balance sheet total}}$$

The Basel I Accord also provided guidelines on how to quantify the amount of regulatory capital that appears in the numerator of the capital ratio. Specifically, regulatory capital consists of two components. The first, core (or Tier I) capital includes equity capital and reserves from post-tax retained earnings. The second, supplementary (or Tier II) capital consists of undisclosed reserves, revaluation reserves, general loan loss reserves, hybrid capital instruments, and subordinated debts.

Appendix 2: Credit Risk Assessment Under the Basel II Capital Accord

Under Basel II, banks have two options to quantify capital requirements for credit risk which differ in terms of their degree of complexity, sophistication, and implementation cost.

The Standardized Approach

The first option, the *standardized approach*, builds on the original risk assessment in Basel I to introduce more differentiation across risk weights. For instance, in contrast to the fixed risk weight of 100% under Basel I, under the standardized approach the risk weights for loans to corporations can range from 20% to 150% depending on the rating of the borrower. More specifically, a loan where the borrower is rated AA– or better attracts a risk weight of 20%, while the higher risk weight is assigned to borrowers with a rating of BB– and below. However, in order to be valid for regulatory risk assessment, only ratings from rating agencies (External Credit Assessment Institutions, ECAI, according to the terminology employed by the Basel Committee) that are recognized by the regulatory authorities qualify. In the case of unrated borrowers, the risk weights remain the same as those under Basel I (100%). Therefore, any differences in the capital requirements under the standardized approach compared with Basel I are only likely to be sizable for banks with many rated borrowers.

Differences in capital requirements might further increase due to a second key difference compared with Basel I: the introduction of a lower weighting scheme for retail credits. These are exposures to individuals or small businesses with a worth of less than €1 million. The exposure includes revolving credits and lines of credit (including credit cards and overdrafts), personal loans and leases (e.g. installment loans, auto loans and leases, student and educational loans, personal finance), and small business facilities and commitments. These exposures receive a risk weight of 75%. Therefore, banks with a business focus on these types of credit benefit from a substantial decline in their capital requirements compared with Basel I.

The Internal Ratings-Based Approach

In contrast to the standardized approach, the *internal ratings-based* (IRB) approach assesses the creditworthiness of borrowers using a bank's internal risk models. This evaluation is then converted into capital requirements on the basis of a risk-weighting function defined by the Basel Committee. In particular, the capital requirements depend on the one-year probability of default of the borrower (PD), the loss given default of the borrower (LGD; that is, the amount that the lender is expected to lose in case of default), the correlation of PD with the rest of the economy (R), the exposure at default (EAD), and the maturity of the loan (M).

The number of parameters that banks need to estimate via internal models differs between the "foundation" IRB approach and the "advanced" IRB approach. In the first case, banks need to estimate internally the PD and the EAD, while the remaining parameters are fixed by the Basel Accord. In the second case, banks need to provide an estimate also for the LGD and the maturity of the loans. Although the inputs necessary to determine capital requirements are the same across credit types, the risk-weighting function differs. Basel II includes adjustments in favor of small and medium-sized enterprises and a specific weighting function for retail credits.

Appendix 3: Capital Requirements for Global Systemically Important Banks under Basel III

The failure of large financial institutions during the financial crisis of 2007–09 has illustrated the need for special policy measures aimed at the so-called global systemically important banks (G-SIBs). These are financial institutions whose failure might undermine the stability of the financial system. As explained by the Basel Committee (2011: p. 1): "The rationale for adopting additional policy measures for G-SIBs is based on the cross-border negative externalities created by systemically important banks which current regulatory policies do not fully address."

Among the policy measures for the G-SIBs that were proposed after the crisis, the Basel Committee suggests the implementation of additional capital requirements. In particular, the Committee proposes to identify these additional capital requirements based on a systemic importance score which reflects the following five characteristics of a bank:

- cross-jurisdictional activity;
- size;
- interconnectedness;
- substitutability;
- complexity.

Finally, G-SIBs will be allocated into several buckets based on their scores of systemic importance, with varying levels of additional capital requirements applied to the different buckets. Specifically, the proposal suggests the categorization shown in Table 1.

Table 1. Categorization of G-SIBs in bucketing approach

Bucket	Score range*	Minimum additional loss absorbency (common equity as percentage of risk-weighted assets)
5 (empty)	>D	3.5%
4	C–D	2.5%
3	B–C	2.0%
2	A–B	1.5%
1	<A (cutoff point)	1.0%

*Scores equal to one of the boundaries are assigned to the higher bucket.

Correcting the Financial Crisis Failures of Asset–Liability Management (ALM) Risk Management

by Jérôme L. Kreuser

RisKontrol Group, Bern, Switzerland

This Chapter Covers

- ALM risk management has been widely accused of failing to anticipate and manage the financial crisis of 2007 and beyond. It did fail—but it didn't have to.
- A risk management framework was available that could have helped to mitigate the impact of the crisis on asset–liability portfolios.
- We discuss the ALM risk management failure factors spawned by the financial crisis and then outline a framework that corrects or mitigates most of them.
- We discuss tools that are under development to integrate into the framework to anticipate the next crisis.
- We provide two examples applied in 2008 and 2009 that mitigated the impact of the crisis.

Introduction

Asset–liability management (ALM) is a term whose meaning has evolved. Its use began in banks and insurance companies and has now extended to most financial institutions and corporations. The term risk management has also evolved. When we use the term "ALM risk management," we do so in the spirit of Zenios and Ziemba (2007).[1] We use the term ALM for managing institutional strategic objectives over a period measured in months and years. A suitable definition, consistent with Zenios and Ziemba (2007), is that:

"ALM is the allocation of financial and real instruments designed and managed to best obtain desired outcomes of measures of institutional strategic objectives."

The measures apply to future outcomes and therefore are defined on a probability distribution. One example of a measure is value-at-risk (VaR). Examples of strategic objectives include pension funds' funding ratios and smoothing of contributions; reinsurance firms' distributions of losses and returns; central banks' asset safety, liquidity, returns, and ratio of reserves to short-term debt; and commercial banks' returns, capital ratios, losses, and regulatory risks.[2]

We consider more than profits and losses or credit and interest rate risk. We consider risks that are aligned to an institution's strategic objectives and are analyzed together—not, as is often the case, in silos. We take a top-down view, looking at the strategic risks of institutions and not just the volatility of returns.

The causes of the crisis spawned factors that impacted asset–liability portfolios and resulted in risk management failures. The crisis was not caused by one factor alone, and it was not relegated to one geographical location. The crisis was a systemic, worldwide failure. The complex financial system had reached a point of instability and several triggers caused the system to fail, resulting in extreme draw-downs. Most existing risk management systems were incapable of handling the resulting factors individually and especially simultaneously.

In the sections that follow we provide a framework that corrects most of the identified risk management failure factors and summarizes the lessons that have been learned from the financial crisis. We show how the framework was applied in 2008 and 2009 and what the results were. Finally, we summarize and conclude.

The Crisis and the Failures

There is no shortage of suspects for causing or facilitating the financial crisis that began in 2007, which we will refer to as the "2007+" crisis. The indicted suspects include subprime mortgages, US spending, world financial imbalances, excess liquidity, the death of the efficient market hypothesis, greed, easy credit, animal spirits,[3] etc. The identity of the most culpable suspects depends on the judge. The main judges with differing views include the International Monetary Fund (IMF), the Bank for International Settlements (BIS) and Basel III, the US Congress, Joseph Stiglitz, etc.

BIS and Basel III on the 2007+ Crisis

According to the BIS and Basel III, the financial crisis was caused by:

- excess global liquidity;
- too much leverage;
- too little high-quality capital;
- inadequate liquidity buffers.

An IMF report (Merrouche and Nier, 2010) on the financial crisis highlights three suspects that contributed to the build-up of financial imbalances. These consisted of rising global financial imbalances due to capital flows, monetary policy that might have been too loose, and inadequate supervision and regulations. Thus, the strong conclusion was that:

> "Capital flows provided the fuel which the developed world's inadequately designed and regulated financial system then ignited to produce the firestorm that engulfed us all."[4]

The result of these imbalances and regulatory inadequacies spawned factors that impacted asset–liability portfolios, including compression of the spread between long and short rates, excessive leverage, excessive risk-taking, widespread moral hazard, and inadequate prudential policies that failed to address the systemic externalities of wholesale funding.

BIS and Basel III, in remarks from the chairman of the Basel Committee,[5] indicated that the causes of the financial crisis were primarily "...excess global liquidity, too much leverage, too little high-quality capital, and inadequate liquidity buffers." These were also factors that impacted asset–liability portfolios.

Other causes and factors included the procyclical deleveraging process, the interconnectedness of the too-big-to-fail institutions, and "shortcomings in risk management, corporate governance, market transparency, compensation practices, and supervision."

The Basel Committee on Banking Supervision also identified shadow banking as a key area where the crisis was propagated with structured investment vehicles (SIVs), the securitization process, off-balance-sheet exposures, hedge funds, etc. These spawned factors like the poor capital treatment for SIVs and other off-balance-sheet conduits, counterparty credit risk, contractual and reputational risks arising from shadow banking into liquidity, and poor regulatory and supervisory standards. Another factor was the inappropriate use of the VaR-based framework.

A BIS report (Basel Committee on Banking Supervision, 2009) identified the impact of weak stress-testing procedures. The factors were failures in scenario selection and failures to sufficiently test specific risks and products. Related factors were that the stress tests did not provide information on how much was likely to be lost, how to aggregate different risks, how to generate stress tests from macroeconomic shocks, and how to formulate the objectives of stress tests.

The Levin–Coburn Report (Levin and Coburn, 2011) on the financial crisis uncovered a "snake pit" rife with greed, conflicts of interest, and wrongdoing. Among these was new evidence showing that Washington Mutual[6] aggressively issued and sold high-risk mortgages to Wall Street, Fannie Mae, and Freddie Mac. There was a lot of evidence of wrongdoing.

The factors impacting asset–liability portfolios consisted of high-risk lending, inflated credit ratings, investment banks pushing structured finance that flooded the markets with high-risk assets, and collateralized debt obligations (CDOs) with low-quality assets.

Joseph Stiglitz said in a talk[7] that economics is supposed to be a science "...but most economists and economic models failed to predict the most important economic event of the last seventy-five years." On the other hand, "even though the mainstream models didn't work well there were many strands of economic theory developed over the last quarter century that I think do provide a lot of insight into what happened, provide alternative advice and better policy advice, and in other respects, better theories and models." He said that one of the examples of what went wrong was the accepted idea that there is no such thing as a bubble and, even if a bubble existed, that its effects could not be contained, and that you can't tell a bubble until after it breaks. In terms of models he suggested that we need to have theories of disequilibrium and of adjustment and learning both for the individual and at the systemic level. Furthermore he indicated the crisis provided clear evidence against the efficient market hypothesis, as well as the hypothesis of rationality. Other theories are needed, including those of "persistent deviations" from equilibrium. He suggested that models need to be constructed that have dynamics, stochastics, and general equilibrium and which include systemic risks.

The implication to be drawn from his talk is the importance of the link between microeconomics, macroeconomics, finance, and risk management.

The Levin–Coburn Report found a "snake pit" in the financial crisis rife with:

- greed;
- conflicts of interest;
- wrongdoing.

Prominent economists such as Brad DeLong, Paul Krugman, and Nouriel Roubini worried about the economy and the unsustainable succession of bubbles over the last decade, but they could not influence Congress, Main Street, or Wall Street. Most top managers did not want the "dancing" to stop, nor did they want to accept the pessimism of their risk departments. The primary factor that impacted asset–liability portfolios in these cases was miscommunication. Risk managers forced their top management to talk in "risk management speak" rather than in "executive speak," causing failures in communication in both directions. This was also facilitated by the poor use of tools like VaR.

René Stulz (2008) identified the main failure factors as the:

- failure to use appropriate risk metrics;
- mismeasurement of known risks;
- mismeasurement stemming from overlooked risks;
- failure in communicating risk to top management;
- failure in monitoring and managing risk.

Is a bubble predictable? The financial crisis has sometimes been characterized as a "black swan" (Taleb, 2010). This is a misdiagnosis. The financial crisis was a "dragon-king" (Sornette, 2009). The dragon-king hypothesis assumes that most crises are in fact endogenous. Dragon-kings are events that are identifiable and predictable in a probabilistic sense. We compare them with black swans in Table 1.

Table 1. Dragon-kings and black swans compared

Item	Dragon-kings	Black swans
Responsibility	Real trigger within or outside system	"Wrath of God"
Event	Identifiable	Unknowable
Impact	Extreme	Extreme
Quantifiable	Yes, probabilistically	No
Predictability	Probabilistically	Retrospectively
Mechanism	Feedback	Unknown
Location	Endogenous	Exogenous
Failure	Multiple	Single
System	Complex	Variable
Strategy	Early warning	Long put option and insurance

For example, bubbles may occur when indicators or prices move faster than exponential and exhibit transient unsustainable growth and then turn down. Professor Sornette[8] proposes that, to understand stock markets, one needs to consider the impact of positive feedbacks via possible technical as well as behavioral mechanisms, such as imitation and herding, leading to self-organized cooperativity and the development of possible endogenous instabilities. Thus the assumption is to explore the consequences of the concept that most of the crashes have fundamentally an endogenous, or internal, origin and that exogenous, or external, shocks only serve as triggering factors. In this sense, the true cause of a crash—and of the 2007+ crash in particular—should be termed a systemic instability. Work is ongoing[9] in the effort to characterize and identify these systemic instabilities and to integrate them into risk management. Other work is ongoing to identify asset bubbles.[10]

In Table 2 we summarize the factors that impacted asset–liability portfolios. There was no portfolio that didn't suffer from several of these factors simultaneously. The banking sector, the insurance sector, pension funds, funds of funds, central banks, sovereign wealth funds, and others all suffered from multiple attacks of these factors. We address the matter of correcting these factors not by suggesting how to improve the measurement of credit risk or equity pricing, but by identifying the framework in which these individual improvements must sit in order to be effective and to do so in a unified way.

Table 2. Summary of crisis factors impacting ALM portfolios

No.	Factor
I1	Spread compression
I2	Excessive leverage
I3	Excessive risk-taking
I4	Widespread moral hazard
I5	Excess liquidity
I6	Too little high-quality capital
I7	Inadequate liquidity buffers
I8	Procyclical deleveraging
I9	Interconnectedness of too-big-to-fail institutions[11]
I10	Poor treatment of SIVs and other off-balance-sheet conduits
I11	Counterparty risk increased
I12	Inadequate measure of liquidity risk and insufficient liquidity
I13	VaR-based framework failed
I14	Poor oversight and regulation
I15	High-risk lending
I16	Inflated credit ratings
I17	Market flooded with high-risk assets
I18	Failure of traditional economic models
I19	Poor communication between risk managers and management
I20	Failure to identify instabilities

In Table 3 we summarize the lessons learned from the financial crisis for ALM risk management and remedies. The bold numbers (e.g. **I5, I15, I17**) in Table 3 refer to the factor listed in Table 2 that is addressed by that lesson and the subsequent remedy.

Table 3. Lessons learned from the financial crisis for ALM risk management

Lesson	Remedy	Comments
K1: Track global imbalances	Use macroeconomic information	These were important and usually left out of risk management systems. (**I5**, **I15**, **I17**)
K2: Old theories failed	New theories or combine theories	EMH and rational expectations theories failed. We need nonequilibrium theories and others. (**I18**)
K3: Need better assessment of leveraging, etc.	Enhance stress-testing methodology	Stress tests and reverse stress-testing methods need improvement, especially in using non-normal processes. (**I2**, **I8**, **I11**)
K4: Poor communication between risk and senior managers*	Risk managers need to learn and apply "executive speak"	It was usually the other way around, resulting in missed or poorly understood messages in both directions. Need to capture "executive speak" in models. (**I19**)
K5: Estimate regime switching	Need to consider changing regimes	Regimes are changing and need to be factored into risk management. Processes need to be dynamic and changing. **(I8 and most others over time**)
K6: Mismeasurement of known risks*	Historical information is not enough	You need additional information such as expert views, theories, implied prices, and changing stochastics. (**I10**, **I12**, **I17**)
K7: Poor assessment of credit risks and high-risk lending	Incorporate extreme movement and non-normal processes	Prices and macroeconomic indicators do not generally follow processes with normal distribution but have fatter tails. (**I3**, **I13**, **I15**, **I16**)
K8: Herding and interconnectedness	Assess imitating and interconnectedness	Imitation in the sense of herding has been implicated in causing crashes in unstable financial systems. (**I9**)
K9: Need better risk measures	Allow processes to change over time and level and capture tails	They change in reality and need to be mimicked probabilistically. (**I10**, **I12**, **I13**)
K10: Assess liquidity buffers and off-balance-sheet exposures	A wider view of risk and risk control	Need to consider more of the risks that impact portfolios, such as uncertainties due to politics, fiscal problems, regulations, liquidity, counterparties, and derivatives, plus new risk measures to capture tail risk, etc. (**I1**, **I5**, **I6**, **I7**, **I13**)
K11: Inadequate supervision and prudential policies	Enhancing the risk culture	The risk culture generally needs improvement and better governance, along with better links to risk management. (**I3**, **I4**, **I14**, **I19**)
K12: Behavioral factors implicated in herding	Need to capture behavioral factors	They played a role in the crisis, such as imitation, herding, irrational behavior, etc. (**I9**, **I18**)
K13: Track and assess potential bubbles	Forecast bubbles	It is possible, and estimates should be incorporated into risk management. (**I13**, **I18**, **I20**)
K14: Improved risk monitoring*	Insight and analysis improvements	Improvements needed in stress-testing, sensitivity analysis, and insight and use of visualization. (**All**)

* Taken in part from Stulz (2009).

Economic instabilities played a major role in the crisis and spawned factors that impacted asset–liability portfolios, precipitating risk management failures. Economic factors and theories, including new ones, need to be integrated into risk management for ALM to prevent future occurrences of these failures.

The Framework and the Corrections

In order to measure and manage the factors that impacted asset–liability portfolios (Table 2), four things are essential: stochastics, dynamics, economic and financial theories, and risk integration. Scenario analysis is insufficient for measurement over a long period. This is because it is unrealistic to suppose that the portfolio decisions would not be revisited and revised over a longer period as new information becomes available.

Stochastics allow the prices, rates, and other factors calculated in the future uncertainty structure to change over time and level and capture extremes and fat tails. This allows changes in financial and economic regimes to be accounted for. These are essential components in calculating interest rates, credit spreads, prices, etc., for correcting the failures in the financial crisis.

Dynamics allow portfolio decisions to be revisited in the future as financial and economic conditions change. These are essential in correcting failures and managing portfolios, with the repricing of instruments based on the uncertainty structure.

Economic and financial theories, including new ones, address one of the most important recommendations made by Joseph Stiglitz: We need new theories as well as some of the old ones and models need to be constructed that have dynamics, stochastics, and general equilibrium, and which include systemic risks.

Risk integration is essential because multiple factors affect asset–liability portfolios at the same time. Without considering integration, the measures will be incorrect and, subsequently, so also the portfolio management.

Figure 1. Example of a scenario tree

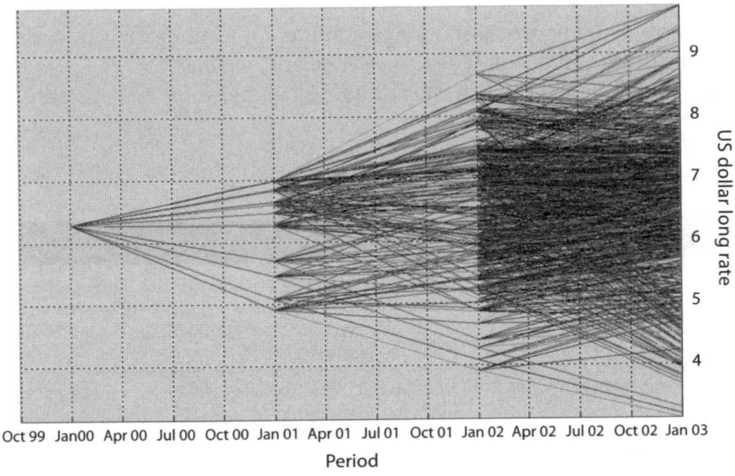

The scenario tree[12] describes the uncertainty structure or stochastics and dynamics of the factors considered. The tree will value the uncertainty in interest rates, exchange rates, equity prices, liquidity requirements, nonperforming assets, contingent liabilities, capital position, etc. The tree maps out the movements of the factors considered, along with their dependencies. An example of one factor from a tree is given in Figure 1.

The scenario tree must be built efficiently. It must be small enough to solve, yet big enough to capture the stochastics with a good collection of fat-tail scenarios. This can be done using variable probability branches, meaning that extremes can be added with fewer branches.

We judge the suitability of a tree by the quality of the decisions it gives and not necessarily by whether or not it matches distributions. The quality of the decisions it gives can be measured by assessing the impact of perturbations in the tree on solutions.

The dynamics of the branching tree are essential in the analysis of the problem. Dynamics matter whenever economic regimes undergo change or liquidity becomes an issue, transaction costs are included, future cash flows become uncertain, rare and special events occur, portfolios contain derivatives, and stochastics change. All of these happen in reality.

A decision model is placed on top of the tree that allows rebalancing of the decision variables at each branching node of the tree. The decision variables can consist of levels of assets and liabilities under consideration plus levels of capital, liquid assets, etc. The model can consist of equations defining the balance sheet and cash flows at each branching node. Constraints are defined for policy and legal issues. The assets and liabilities are repriced in the future based on the values in the tree. An optimizing objective function is usually specified.

Risk constraints are defined in a variety of ways. One way is conditional value-at-risk (CVaR) constraints that limit the expectation on the tail of the distribution and only on the downside. There can be multiple constraints of this kind.

We use the term dynamic stochastic programming (DSP) to describe a decision model with risk constraints that combines dynamics and stochastics. The use of theories is essential in building the stochastics, and risk integration is necessary in getting realistic results.

Table 4. Summary of how DSP handles the remedies

Remedy	How DSP can address it
Use macroeconomic information	These are entered as additional stochastic processes. When the tree is created, values of these macroeconomic indicators will be generated with dependencies on other factors, including prices.
New theories, or combine theories	Non-equilibrium theories and others can be entered via stochastic equation parameters or through econometric equations.

Remedy	How DSP can address it
Enhance stress-testing methodology	Stress tests and reverse stress-testing methods with stochastics and dynamics or stress scenarios can be entered.
Risk managers need to apply "executive speak"	It is easy to translate executive speak because you can define it in terms of objectives and risk constraints.
Need to consider changing regimes	Enter changing regimes by time and level on the scenario tree.
Historical information is not enough	You can enter expert views, theories, and implied prices by putting additional constraints on the parameters that generate the tree.
Incorporate extreme movement and non-normal processes	These can be done by triggering on processes depending on their time and level on the tree.
Assess imitation and interconnectedness	A DSP model is tailored to each individual institution and naturally avoids imitation.
Capture tails	This can be done to mimic correlation convergence, herding, concentration (in the case of multiple institutions), etc.
A wider view of risk and risk control	Uncertainties can be entered by changing stochastics and addressing issues such as political and other risks, including contingent liabilities; multiple risks can be controlled using CVaR constraints.
Enhancing the risk culture	The incorporation of DSP into the risk culture is easier because the terminology is oriented toward "executive speak."
Need to capture behavioral factors	This can be done by adjusting tree-generation factors.
Forecast bubbles	See references at end of chapter and incorporate scenarios coming from external sources.
Insight and analysis improvements	There is considerable flexibility because you have the complete set of stochastic scenarios.

Applying the Framework

When applying the framework, there are several points to consider.

- Ziemba points[13] to consider:
  - mean–variance is useful as a guideline, but do not use for ALM models;
  - need scenario-dependent correlations when you have extremes and a large drop;
  - use DSP when you have assets, liabilities, liquidity, taxes, etc., and a lot at stake;
  - do not be concerned with getting all the scenarios right, but try to cover the tails.
- Translate manager risk speak to analytics and not the other way around.
- Establish a robust risk culture that is mirrored by the analytics.
- Include more than history to create trees. For example, add in theories, implied values, and expert views.
- Need to consider regime changes and short- and long-term views.
- Assess bubbles/dragon-kings and include external stress scenarios.

- Add extremes or stress scenarios as contaminations to an existing tree.
- Need excellent visualization tools to build intuition and insight.
- Move slowly to a full DSP from, for example, mean–variance.

DSP has not become ubiquitous because of a number of myths that have wrongly hampered its general acceptance.

- *The "curse of dimensionality"*: It is usually assumed that only a tree of a few factors can be built. The reality is that using scenario reduction, large-scale solvers, efficient techniques to generate trees, and large workstations, a large number of factors can be included.
- *Underlying distributions must be righ*t: The reality is that it is not the distributions that are important but rather the solution and its stability.
- *Optimization solutions are uncontrollable*: The reality is that DSP models are very stable. Perturbations in the data do not usually cause major perturbations in the solution.
- *Long time to build a DSP model*: The reality is that with new technology and modeling languages it can be done quickly and the technology can be absorbed in-house.
- *DSPs are black boxes*: The models written in a modeling language are easily readable by a human and by a computer.
- *DSPs are not tractable*: They are easily built and solved with the technological advances now available. The examples here were solved on a PC.
- *DSPs are too complex*. In the past this may have been true, however advances in modeling languages, solvers, computing, and visualization techniques have greatly simplified them. Visualization and moving slowly from old frameworks to DSP are the keys to absorbing it.

Many applications of DSP in all financial sectors, including banking, can be found in the references at the end of the chapter. What makes the examples here especially interesting is that they were run during the height of the crisis and we can now look back and see how they performed.

DSP Myths

- The "curse of dimensionality."
- Underlying distributions must be right.
- Dynamics are not important.
- Optimization solutions are uncontrollable.
- Takes a long time to build a DSP model.
- A DSP model is a black box.
- Scenarios need to be correct.
- DSP is not tractable.
- DSPs are too complex.

We applied the framework to Norway's sovereign wealth fund, the Government Pension Fund Global of Norges Bank. As the name implies, it behaves much like a pension fund but there are a number of additional considerations. A different objective function is employed, which maximizes overall country welfare, and different constraints came into play. Another requirement is the need to include macroeconomic and micro-based concerns and constraints on sovereign wealth management. Macroeconomic concerns include issues arising from the country's currency management, debt management, and stability of the domestic financial sector. Microeconomic concerns arise from legal or disclosure constraints and constraints on the capacity of the institution. Specifically, this means that one may need to include commodity price behavior, resource depletion, import and export levels, fiscal issues, GDP, population growth/decrease, benchmarks, asset universe, or other factors.

Figure 2. Graph of predicted oil price for tree in the DSP for the Government Pension Fund Global of Norges Bank

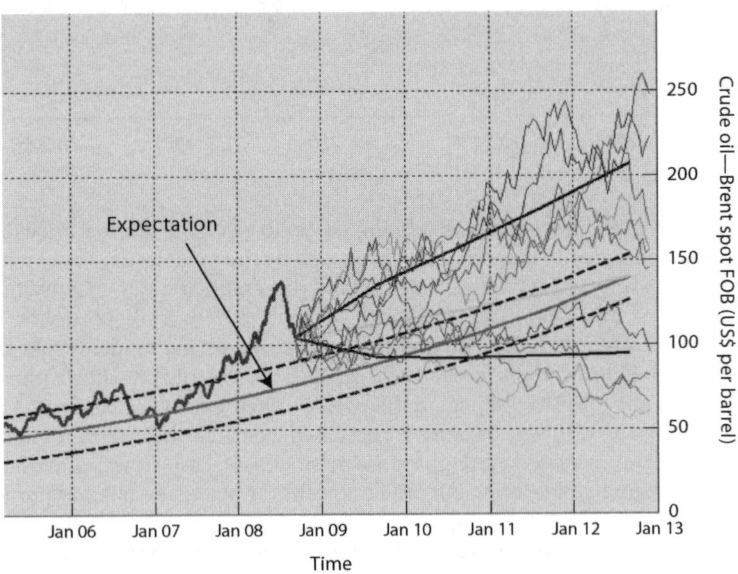

Projections cannot be based on history alone. In this model we added in two theories that have been widely considered. These are short-term momentum and long-term mean-reversion. In Figure 2 we see the resultant graph as it was projected on September 5, 2008, for the Brent crude oil price. The curve representing the expected price is indicated in Figure 2. The expectation generated for February 7, 2012, is US$125. The actual spot price on that date was US$117. These theories captured nicely the stochastics of the spot price and can be used for other instruments in asset–liability portfolios. We can even see a suspected bubble in the graph.

The objective function was expected wealth denominated in a currency basket designed to preserve the purchasing power of imports. Four currencies and 18 instruments along with oil flows, prices, and swaps were tracked on a tree over four periods. The instruments included bonds, equities, real estate, private equity, and inflation-linked instruments, all in currencies of euro, sterling, the US dollar, and yen.

Figure 3. Portfolio value comparison for Norges Bank Government Pension Fund Global

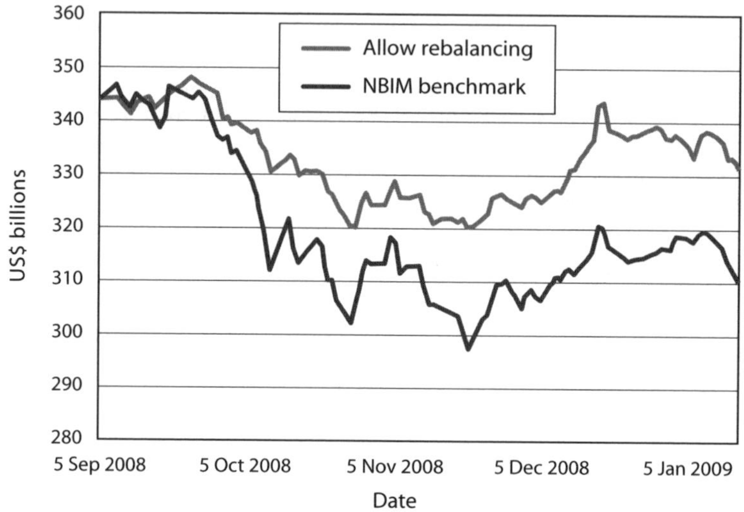

The graph in Figure 3 tracks the value of the portfolio given the original allocation (NBIM benchmark) compared to the allocation proposed by the model run (Allow rebalancing). The model was run on September 5, 2008, and presented at a BIS–ECB–WB conference in November of that year (Claessens and Kreuser, 2010). Both portfolios were then tracked to mid-January 2009. The allocation proposed by the model would have saved about US$20 billion over that period and with lower volatility. It didn't prevent a loss, but it strongly mitigated the impact of the crisis following the Lehman Brothers collapse. The reason it did so well was because it combined transient short-term momentum with longer-term mean-reversion, integrated risks, stochastic cash flows, downside risks on tails, and appropriate objectives. All are important for any asset–liability portfolio.

The next case study[14] is for India's central bank, the Reserve Bank of India (RBI). This focuses on translating executive speak into risk management speak to get results that are more understandable and usable by senior management. The RBI's institutional strategic objectives for holding reserves include:

- maintaining confidence in monetary and exchange rate policies;
- enhancing the capacity to intervene in foreign exchange markets;
- limiting external vulnerability by maintaining foreign currency liquidity to absorb shocks during times of crisis;
- providing confidence to the markets—especially credit rating agencies—to the effect that external obligations can always be met, thus reducing the overall cost to the economy or market participants;
- adding to the comfort of market participants by demonstrating the backing of the domestic currency by external assets.

Figure 4. Mean-reverting branching tree used in RBI study

Mean-reverting branching tree

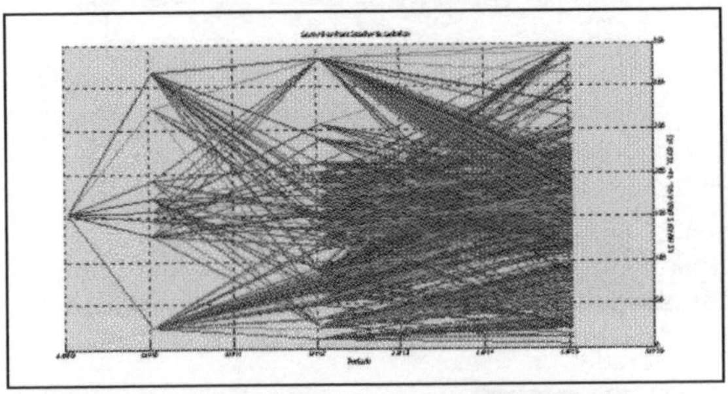

Reserve Bank of India application

- Seven risk constraints over three periods = 21!
- 27 factors estimated with dependencies
- Smart tree

Factors on tree (prices)

Australian money market fund
Cash in euros, sterling, US dollars, yen
Short bonds in euros, sterling, US dollars, yen
Long bonds in euros, sterling, US dollars, yen
Corporate bonds in euros, sterling, US dollars, yen
Deposits with Central Bank and Bank for International Settlements
Exchange rates (four)
External debt by residual maturity
Total external debt
Net domestic assets
Liquidity requirements
GDP

The model consisted of developing a tree of 27 factors over three periods with seven risk constraints, listed below, giving a total of 21 risk constraints. An example of a mean-reverting tree and a summary of the factors are given in Figure 4. The model optimized the level of reserves given the uncertainty structure on the tree and the risk constraints.

The institutional objectives were formulated as the following set of risk constraints:

- lower limit on the size of reserves—US$200 billion, adjusted for nominal GDP growth (%);
- lower limit on the ratio of NFA to (NFA + NDA) (where NFA is net foreign assets, NDA is net domestic assets);
- upper limit on the fall in value of reserves (%) in any period in US dollars;
- mark-to-market value of reserves not to lag behind the expected value, as measured in the composite currency aligned to its imports;
- foreign currency assets should exceed the amortization of external debt over the next 12 months;
- ratio of short-term external debt to reserves should not exceed a preset level;
- limit the liquidity at risk.

Figure 5. RBI study: histogram of shortfall in ratio of NFA/(NFA + NDA) for 2015

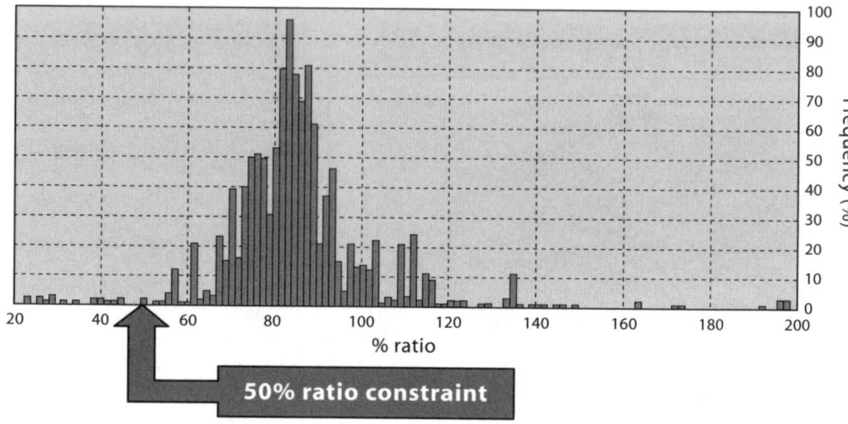

All the risk constraints were specified to limit the expectation on the tail with a given confidence level (CVaR constraint) and all were required to hold simultaneously at each period into the future. In Figure 5 we exhibit a characteristic histogram of a CVaR constraint that sharply cuts off the ratio at the lower end of 50%.

The model was run in January 2009 and the results published. We see in Figure 6 the distribution of reserves the model predicted for January 2012. The expected value was $US284.92 billion. The actual reserves were $US270.07 billion.[15] If we pick from the tree the scenario that closely matches what happened, we get a possible return of $US312.30 billion. Why did the model do so well?

Figure 6. Distribution of RBI reserves predicted by the model for January 2012

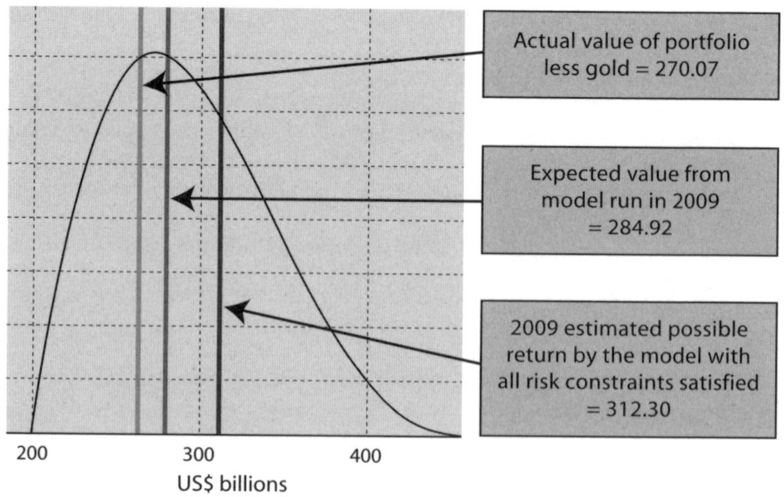

The better return was likely[16] caused by the model holding a larger percentage of assets in US dollars than was actually the case as the dollar appreciated and by a larger percentage in longer-dated US Treasuries than were likely held by the RBI. The model for 2012 posited an expectation of 3% of the portfolio in Treasuries with less than one-year maturity, 11% in one to three years, and 15% in three to five years. This turned out to be a good choice. This occurred because of upward momentum in Treasury prices, mean-reversion, and uncovered interest parity (UIP)[17] in exchange rates that were captured in the model. These factors and capturing "executive speak" are important in any asset–liability portfolio.

Several additional examples are given in the resources at the end of the chapter. The implementation of dynamic stochastic programming models even in the banking sector goes back to 1971 (Crane, 1971). A version of that model[18] was implemented in the World Bank by Kreuser and Lane in 1977. Many advances since then have made DSP much more tractable.

A banking sector model might be constructed as follows based on the RBI model.

1. Define the instruments used (assets, liabilities, and off-balance-sheet items).
2. Generate a stochastic tree of prices, rates, yield curves, cash flows, liquidity and capital requirements, and other economic factors (such as employment to compute default rates, for example) incorporating history, expert views, implied prices,[19] and theories (economic and financial).
3. Create a model of the instruments, pricing or evaluating them on the tree with a balance sheet and cash flows at the branching nodes, including transaction costs and taxes.
4. Create an objective, such as maximizing net equity with discounting over time on the tree.
5. Replace the risk constraints (CVaR) listed for the RBI model by:
   a. a limit on regulatory capital;
   b. a limit on systemic risks due to GDP and employment fluctuations with their impacts on default rates;
   c. a limit on liquidity risks;
   d. a limit on earnings-at-risk;
   e. a requirement for return on equity.
6. Add in policy, legal, accounting, and regulatory constraints.

DSP: A Summary

Some of the most important points regarding DSP are that it:

- provides a framework to address all the ALM risk management failures of the crisis;
- enables CEO strategic speak to be formulated with risks and results communicated back;
- tailors strategic objectives and constraints to each institution;
- emphasizes long-term performance over short-term gains;
- controls and integrates several risks simultaneously;
- incorporates extreme movements and non-normal processes;

- integrates multiple risk factors with history, views, theories, and implied prices;
- facilitates the inclusion of multiple new economic theories;
- is dynamic with assets, liabilities, and derivatives;
- allows processes to change over time and level as regimes change;
- allows you to shape the risk profiles of multiple integrated risks simultaneously;
- can handle all kinds of institutional strategic objectives, simultaneously if required;
- separates downside risks from upside opportunities;
- facilitates the formulation of models that are countercyclical.

Both models discussed here performed very well over time and corrected many of the ALM risk management failures of the crisis. Other examples of DSP models can be found in Zenios and Ziemba (2007) and in Zenios and Mulvey (1998), Ziemba (2003), and other resources listed at the end of the chapter.

Summary and Further Steps

- The failure of economics and of economic theories played a major role in the failure to predict the 2007+ financial crisis. These failures spawned many factors that caused ALM risk management to fail. No financial sector escaped.
- Implementation of the mitigation of the impact of these factors in ALM risk management requires models with stochastics, dynamics, various financial/economic theories, and risk integration.
- DSP is the ideal framework to incorporate all of these.
- Models with stochastics and dynamics allow the inclusion of theories of dragon-kings for predicting bubbles and regime changes.
- There are several risks, stresses, and dragon-kings that can impact ALM risk management in 2012. Major examples include unrest in the Middle East and North Africa, spiking oil prices, food cost spikes, debt crises in the United States and Europe, exchange rate problems, economic slowdowns in the world, economic distortions, inflation and deflation, bank failures, government risks and political risks, regulation changes, worldwide systemic risks, etc.
- All these require new strategic risk management tools for ALM. DSP provides the framework to implement these tools.

If you want to take the steps to move from mean-variance (for example) to DSP you should move slowly to absorb the technology. Below is a sequence of steps you can follow:

1. Change from mean-variance to generating scenarios. You can use means and co-variances to do so.
2. Modify scenario generator to include non-normal processes and adverse or extreme scenarios.
3. Modify scenario generator to get scenarios that change their stochastics over time and capture changing regimes (for example, correlations can change depending on time and level).
4. Add rebalancing dates and create a decision model based on the scenarios.
5. Create a scenario tree directly or by aggregating scenarios and you have full DSP.

More Info

Books:

Taleb, Nassim Nicholas. *The Black Swan: The Impact of the Highly Improbable*. 2nd ed. New York: Random House, 2010.

Zenios, Stavros A., and William T. Ziemba (eds). *Handbook of Asset and Liability Management*. Vols 1 and 2. Amsterdam: Elsevier, 2007.

Ziemba, William T., and John M. Mulvey (eds). *Worldwide Asset and Liability Modeling*. Cambridge, UK: Cambridge University Press, 1998.

Articles and Reports:

Basel Committee on Banking Supervision. "Principles for sound stress testing practices and supervision." Bank For International Settlements, May 2009. Online at: www.bis.org/publ/bcbs155.htm

Bhattacharya, Himadri, Jérôme Kreuser, and Sivaprakasam Sivakumar. "A sovereign asset–liability framework with multiple risk factors for external reserves management—Reserve Bank of India." Paper presented at the conference on "Portfolio and risk management for central banks and sovereign wealth funds" held jointly by the Bank for International Settlements, the European Central Bank, and the World Bank, November 2009.

Claessens, Stijn, and Jérôme Kreuser. "Strategic investment and risk management for sovereign wealth funds." In Arjan B. Berkelaar, Joachim Coche, and Ken Nyholm (eds). *Central Bank Reserves and Sovereign Wealth Management*. Hampshire, UK: Palgrave MacMillan, 2010. Paper first presented at the conference on "Strategic asset allocation for central banks and sovereign wealth managers" held jointly by the Bank for International Settlements, the European Central Bank, and the World Bank, November 2008.

Crane, Dwight B. "A stochastic programming model for commercial bank bond portfolio management." *Journal of Financial and Quantitative Analysis* 6:3 (June 1971): 955–976. Online at: dx.doi.org/10.2307/2329914

Lane, Morton, and Jérôme Kreuser. "Designing investment strategies for fixed-income portfolios." In A. V. Fiacco and K. O. Kortanek (eds). *Extremal Methods and Systems Analysis*. New York: Springer Verlag, 1980.

Levin, Carl, and Tom Coburn. "Wall Street and the financial crisis: Anatomy of a financial collapse." US Senate Permanent Subcommittee on Investigations, Washington DC, April 2011. Online at: tinyurl.com/6dhewck

Merrouche, Ouarda, and Erlend Nier. "What caused the global financial crisis?—Evidence on the drivers of financial imbalances 1999–2007." Working paper WP/10/265. IMF, December 2010. Online at: tinyurl.com/7x9zjzb

Sornette, Didier. "Dragon-kings, black swans and the prediction of crises." *International Journal of Terraspace Science and Engineering* 2:1(July 30, 2009): 1-17. Online at: arXiv.org/abs/0907.4290

Stulz, René M. "Risk management failures: What are they and when do they happen?" *Journal of Applied Corporate Finance* 20:4 (Fall 2008): 58–67. Online at tinyurl.com/yhdgahn [PDF].

Ziemba, William T. "The stochastic programming approach to asset, liability, and wealth management." Research Foundation of the Association for Investment Management and Research (AIMR), Charlottesville, VA, 2003.

Websites:

General

Cornerstone Research (see "Publications"): www.cornerstone.com

RisKontrol Group ("Papers" section has publications with further references): RisKontroller.com

See also the IMF, BIS, and World Bank websites.

More on DSP and CVaR

Committee on Stochastic Programming (COSP) stochastic programming community home page: stoprog.org

Stan Uryasev's "Publications" page on his University of Florida site has many papers on CVaR, all downloadable: www.ise.ufl.edu/uryasev

Crisis Prediction and Analysis

Financial Crisis Observatory, ETH Zürich: www.er.ethz.ch/fco

Financial Stability Board (FSB), Basel: www.financialstabilityboard.org

International Monetary Fund (IMF)—"IMF–FSB early warning exercise": www.imf.org/external/np/exr/facts/ewe.htm

NYU Stern systemic risk rankings: vlab.stern.nyu.edu/welcome/risk

Modeling Languages

AIMMS: www.aimms.com/aimms

AMPL: www.ampl.com

GAMS: www.gams.com

Webinars

Henry Stewart Talks—online seminars on "risk management for sovereign institutions": hstalks.com

Notes

1. The handbooks by Zenios and Ziemba (2007) describe theory (Vol. 1) and practice (Vol. 2) applied to banks, insurance companies, pension funds, personal finance, and general institutions.
2. For additional measures in the banking sector, see Jean Dermine in Chapter 11, Volume 2, of Zenios and Ziemba (2007).
3. "Animal spirits" is a term first used by John Maynard Keynes in 1936 to describe emotions that influence human behavior which can be measured in terms of consumer confidence. The term has been popularized in recent books describing how human psychology impacts the economy, finance, and the crisis. A new field of behavioral finance has evolved.
4. Speech by Mervyn King at the University of Exeter, January 19, 2010, and referenced in the report.
5. Remarks of Nout Wellink, chairman, Basel Committee on Banking Supervision, Kuala Lumpur, Malaysia, January 17, 2011.
6. Washington Mutual was a savings bank holding company and owner of the largest US savings and loan association until its collapse in 2008.
7. Address by Joseph E. Stiglitz entitled "Agenda for reforming economic theory" at the Inaugural Conference on "The economic crisis and the crisis in economics" held at King's College, Cambridge, Institute for New Economic Thinking, April 8–11, 2010. Online video at: tinyurl.com/6tr7v77
8. Head of the Financial Crisis Observatory and professor at ETH Zurich. See the Observatory's "Financial bubble experiment" online at: www.er.ethz.ch/fco
9. See www.er.ethz.ch/fco, RisKontroller.com and the Sovereign Crises Alert Transmitter (SCAT) initiative.
10. See for example, Robert Jarrow, Younis Kchia, and Philip Protter (2011). "How to detect an Asset Bubble." Online at ssrn.com/abstract=1621728
11. This issue is being addressed by the New York University Stern global systemic risk rankings under the direction of Nobel laureate professor Robert Engle (see tinyurl.com/89hb4zf). It can be incorporated into our framework.
12. Methods for building these trees are beyond the scope of this chapter but can be found in the More Info section.
13. These points are taken from Ziemba (2003). See the same reference for additional points to consider.
14. This is detailed in the paper by Bhattacharya, Kreuser, and Sivakumar (2009) and presented at a BIS–ECB–WB conference and subsequent publication.
15. See Reserve Bank of India website: www.rbi.org.in
16. "Likely" because we do not know the exact composition of the RBI portfolio, which is confidential.
17. Uncovered interest parity (or uncovered interest rate parity): if the interest rate on US dollar deposits drops relative to the euro, for example, then the exchange rate on the dollar will increase to move to parity and prevent arbitrage.
18. See Lane and Kreuser (1980).
19. These are prices whose values are implied by derivative valuation or other instruments.

Formulating a Contingency Funding Plan to Manage Liquidity Risks

by Gary Deutsch

BRT Publications LLC

This Chapter Covers

- How financial institutions can use their liquidity risk management program as the launch point for developing a comprehensive contingency funding plan (CFP) to address potential adverse liquidity events and emergency cash flow requirements.
- Guidance on establishing a CFP, management strategies for implementing a CFP, and steps for developing CFP liquidity needs and availability based on stress-testing.
- Conclusions and next steps, as well as an extensive list of reference sources for those looking to delve into this topic in more detail.

Introduction:

Managing the funding activities of a financial institution has become quite challenging as the global economy continues to develop economic linkages that can lead to unexpected volatility and systemic problems. The European Union, the United States, Asia, and other world economies have become connected through trade and currencies, and changing cultures and demographics such that it is no longer possible to focus solely on local or regional markets when planning for liquidity risk management.

Liquidity risk measurement and monitoring systems must, of necessity, look to worldwide economic linkages to understand how to assess current and prospective cash flows and to establish plans for funding sources and uses. Financial institutions need to establish a forward-looking approach to developing liquidity management strategies, policies, procedures, and limits to ensure that they draw on a diverse mix of existing and potential future funding sources.

Moreover, to protect against unexpected economic volatility and systemic problems, financial institutions need to hold adequate levels of highly liquid financial instruments free of legal, regulatory, or operational impediments to meet liquidity needs in stressful situations.

The Importance of a Contingency Funding Plan

A contingency funding plan (CFP) should describe the procedures that a bank or financial institution will implement to fund cash flow shortfalls that could occur in situations of stress or liquidity crises. To develop effective stressed or crisis-based CFP procedures, institutions must create plausible scenarios that simulate what could happen in various stress or crisis conditions.

CFP procedures must outline in sufficient detail areas such as:

- specific tasks and responsibilities, including decisions that must be made;

- timely and detailed liquidity information;
- alternative contingency funding measures.

CFP procedures cannot be passive. The procedures have to be tested, adjusted, and updated as market conditions, regulations, funding sources, business operations, and the capabilities of internal systems change over time.

Furthermore, because CFP procedures are derived from a financial institution's liquidity risk management (LRM) program, the procedures must be coordinated with the institution's overall asset–liability management program as well as with its central bank to avoid possible contagion effects that could disrupt the efficiency and stability of money market channels.

Consider the scenario presented in the case study as an example of how a minor problem can grow into a liquidity crisis if not handled according to a properly developed and executed CFP. This example will then be discussed in the remainder of the section.

Case Study

Bank Without an Effective Contingency Funding Plan

Bank A did not have an effective CFP. Negative news related to the bank's capital position caused sufficient concern about its viability that some depositors decided to move their accounts to a more stable bank. Although Bank A had plans approved by its regulator to raise additional capital, the limited run on its deposit base left it with a funding shortfall for which it had no prepared response. As a result, the press reported that the bank might not be able to fund a new loan to XYZ Corporation. As a result of the latest new report, the bank pressured its correspondents to assist with temporary credit lines, but since it did not have prior arrangements in place for this funding, it had to turn to its central bank for emergency funding. However, without an emergency funding plan, Bank A did not have sufficient collateral to support its funding shortfall.

More negative news was published and deposit withdrawals began to accelerate. Without an emergency funding source, the bank's correspondents were not able to support its deposit clearing activities or overnight cash needs. With matters growing worse by the day, and without detailed procedures to handle the growing funding shortfall, negative news prompted still more depositors to move their accounts and a run on the bank ensued. The run escalated and created a public relations problem for other banks in Bank A's markets. Bank A, unable to find funding sources to deal with its liquidity crisis, resorted to selling assets at fire-sale prices. What started as a minor capital problem for the bank became a liquidity crisis in its wholesale and retail markets and led to increasing uncertainty as to the viability of the bank.

In the example described in the case study, Bank A did not have a plan to contain the liquidity risk that it encountered. In developing CFPs, many institutions focus on methods to contain or limit liquidity risks so that they will not grow and get out of hand, as they did for this bank. Ideally, Bank A should have expanded its liquidity risk limits to go beyond just containing the risks that it encountered. It should have considered various types of liquidity shocks and how it could set CFP procedures in motion to absorb those shocks.

An effective CFP will consider the types of shock that could result in a liquidity crisis using scenarios like the one in the example. Often, describing possible scenarios can help management to think through what it would do if specific events occurred. For instance, when Bank A had a capital shortfall and obtained regulatory approval to seek new capital, it is unlikely that it would have associated a liquidity crisis with its capital plan. Yet, if it had used its cumulative experience to describe a sequence of events that could lead to a liquidity crisis stemming from a capital event, it would have been able to evaluate plausible ways to limit the impact of a minor liquidity problem and avoid a more severe problem that could lead to contagion effects. Each step in this process can be balanced against the institution's tolerance for dealing with related risks.

Overall, a CFP should address two major questions:

- Does management have a strategy for handling a crisis?
- Does management have procedures in place for accessing funds in an emergency?

A CFP should be required as part of a comprehensive liquidity risk management (LRM) program. A financial institution's LRM program should be based on comprehensive cash flow projections together with a funding plan that forecasts funding needs and funding sources under various market scenarios. If the LRM is forward-looking, a CFP will also be designed to deal with future events. Past liquidity crises are important to gaining an understanding of what could happen, but future events may not follow the same pattern. CFPs that are derived from forward-looking LRM programs work much better in the real world.

Given a forward-looking approach, the CFP should evaluate an institution's estimate of potential balance sheet changes that may result from various liquidity or credit events. The idea is to develop specific plans that uncover early warning signals of a potential liquidity crisis. Early warning signals are essentially a way to anticipate what could happen if events A, B, C, or D occur.

For instance, in the above example scenario for Bank A, event A was a capital deficiency. What could happen if Bank A experienced a capital deficiency was probably not a question that arose because the bank did not create a CFP. If it had, it would have explored the possible scenarios that could arise if a capital deficiency occurred. Although it may seem unlikely that a capital deficiency would trigger a liquidity crisis, one seemingly controllable event led to another which, in a short time, progressed into a serious liquidity crisis. It is the steps that lead to this possible progression that institutions must discuss and evaluate when formulating their CFP.

Once possible events and steps leading to a potential liquidity crisis have been evaluated, financial institutions should develop detailed strategies and tactics to prevent the escalation of liquidity concerns. If Bank A had initiated a public relations campaign to proactively dispel rumors of financial problems, it might have prevented the build-up of negative market impressions that eventually led to its liquidity crisis.

There should always be more than one alternative for dealing with events, especially considering that liquidity events may be taking an institution into uncharted waters. CFPs should highlight possible strategies for dealing with different levels of severity and types of liquidity stress events that may cause liquidity shortfalls. Ideally, institutions will link their CFP to specific stress-testing scenarios and proposed actions for accessing liquidity under each scenario. The proposed actions should be translated into specific procedures that should be followed in the attempt to close liquidity shortfalls, particularly in emergency situations.

Management Strategy for Implementing CFP Procedures

There are five key areas that management must focus on when developing a CFP implementation plan.

- *Policies and procedures* to ensure that information-flows to senior management remain timely and uninterrupted.
- *Division of responsibility* to ensure that all personnel understand exactly what is required of them during a period of liquidity strain or a stress event.
- *Information provided to markets and relevant parties* should be covered in a clear and decisive strategy that ensures a continuous stream of information to manage perceptions during times of stress.
- *A press and broadcast media communications strategy* should cover how management is to deal with press and broadcast media when negative information about the institution is disseminated.
- *A public relations strategy* should set out how management can deploy an effective program to counter rumors about the financial institution that may result in significant withdrawals of deposits.

When considering the division of responsibility, one alternative is to establish a crisis management team chaired by the institution's treasurer or chief financial officer or as part of the institution's asset and liability management committee (ALCO). Functional participants could include representatives from treasury, finance, risk management, ALCO, funding desks, and other significant business functions or geographic areas. This team should be responsible for implementing liquidity stress scenario simulations, developing market insight reports, conducting liquidity monitoring, and analysis and updating of the institution's liquidity management strategy.

Good communications are essential to ensuring that this team functions effectively and is prepared to defend the institution against a potential liquidity crisis. Therefore, the CFP should include the following information in the section on administrative policies and procedures:

- specific senior management responsibilities during a funding crisis;
- names, addresses, and telephone numbers of members of the liquidity crisis team;
- team members' assignments based on their office locations and functions.

If the liquidity crisis management team has to be activated, designated members should be contacted to initiate actions included in the CFP procedures. It may also be beneficial to conduct periodic tests or "dry runs" so that everyone has the opportunity to practice their role in the event of a liquidity crisis.

Steps for Developing CFP Liquidity Needs and Availability

Developing a CFP is a relatively new requirement for many financial institutions. As an extension of liquidity risk management practices, a CFP should be designed to help an institution to deal with both pre-crisis and crisis situations. Therefore, there are some basic concepts that need to be included in a CFP. These include determining how to measure the current availability of liquidity and routine needs, identifying and generating stress scenarios that could adversely impact the institution's funding availability and needs, and identifying indicators that can be used to establish an early warning system consistent with the stress scenarios.

Determining How to Measure Current Liquidity Availability and Routine Needs

When evaluating how liquidity should be measured, a financial institution can start by looking to its liquidity risk management (LRM) program to assess current risks. Here are some risk assessment questions to consider:

- Are liquidity needs and availabilities clearly identified and reported?
- Do reports related to liquidity needs and availabilities assist management with identifying liquidity vulnerabilities?
- Does the liquidity reporting system address how credit risk exposure, spread, and spread volatility impact market, funding liquidity, and counterparty risks?
- Are collateral, counterparty, regulatory, and legal entity issues updated routinely?
- Does the LRM program look to capital as a potential means of correcting or mitigating exposure to liquidity risk?

Expanding the risk assessment into the development of a CFP, here are some additional questions to address:

- Does the CFP stress-testing consider how financial and nonfinancial risks are often interconnected in unexpected, but significant, ways?
- Do scenario analyses and stress-testing analyses consider plausible but extreme circumstances?

When determining how to measure current liquidity availability and routine needs, institutions must consider their unique internal and external environment as well as the interconnectedness of financial markets. Despite the complexities that can arise, the measurement process ultimately is focused on an institution's ability to raise cash quickly at a reasonable cost. If asset sales are involved, there should be minimal loss of principal.

As stated earlier in this chapter, when measuring liquidity risks during development of a CFP, an institution is best served by adopting a forward-looking approach. An effective liquidity measurement process should therefore start with the institution's balance sheet and capture the following monthly and quarterly data:

- overnight funds sold;
- short-term investments;
- market value of securities less securities pledged;
- overcollateralized securities;
- government- and agency-guaranteed loans;
- cash flow due in 30 days or less from other securities;
- other liquid assets, such as interest-bearing deposits or money-market mutual funds.
- *Less:* Funds purchased, contingencies for deposit withdrawals (maturing certificates of deposit (CDs) and other withdrawals), and other liquidity reserves needed.

These balance sheet items represent the institution's core surplus or deficit of available funds to meet routine or emergency cash needs. When considering emergency needs in a CFP, the core surplus or deficit can then be enhanced with such items as:

- additional borrowing capacity;
- available board-authorized broker deposits;
- secondary collateral (municipal securities, corporate securities, equities);
- borrowing capability from the central bank.

Once the core and enhanced surplus or deficit are known, the next step is to determine how this number could change in the future. To address this issue, consider the following analysis of cash flow and availability of funds.

Cash Inflows

These balance sheet items are the core cash inflows that impact most financial institutions:

- loan payments and prepayments;
- loan sales;
- investment coupon payments and maturities;
- investment sales;
- new nonmaturity deposit balances;
- new CD balances;
- wholesale funding drawdowns.

As institutions grow larger, the list may become more detailed and complex, but the cash flow concepts remain the same. These cash inflows must be tracked over time and under various economic conditions to determine their sensitivity to market liquidity risks. This tracking could be as simple as producing graphs of these transactions, or the transaction data (cash flows) could be correlated with economic data to determine if there is a positive or negative correlation between the institution's cash flows and specific economic factors. Institutions often rely on judgment in this analysis process, especially since liquidity risk management should be forward-looking and not be solely based on historical data that may be misleading should market conditions shift beyond what the institution has previously experienced.

Cash Outflows

The same type of analysis as described above should be conducted for cash outflows. Here are the core cash outflow transactions to consider:

- investment purchases;
- loan originations and purchases;
- the decay of nonmaturity deposits (annual decay as a percentage);
- CD withdrawals;
- CD maturities less retention of CD maturities;
- wholesale funding maturities (borrowings with bond or loan collateral, brokered CDs, other borrowings).

When the cash inflows and outflows are added together, they reflect the institution's proforma cash surplus or deficit. These data should be tracked monthly and quarterly and on a cumulative basis.

The proforma net cash flow can then be compared to the institution's primary, secondary, and other funding sources. For instance, primary funding sources may include the cash inflows described above plus any collateral available to support additional funding or any remaining approved broker deposit cap. This availability of primary funds can be calculated as a percentage of the institution's total assets to provide management with a benchmark that can be tracked over time and possibly tied to the institution's liquidity risk management policy guidelines.

Secondary funding resources can include the current line availability and maximum line capacity for borrowing sources and availability of funding from the central bank. In addition, institutions may receive funding support from their holding company if the organization is so structured.

Any other borrowing capacity not mentioned above should also be factored into the funds availability analysis process.

Identifying Indicators that Can Be Used to Establish an Early Warning System Consistent with the Stress Scenarios

Stress scenarios are discussed later in this chapter, but before evaluating what to stress-test, institutions must settle on how they will interpret what they learn. For instance, if under stressed conditions it appears that the institution would deplete its available collateral to support wholesale borrowing, should management consider the collateral situation as a warning sign that CFP procedures should be invoked? Or are there other cash flow trends and fund availability issues that need to be considered before CFP procedures are initiated?

Warning signals or risk indicators can be triggers for CFP actions, but institutions must think through which indicators work best for them and when an indicator represents a trigger or call to action. There is no one-size-fits-all approach that management can use to decide on indicators and triggers. This is because a CFP should not be a boilerplate rehash of what another institution decided worked for them. CFPs should be institution-specific and be tailored to operating systems, management philosophies, local, regional, national, and international market conditions, and customer demographics. Each institution will have a unique balance sheet risk profile, so choose measures that work best in your environment.

In fact, appropriate indicators and triggers may already be in use in your management and board meeting reports. For instance, a liquidity early warning system could consider such operating liquidity measures as loan and investment collateral levels, as discussed in the previous section. Institutions that need to maintain access to brokered deposit markets should track their regulatory capital status. If increased funding needs are projected in stress scenarios, then deposit trends compared to loan growth could be a useful indicator and potential trigger within the CFP.

Here are some sample indicators to consider when evaluating liquidity risk stress tests to use in developing and updating an institution's CFP.

Cash flows:

- cash flow surplus plus additional availability from wholesale borrowing and brokered deposit lines;
- cash flow surplus plus available loan collateral;
- net cash flow surplus as a percentage of total assets.

Investment securities:

- total available investment securities collateral plus short-term investments divided by total assets;
- increases or decreases in the fair value of investment securities available as collateral.

Loans:

- total available loan collateral for wholesale borrowing divided by total assets;
- material short-term increases in the loan-to-deposit ratio;
- significant increases in loan line of credit utilization as a percentage of committed amounts;
- significant increases in the amount of adversely classified loans for regulatory purposes;
- material increases in the amount of nonperforming loans as a percentage of total loans by category;
- material increases in the amount of nonperforming loans as a percentage of tangible capital.

Deposits:

- material increases or decreases in nonmaturity deposit balances.

Capital:

- Basel II, Basel III, and regulatory capital ratios.

On the negative side of stress tests, if credit conditions are projected to worsen, then track loan impairment, loan loss provisions, troubled debt restructurings, foreclosures, and related collateral sales and charge-offs and include them in your liquidity risk management analyses.

> Stress tests should be updated when market and economic conditions change and the CFP should be modified to include the results of these new stress tests when warranted.

Institutions that show net operating losses in stress scenarios should consider the possibility that they may also suffer from a reduced availability of funds due to a decline in the value of collaterals, among other factors. When the quality of assets on an institution's balance sheet deteriorates, there is often a greater potential for regulatory intervention. If stress scenarios indicate this potential, this situation could represent a red-flag trigger that should be integrated into the CFP, along with detailed procedures for risk mitigation alternatives. Some early warning indicators that could be considered red-flag indicators that may significantly reduce fund availability include:

- material adverse changes in wholesale borrowing lines, such as line reductions, increased collateral restrictions, or term-to-maturity restrictions;
- a downgraded credit rating or regulatory risk rating;
- inability to access the brokered CD market.

Institutions will need to experiment with the above indicators by conducting multiple stress tests to determine which represent the best triggers to use when implementing CFP emergency procedures. Also, stress tests should be updated when market and economic conditions change, and the CFP should be modified to include the results of these new stress tests when warranted.

Creating Stress Scenarios that Could Adversely Impact the Institution's Funding Availability and Needs

Stress tests should be conducted to determine how and when the institution's liquidity position may become impaired. Guidelines for developing stress tests will depend on the institution's risk profile based on current assessments of interest rate risk, liquidity risk, earnings performance, and regulatory capital position. Tests should be designed to review the impact of specific liquidity events that may occur at various crisis levels, such as moderate, significant, and severe. To do this, one liquidity assumption at a time is input into the institution's asset–liability management (ALM) model. This is called sensitivity testing—only one assumption is changed and all other model assumptions remain the same. Therefore, the model output tests the sensitivity of the institution's liquidity to that single assumption.

Here are some examples of assumptions that can be changed in an ALM model:

- a significant decline in investment security collateral values;
- credit issues that result in the need to sell loan assets at a substantial loss;
- significant tightening by wholesale lenders of collateral standards that reduce borrowing capacity;
- a material increase in deposit outflows;
- a significant reduction in capital that reduces access to brokered CD markets.

In addition to changing just one assumption at a time to conduct sensitivity stress-testing, consider inputting several of the types of assumptions listed above to determine if and when the institution may have a severe liquidity need that would require borrowing from the central bank.

Other sample stress test assumptions to consider are as follows:

- reductions in the correspondent credit lines available and counterparty limits;
- inability to draw down on precommitted lines;
- increased "haircuts" and collateral calls;
- increased utilization of credit commitments;
- currency conversion issues.

According to the European Central Bank's (2008) report "EU banks' liquidity stress testing and contingency funding plans," institution-specific assumptions should be supplemented with stress assumptions related to market-wide events such as:

- geographical liquidity issues during local, regional, and global liquidity crises;
- systemic issues in major financial centers, emerging markets, local money markets, or retail deposit markets such as the closure of key funding markets—including bond and covered bond markets, unsecured and secured interbank markets, and securitization markets;
- negative economic indicators related to an increase in bond yields, a drop in stock prices, a rise in credit spreads, a rise in short-term interest rates, or appreciation/depreciation of the domestic currency;
- a market perception that can lead to an acceleration of stress severity from mild to severe without a clear underlying cause;
- a clarification in the market perception of causes of stress based on such events as a subprime market liquidity crisis, government crisis or change in monetary policy, sudden and deep economic recessions, or the default of a primary market counterparty.

Furthermore, as liquidity risk increases, an institution may be faced with stress assumptions such as:

- repo markets and unsecured interbank markets are closed;
- marketable securities cannot be sold immediately—and when a sale takes place the price is lower than a recent fair-market value estimate;

- credit lines granted are drawn by corporate clients;
- loan securitizations cannot be completed;
- the commercial paper and certificate of deposit markets are in turmoil and not accessible as a source of funds;
- large demand deposit accounts are drawn down;
- the stability of retail deposits decreases substantially;
- foreign exchange markets create cross-border liquidity risk issues;
- no access to capital market funding.

The time horizon for stress tests with the types of assumptions described above should cover from one month up to 12 months in the future. Generally, a CFP should look out over a one- to six-month time period since that time horizon defines the amount of time it may take to evaluate CFP indicators, identify a trigger, and initiate procedures as defined in the CFP. It is important to be prepared to take quick, decisive actions based on predetermined and preapproved CFP plans that have been tested often to ensure their viability should there be a call to action.

Assumptions for longer time periods will become more strategic and should only be considered in the context of the institution's liquidity risk management program and strategic plans.

Overall, the information you should expect to derive from stress-testing is rooted in what can go wrong, how it can go wrong, and how badly can it go wrong in terms of your institution's liquidity. Through stress-testing, you should be able to determine what your institution can do well in advance of a severe liquidity crisis to minimize the damage that may result from even the worst-case scenario. The CFP should use stress-test results together with risk indicators, red flags, and triggers to identify opportunities for rapid and effective responses to liquidity risks. This process should assist management in making a smooth transition from benign conditions to stress conditions and help to identify the suitability and adequacy of resources available to deploy during a stress event until planned remedial actions are implemented.

Summary and Further Steps

Developing an effective CFP is an important extension of an institution's liquidity risk management program. Issues that should be considered in structuring a CFP include the following.

- Ensuring that the organizational level at which the CFP is set up does not leave any gaps in the coverage.
- Establishing procedures that stress the importance of prompt decision-making.
- Making sure that decision-makers have quick access to timely and detailed liquidity information.
- Including diversified funding sources and funding maturities in the CFP.
- Giving consideration to the potentially destabilizing second-round effects on markets from liquidity-saving measures and asset sales.

- Reducing or avoiding potential contagion effects at the money-market level that stem from liquidity problems at money-center banks by maintaining the institution's role at the money-market level even in times of stress.
- Providing for and testing credible communication strategies and effective internal procedures consistent with cash flow projections and stress tests.
- Ensuring timely and comprehensive communication with regulators and central banks in periods of stress.

According to the ECB (2008) report referred to earlier in the chapter, experiences with liquidity stress tests and CFPs during the severe recession indicated that there was substantial room for improvement. Some of the areas where improvement was warranted are listed here.

- Recourse to central bank liquidity facilities in CFPs should be limited only to those which are routinely provided. Emergency facilities should not be relied on in CFPs. In addition, potential reputational costs associated with borrowing from the central bank in stress situations should be taken into account.
- When identifying "fail-safe" refinancing sources for inclusion in CFPs, the necessary operational arrangements have to be in place in order to access those sources easily during episodes of market turbulence. This implies regular and thorough testing and plausibility checks, with a view to potentially revising and updating the CFP in the light of changing conditions inside or outside the bank.
- During the recent turmoil some banks encountered difficulties in selling assets or pledging assets in secured lending. Regularly testing the capacity of liquid assets to actually generate positive cash flows might not only prove useful in its own right, but should also improve the identification of available and easily locatable liquid assets within a banking group in times of stress.

Institutions that are creating or updating their CFPs should give consideration to these liquidity risk issues. More resources are given in the More Info section to assist readers in developing an effective CFP.

More Info

Articles:

Longstaff, Francis A. "The flight-to-liquidity premium in U.S. Treasury bond prices." *Journal of Business* 77:3 (July 2004): 511–526. Online at: www.jstor.org/stable/10.1086/386528

Huberman, Gur, and Dominika Halka. "Systematic liquidity." *Journal of Financial Research* 24:2 (Summer 2001): 161–178.
Online at: www.gsb.columbia.edu/whoswho/getpub.cfm?pub=1815 [PDF].

Reports:

Basel Committee on Banking Supervision. "Principles for sound liquidity risk management and supervision." Bank for International Settlements, September 2008.
Online at: www.bis.org/publ/bcbs144.htm

Basel Committee on Banking Supervision. "Principles for sound stress testing practices and supervision." Bank for International Settlements, May 2009.
Online at: www.bis.org/publ/bcbs155.htm

Biais, Bruno, Fany Declerck, James Dow, Richard Portes, and Ernst-Ludwig von Thadden. "European corporate bond markets: Transparency, liquidity, efficiency." Centre for Economic Policy Research report. City of London Corporation, May 2006. Online at: www.cepr.org/PRESS/TT_CorporateFULL.pdf

Bühler, Wolfgang, and Monika Trapp. "Time-varying credit risk and liquidity premia in bond and CDS markets." Working paper no. 09-13. Centre for Financial Research, October 2009. Online at: tinyurl.com/7k629v7 [PDF].

Chen, Long, David A. Lesmond, and Jason Wei. "Bond liquidity estimation and the liquidity effect in yield spreads." December 2002. Online at: tinyurl.com/86bjlxh [PDF].

Chen, Yaru. "What explains credit default swaps bid–ask spread?" Master's thesis. Singapore Management University, 2007. Online at: tinyurl.com/796637c [PDF].

Erigero, David, Rick Miller, Bonn Phillips, and Michael Cawthorn. "Sound liquidity risk management in a challenging environment." Federal Reserve Bank of San Francisco and Federal Deposit Insurance Corporation, October 2008. Online at: tinyurl.com/6tcdzco [PDF].

European Central Bank. "EU banks' liquidity stress testing and contingency funding plans." November 2008. Online at: tinyurl.com/84q2efd [PDF].

Financial Services Authority. "Strengthening liquidity standards, including feedback on CP08/22, CP09/13, CP09/14." Policy statement 09/16. October 2009. Online at: www.fsa.gov.uk/pubs/policy/ps09_16.pdf

Fragnière, Emmanuel, Nils S. Tuchschmid, and Qun Zhang. "Liquidity adjusted VaR model: An extension." Haute Ecole de Gestion de Genève, 2008. Online at: campus.hesge.ch/tuchschmidn/pdfs/LiquidityVaR.pdf

Friewald, Nils, Rainer Jankowitsch, and Marti Subrahmanyam. "Illiquidity or credit deterioration: A study of liquidity in the US corporate bond market during financial crises." July 2009. Online at: archive.nyu.edu/bitstream/2451/28293/2/wp9.pdf

Han, Song, and Hao Zhou. "Nondefault bond spread and market trading liquidity." Federal Reserve Board, April 2007. Online at: www.fdic.gov/bank/analytical/cfr/2007/apr/liq.pdf

Kunghehian, Nicolas. "Stress testing for liquidity risk: The impact of the new regulations." Moody's Analytics, November 2010. Online at: tinyurl.com/7zdecqo [PDF].

Matten, Chris. "Stress testing liquidity and the contingency funding plan." PricewaterhouseCoopers, PRMIA members' meeting, February 2009. Online at: tinyurl.com/cyq73p [PDF].

Molitor, Philippe. "The development of robust and internationally consistent approaches for liquidity supervision: The current state of international initiatives." Money Market Contact Group, European Central Bank, September 2009. Online at: tinyurl.com/7eovddc [PDF].

Muranaga, Jun, and Makoto Ohsawa. "Measurement of liquidity risk in the context of market risk calculation." In "The measurement of aggregate market risk." CGFS publication no. 7. Bank for International Settlements, November 1997; pp. 193–214. Online at: www.bis.org/publ/ecsc07.htm

Office of the Comptroller of the Currency, Board of Governors of the Federal Reserve System, Federal Deposit Insurance Corporation, Office of Thrift Supervision, and National Credit Union Administration, with the Conference of State Bank Supervisors. "Interagency policy statement on funding and liquidity risk management." March 2010. Online at: tinyurl.com/77wq8hh [PDF].

Schwarz, Krista. "Mind the gap: Disentangling credit and liquidity in risk spreads." October 2010. Online at: finance.wharton.upenn.edu/~kschwarz/Spreads.pdf

Stragiotti, Franco. "Stress testing and contingency funding plans: An analysis of current practices in the Luxembourg banking sector." Working paper no. 42. Banque Centrale du Luxembourg, December 2009. Online at: tinyurl.com/85pfpgk [PDF].

Zhen Qi, Claudia, K. R. Subramanyam, and Jieying Zhang. "Accrual quality, bond liquidity, and cost of debt." Marshall School of Business, University of Southern California, August 2010. Online at: tinyurl.com/6ngrje9 [PDF].

Funds Transfer Pricing: Beyond the Global Banking Crisis

by Jean Dermine

INSEAD, Fontainebleau, France

This Chapter Covers

- The evaluation of profit on bank loans and deposits.
- A review of the standard methodology used to identify the funds transfer price.
- A call to move to a more advanced funds transfer pricing methodology to take into account:
  - rationing on the interbank market;
  - the build-up of a costly Basel III contingency portfolio of liquid assets;
  - the credit risk of specific assets.
- As opacity of banking transactions disappears over time, a call to distinguish short-term profit evaluation from long-term evaluation.

Introduction

Funds transfer pricing (FTP) is used to evaluate the profitability of deposits and loans. The issue that concerns on-balance sheet banking is as follows. When one evaluates the profitability of deposits one knows the cost, the interest paid on deposits, and the operating expenses allocated to deposits such as employee time and IT expenses. However, the choice of a return on deposits is more problematic because deposits are used to finance various types of assets: consumer loans, corporate loans, interbank assets, bonds, and fixed assets. A revenue, a funds transfer price, must be identified to remunerate deposits. The problem for loans is symmetrical. One knows the return on loans—that is, the interest income net of expected bad debt expense—but not their funding costs. The reason is that banks use several sources of funds to finance assets: demand deposits, savings deposits, time deposits, corporate deposits, interbank deposits, bonds, and subordinated debt. Again, there will be a need for a specific funds transfer price to evaluate the cost of funding loans.

A *foundation* approach, which is used around the banking world, is presented first. Next, we argue that the global financial crisis has focused attention on issues that hitherto have often been ignored: rationing on the interbank market, the creation of a Basel III contingency liquidity buffer, and the necessity to adjust funds transfer prices to take into account the credit-riskiness of the assets. An *advanced* approach to FTP is needed, and a methodology to do this is presented in the second part.

Foundation Approach to Funds Transfer Pricing

The foundation approach to funds transfer pricing used around the world can be represented as in Figure 1. Here, the horizontal line represents the market rate—that is, the interest rate observed on the interbank market (Libor).[1] The line is horizontal as this interest rate is set on large international markets and is independent of the volume of transactions initiated by the bank. The other two lines represent the marginal income on loans and the marginal cost of deposits. When a bank wishes to increase its loan portfolio, the expected income on an additional dollar of loan (the marginal or incremental income) goes down because the bank needs to reduce the interest rate to attract that additional dollar of loan, or because the bank is willing to accept loans of decreasing quality.[2] Similarly, the cost of an additional dollar of deposits (the marginal or incremental cost of deposits) goes up because the bank needs to raise the deposit rate to attract the additional dollar of deposits, or because the bank needs to open more expensive branches in remote areas.[3]

Figure 1. Funds transfer pricing in liquid markets

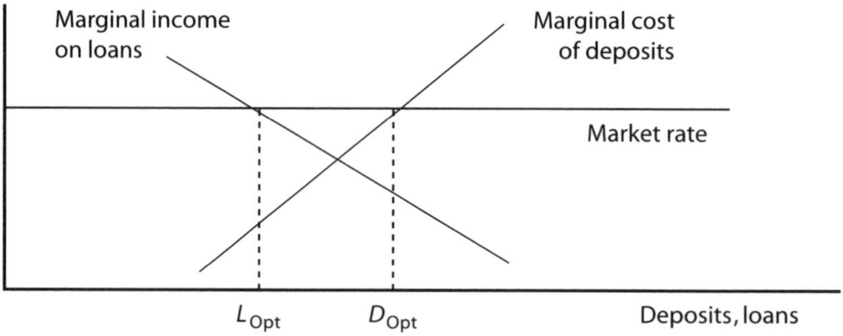

In Figure 1 the optimal volume of deposits, D_{Opt}, is reached when the marginal cost of deposits is equal to the opportunity market rate. You would not want to go beyond D_{Opt} because the incremental cost of deposits would be higher than the return earned on money markets.[4] Similarly, the optimal volume of loans, L_{Opt}, is reached when the marginal revenue from loans is equal to the marginal investment return, the market rate.[5] One would not go beyond L_{Opt} because the incremental expected return on new loans will be lower than the return available on money markets.

Thus, one sees a *separation* between the lending and funding decisions. The separation theorem states that one must price loans and deposits with reference to the market rate and these decisions are independent of one another. The difference between the optimal volumes of deposits and loans, $D_{Opt} - L_{Opt}$, is the net position in treasury assets and interbank assets (or bonds). In Figure 1 it is positive, with deposits exceeding the volume of loans. The bank is a net lender in the market. But it could be negative, with the bank being a net borrower. This is illustrated in Figure 2. Here the difference between the volume of loans and that of deposits, $L_{Opt} - D_{Opt}$, must be funded in the money market.

During the economic expansion observed in many countries of the world from 2003 to 2007, banks expanded their loan books massively, relying on market funding when the loan book exceeded the deposit base. The loan-to-deposit ratio exceeded 100% in quite a few countries, such as the United Kingdom, Greece, Portugal, and Spain. The underlying assumption was that market-based funding, such as interbank deposits or certificates of deposit (CDs), would always be available to finance the illiquid loan books.

Figure 2. Funds transfer pricing in liquid markets

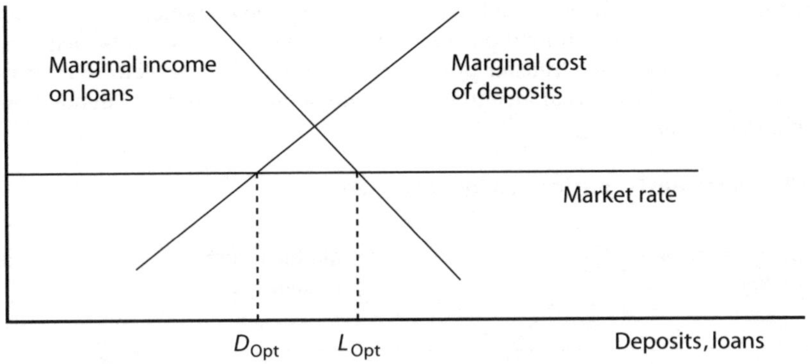

The global financial crisis that started in July 2007 proved this assumption wrong when the interbank markets froze after Bear Stearns' announcement that it had to refinance two of its structured investment vehicles. Banks rediscovered liquidity risk and the need to price this source of risk, and this led to a review of the funds transfer pricing methodology.

Advanced Approach to Funds Transfer Pricing

The interbank (or bond) rate has been in use around the world as the relevant funds transfer price for more than 20 years. The global financial crisis has brought to attention the fact that in specific circumstances an *advanced* funds transfer pricing system is needed. Three such situations are analyzed below: rationing on the interbank market, the need to build up a Basel III contingency liquidity buffer, and the need to adjust to the credit-riskiness of the asset.

Rationing on the Interbank Market

In Figure 2, the optimal volume of loans is larger than that of deposits. This implies a net borrowing on the interbank market. The crisis has called to attention that interbank funding is volatile, and in some countries, such as Greece or Ireland, that face a sovereign debt crisis, local banks have been excluded from the international money markets. In such a situation, loans cannot exceed deposits unless a central bank is willing to fund the gap. It must be noted that this situation of rationing on the interbank market is quite novel in countries belonging to the Organization for Economic Co-operation and Development (OECD), but that it has been frequently observed in emerging markets with less developed liquid interbank markets.

In Figure 3, the starting position is identical to that of Figure 2. If deposits and loans are chosen with reference to the market rate, the optimal volume of loans exceeds that of deposits, the shortfall of funds being met on the interbank market. As this will not be feasible in a situation in which no lender is willing to provide funds at a reasonable market rate, the bank needs to increase its volume of deposits and/or reduce its volume of loans. The optimal point is achieved where the line representing the marginal income on loans crosses that of the marginal cost of deposits. At this point, the volume of loans matches the volume of deposits, and there is no reason to seek further deposits as the marginal cost would exceed the marginal income on loans. As shown in Figure 3, the optimal portfolio of loans and deposits can be achieved by artificially raising the funds transfer price, i.e. the straight line labeled "market rate," thus creating the right internal incentives to ensure a larger volume of deposits and a lower volume of loans.

Figure 3. Funds transfer pricing in illiquid markets

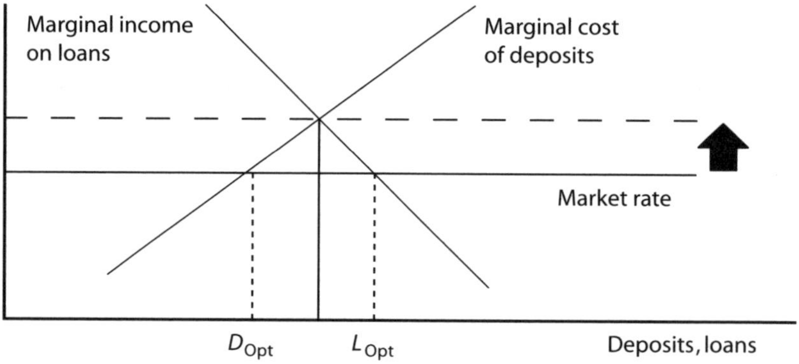

To summarize: in a situation of rationing on the interbank market which is closed to the bank, or in a situation where the loan-to-deposit ratio is binding, an adjusted funds transfer price can be found by *grossing up* the "market rate." This creates internal incentives to raise additional deposits and reduce the volume of loans, ensuring the desired equality of loans and deposits. As in real life the locations of the deposit and loan marginal lines are not known with certainty, some experimentation will be needed. The setting up of a higher funds transfer price meets the intuition of better remunerating the collection of stable deposits and charging a higher cost for illiquid bank loans. It preserves the logic of maximization of profit on loans evaluated against an adjusted funds transfer price and the maximization of profit on deposits invested at an opportunity rate. An alternative to raising the funds transfer pricing would be to set directly deposit and loan volume targets at the level where the volume of deposits equals that of the loans.

In this first case, we considered rationing on the interbank market. That is, banks cannot fund themselves on this market, often due to a fear that they will become insolvent or fear of sovereign risk resulting from the insolvency of a country. In the second case we analyze below, banks have access to an interbank market but they must fund a Basel III contingency liquidity buffer.

Basel III Contingency Liquidity Buffer

Consider the following balance sheet. At the initial stage, a loan portfolio is funded partly by deposits and interbank funding. The interest rate on the interbank deposits is denoted by *i*.

Loans, L	Deposits, D
	Interbank deposits, I (rate, i)
Liquid bonds, B (return, b)	Long-term debt, F (cost, f)

During the global liquidity crisis that started in July 2007, the interbank market dried up and banks turned to governments or central banks to obtain liquidity. For example, in December 2011 30% of the funding of Greek banks was obtained from the European Central Bank. As a result, bank regulators have decided to put into place a new regulation that ensures self-sufficiency with respect to liquidity in the future. This requires banks to create a portfolio of contingency liquid bonds, B, funded by long-term funds, such that $F = B$.[6] We will denote the return on liquid bonds and the cost of long-term funding by b and f, respectively. The objective is that the banks can liquidate the bonds or use them as collateral if the interbank market dries up. The contingency portfolio of liquid bonds has to meet cash outflows in a stress scenario that lasts 30 days. It is assumed that α% of clients' deposits would be withdrawn in a crisis and that β% of more volatile interbank deposits (with $\beta > \alpha$) would leave the bank. As long-term funding, F, is expensive, the cost of the liquidity buffer—the difference between the cost of long-term funding and the return on contingent liquidity assets—is equal to:

$$(f - b) \times B$$

We can write: $B = F = (\alpha \times \text{Deposits}) + (\beta \times \text{Interbank deposits})$

It can be shown (Dermine, 2009) that in this case we need two different funds transfer prices, one for loans and one for deposits. This takes into account not only the impact of collecting deposits and loans on the interbank position, but also the impact on the cost of the contingency liquidity buffer:

Loan – FTP = Marginal income on loan $= i + [\beta \times (f - b)]$
= Interbank rate + Liquidity cost

Deposit – FTP = Marginal cost of deposit $= i + [(\beta - \alpha) \times (f - b)]$
= Interbank rate + Liquidity revenue

The intuition behind this is as follows. In a first step, an increase of one dollar in the loan portfolio requires additional interbank funding as there is a lack of deposits. The first part of the funds transfer price is the usual interbank rate. But, in a second step, the increase in interbank funding requires, due to the new liquidity regulation, an increase in the costly contingency buffer. This is the added liquidity cost $[\beta \times (f - b)]$. By similar reasoning, an increase in its stable deposits allows the bank to reduce its need for interbank funding. The first part of the funds transfer price for deposits is, thus, the usual interbank rate. But, due to the contingency liquidity regulation, an increase in stable deposit funding accompanied by a decrease in volatile interbank funding leads to a reduced contingency liquidity buffer $(\beta - \alpha)$ and an additional revenue—the reduced cost of the liquidity buffer $[(\beta - \alpha) \times (f - b)]$—is added to the funds transfer price for deposits. It must be noted that a higher funds transfer price for loans will lead to higher lending rates. This is justified to price correctly the cost of liquidity risk.[7]

The global crisis has called to attention a third type of situation that creates the need for an advanced funds transfer pricing methodology: the case where the credit-riskiness of a specific asset differs from the average credit-riskiness of the assets of the bank.

Asset Risk-Adjusted Funds Transfer Price

In many situations, the credit approval committee of a bank will consider a loan whose riskiness differs from the average riskiness of the bank's assets. Let us consider an example:

Assets	Deposits
	Interbank debt (A-rated, 5.6%) Equity (10%)

A bank's assets are funded with deposits, interbank debt, and equity. The rating of the bank is A, with a cost of interbank debt of 5.6%.

Consider the following loan proposal: the funding of a very safe (AAA-equivalent) loan of 100 units yielding an expected return of 5.5%. The new very safe asset is funded with 2 units of equity and 98 units of interbank debt. The overall cost of equity is 10% and the corporate tax rate is 40%. In capital markets, the expected return on an AAA-rated corporate bond is 5%.

If we use the overall cost of debt and cost of equity of the bank, the *standard* economic profit used to evaluate performance would be measured as follows:

Standard economic profit = Profit – Cost of allocated equity

$$= (1 - 0.4) \times [(5.5\% \times 100) - (5.6\% \times 98)] - (10\% \times 2) = -0.1928.$$

Since the economic profit is negative, the loan would not be accepted.

In this example, the standard economic profit would underestimate the value created by the safe loan because it would charge too high an *average* cost of interbank debt and equity. There are two flaws in this approach. The first, and more significant one, is that it fails to recognize that taking a very safe (AAA-equivalent) asset (partly funded by equity) reduces the overall risk of the debt of the bank. The marginal cost of debt funding should be less than 5.6%. The second is that the overall cost of equity of 10% does not recognize the specific risk of the loan.

If a bank is not careful, it can lead itself into a vicious circle, avoiding safe loans and funding risky loans that lead, later, to a further downgrade. One can argue that the funding of a safe asset would not change the market perception of the riskiness of the bank in the short term. This may well be true in the short term as an opacity of accounts could hide the change in the riskiness of the bank. However, in the longer term, the opacity disappears and the market would recognize the improved safety.[8] Proper bank corporate governance rules are calling for long-term value creation (Dermine, 2011) and one needs a funds transfer pricing methodology that can recognize changes in the riskiness of the bank. The advanced economic profit approach allows one to respond to these flaws.

An intuitive introduction to asset-based funds transfer pricing might go as follows. It is based on a bank valuation model developed by Dermine (2009). The traditional balance sheet of the new loan is rewritten as the sum of two equity-funded positions:

Traditional balance sheet

New safe loan, 100 units (5.5%)	Debt, 98 units Equity, 2 units

In the traditional balance sheet the loan is funded by debt and equity. One refers to "levered" equity as some debt is used in the funding of the asset. This traditional balance sheet can be expressed in a revised manner:

Revised balance sheet (sum of unlevered 100% equity-financed positions)

New safe loan, 100 units (5.5%) –Debt, 98 units (5% – ε) (*Short position*)	Equity, 100 units (5%) Equity, 98 units (5% – ε)

Under the revised balance sheet, the leveraged loan is identical to (equivalent to) the sum of a 100% equity-funded loan and a short position in debt—indeed, the debt of a company, the obligation to pay out cash, is equivalent to shareholders having a short position in a bond.[9] The opportunity cost for the first position—equity funding the safe loan—is the expected return on corporate bonds with similar risk, 5%. Indeed, instead of making the safe loan, the bank can return the funds to shareholders, who can buy on the market corporate bonds with similar risk. The expected cost of the marginal debt used to fund the loan is 5% – ε. Protected by the equity cushion of 2, the expected marginal cost of debt funding should be slightly less than the expected return on the new asset, 5% – ε.

In the revised balance sheet (the sum of two 100% equity-financed positions), the *advanced* economic profit is approximately equal to:

$$\{[(1 - 0.4) \times 5.5\% \times 100] - [5\% \times 100]\}$$

$$+ \{[-(1 - 0.4) \times (5\% - \varepsilon) \times 98] - [-(5\% - \varepsilon) \times 98]\} \approx 0.26$$

The first part of the expression represents the economic profit on the loan funded 100% with equity (that is, the after-tax return on the loan net of the cost of equity, i.e. the opportunity return available to shareholders on the corporate bond market). The second part represents the economic profit on the debt (that is, the after-tax cash outflow on the debt net of an opportunity cost of equity, i.e. the borrowing opportunity cost available to shareholders on the market).[10]

In the advanced approach we ignore the overall cost of debt and the overall cost of equity, but rather focus on the marginal/incremental risk-adjusted specific opportunity rate. The advanced economic profit being positive in this example, the loan should be accepted.

One could argue that financial markets are not so well informed and that they will not recognize the change in riskiness of the bank when it funds a safe asset. As said above, this might well be the case in the short term, but boards of banks should be concerned with long-term value creation and accept that the market will soon enough understand the change in riskiness of the bank. As this might take time, it is advisable to conduct two evaluations of the economic profit of a transaction: a short-term evaluation based on *traditional* economic profit (based on the current average cost of funds), and a long-term *advanced* economic profit that recognizes the marginal risk of the new transaction.[11]

Summary and Further Steps

Following up on the global banking crisis, there is a pressing need to review the methodology used to evaluate the profitability of loans and deposits. This is indeed fundamental to evaluation of the profitability of on-balance sheet products and for pricing. Attention has been called to three issues that arose during the recent crisis: rationing on the interbank market, the need to create a costly Basel III contingency liquidity buffer, and the need to adjust the funds transfer pricing method to take into account the riskiness of the asset. An old issue, funds transfer pricing, has been revisited. Rightly so, as it is a major driver of performance evaluation, pricing, and value creation.

Further steps:

- Banks need to identify whether or not the current environment they face requires a move to advanced funds transfer pricing. Do they face rationing in illiquid interbank markets? Do they need to build up a costly Basel III contingency portfolio of liquid bonds?
- When banks finance loans the risk of which differs significantly from the average riskiness of the portfolio, they need to ensure that the cost of funds recognizes the incremental risk on new loans.
- Due to opacity of loan transactions, markets will take time to understand and price correctly the risk incurred in funding banks. In such a case, one has to be careful that short-term profit evaluation of loan transactions does not ignore some costs that will only become apparent over time.

More Info

Book:

Dermine, Jean. *Bank Valuation and Value-Based Management: Deposit and Loan Pricing, Performance Evaluation, and Risk Management*. New York: McGraw-Hill, 2009.

Articles:

Dermine, Jean. "Bank corporate governance, beyond the global banking crisis." Faculty and research working paper 2011/33/FIN. INSEAD, March 2011. Online at: www.insead.edu/facultyresearch/research/doc.cfm?did=47338

Financial Services Authority. "The failure of the Royal Bank of Scotland. Financial Services Authority board report." December 2011. Online at: www.fsa.gov.uk/pubs/other/rbs.pdf

Swiss Federal Banking Commission. "Subprime crisis: SFBC investigation into the causes of the write-downs of UBS AG." September 2008. Online at: tinyurl.com/cuj9ty6 [PDF].

Notes

1. In some countries with illiquid interbank markets the relevant market rate is the interest rate on government bonds.
2. It must be observed that the marginal income on a loan portfolio is smaller than the interest rate charged on the loan portfolio. The marginal income on an extra dollar of loan is the interest reduced by the cost of the action needed (such as marketing) to attract the extra dollar of loan.
3. The marginal cost of deposits is higher than the interest paid on the deposit base. The additional cost of an extra dollar of deposit is the interest paid augmented by the cost of the action needed to attract the extra dollar of deposit.
4. We ignore reserve requirements with central banks, which reduce the revenue earned on deposits.
5. The maturity of the market rate should correspond to the maturity of the deposit or loan.
6. The report of the Financial Services Authority on the failure of the Royal Bank of Scotland (FSA, 2011, p. 106) shows that the FSA liquidity rules did not cover the firm's dependence on nonsterling-denominated wholesale funding, nor did they capture off-balance sheet liquidity risk, for example as a result of committed liquidity facilities. For sterling deposits, banks had to be able to meet a five-day stress scenario.
7. The FSA report on the failure of the Royal Bank of Scotland (FSA, 2011, p. 97) states that "the internal transfer pricing obtained by businesses did not reflect the liquidity cost of the Group."
8. An official Swiss enquiry observed that one of the reasons UBS encountered problems during the crisis was the evaluation of very risky assets booked in New York with a funds transfer price that reflected the high rating of the overall bank (Swiss Federal Banking Commission, 2008).
9. It must be observed that the technique of replacing a leveraged position by an equivalent sum of unlevered (100% equity-financed) positions is used to evaluate investments in project finance.
10. In this example it is assumed that large shareholders face the same cost of funds as the bank for the marginal funding of the new asset, $5\% - \varepsilon$. The calculation of the advanced economic profit is an approximation as the very small ε has been ignored.
11. Two financial techniques can be used by the bank to ease the short-term effect resulting from opacity. The first is securitization of the safe asset. Securitization will force the market to evaluate the riskiness of the specific safe asset. A second technique is to use collateralized funding. The safe asset being used as a collateral should allow the bank to access lower-cost funding.

The Importance of Detail

Analyzing a Bank's Financial Performance

by Jyothi Manohar

Accounting, Audit and Consulting Professional, Philadelphia, Pennsylvania, USA

This Chapter Covers

- The key components of a bank's basic financial statements.
- A description of each of the components.
- How relationships between components are measured and analyzed.
- The conclusions that can be reached as a result of analyzing these relationships.
- The capital, asset, management, earnings, liquidity (CAMEL) methodology of analyzing a bank's financial performance.

Introduction

Individually and collectively, the financial health of banks and the banking system is critical to national and global economies. Central banks or other regulators in various countries monitor financial institutions using rating and evaluation systems that may be unique to those countries. However, there are certain common measures of financial performance and the safety and soundness of a financial institution. No one measure, by itself, is an indicator of the financial health of a bank. It is important to understand each and the interplay among all or many of these measures to properly evaluate a bank's financial performance.

Analyzing a Bank's Financial Performance

It is necessary to understand the composition of a bank's basic financial statements (this is itemized in detail in the Appendix to this chapter) and the business of banking (described in the section "Earnings" below). It is difficult to analyze a bank's financial performance merely by looking at financial information at a particular point in time. Essential to this analysis is a review of how similar components of a bank's financial information have trended over time, compared to its own past performance as well as the performance of its peers.

> Common measures of financial performance are capital adequacy, asset quality, liquidity, earnings, management capability, risk management, and critical key ratios that serve as tools to analyze a bank's financial performance.

Common Measures of Financial Performance

Capital Adequacy

How do banking regulators measure, evaluate, and rate the quality of a bank's financial stability or, in industry parlance, the safety and soundness of a bank? Capital adequacy is a keystone. The Basel Committee on Banking Supervision of the Bank of International Settlements (BIS) has established minimum capital standards that are widely followed by banks across the world. (In September 2010 higher global minimum capital standards were announced that will be phased in over a period of time.) Capital adequacy is generally measured in the following categories.

- *Tier I capital* generally consists of common equity, disclosed reserves, and retained earnings (excluding other comprehensive income) and is calculated as Tier I capital/Total risk-weighted assets. All assets on a bank's balance sheet are risk-weighted based on the respective credit risk as defined by the respective central banks; for instance, cash on hand has a risk weight of 0, whereas a commercial advance may carry a risk weight of 100%. Tier I minimum capital ratios are generally established at 4%.
- *Total risk-based capital* includes Tier I capital plus certain other eligible items up to limits specified by regulatory guidance. Minimum capital ratios are generally established at 8%.
- *Leverage ratio:* Calculated as Tier I capital/Average total assets, with the minimum established at 4%.

Capital adequacy helps to sustain a bank's growth and protect it from the consequences of the risks represented by its various lines of business. For instance, if a bank makes a strategic decision to expand its lending operations in a new geography, it will need to ensure that any impairment losses inherent in the new operations can be adequately absorbed by retained earnings while still maintaining healthy capital ratios.

These ratios are a necessary disclosure in any bank's financial statements. Once a bank's key capital ratios start to hover near or sink below the minimums required, alarm bells sound, hinting to analysts and regulators that the financial institution requires closer monitoring. In the United States, starting in 2009, peaking in 2010, and continuing today have been numerous bank failures that resulted in closure by the Federal Deposit Insurance Corporation (FDIC). A common thread among these failures is credit losses so excessive that they eroded retained earnings, and hence capital, to below the minimum or to such critically deficient levels as to threaten the very existence of the financial institution. Analyses of several of these bank failures can be read on the FDIC's website (see More Info section at the end of the chapter).

Asset Quality

The asset quality measure largely addresses the quality of the loans and advances of a bank, although the quality of investment securities has also come into play. While all banks have credit policies that provide a framework within which the bank limits its lending operations, the varied nature of the loans made by a bank, the vast geographies over which they are spread, the varied nature, characteristics, and demographics of the borrowers, and the collateral underlying the loans present risks of nonperformance and collectability that are difficult to measure and quantify. Hence, credit risk is among the most critical risks that a financial institution must manage. Banks must necessarily have risk management systems in place to continuously monitor their loan portfolios.

The notes to a bank's financial statements detail a bank's credit risk management policies, the types of loans it makes, policies related to when nonperforming loans (NPLs) are placed on nonaccrual status (usually at 90 days of delinquency), charge-off (write-off as losses) policies, when loans are deemed impaired, policies related to the evaluation and measurement of impaired loans, and what factors are considered by the bank in establishing reserves (or allowances) for credit impairment and losses. Key asset quality ratios include the following.

- *Loan by type/Total loans and advances*. Reflects the composition of the loan portfolio and growth rate of each in relation to total loans and advances, showing which sector of the portfolio is increasing rapidly and how credit risk might be impacted as a result.
- *Reserve (allowance) for credit losses/Total loans and advances*. Presents the reserve for loan losses as a percentage of total loans.
- *NPL/Total loans and advances*. Presents the proportion of the total loan portfolio that is nonperforming, i.e. no longer accruing interest since collection is in doubt.
- *Loans and advances charged off (written off)/Average total loans and advances*. Represents actual losses incurred as a result of loans written off in proportion to average total loans.
- *Reserve for credit losses/NPL*. Coverage represented by the reserve or allowance for credit losses to the existing level of nonperforming loans.

Liquidity

At any given point in time, a bank must have the necessary funds to make loans and advances to borrowers, meet the demands of customers for deposit withdrawals, and pay other obligations. Although a bank can project some of these requirements based on loan commitments in the pipeline, upcoming maturities of loans and deposits, and known obligations, unanticipated demands and contingencies must be met as well. A necessary byproduct of asset liability management processes is liquidity management. All banks have liquidity policies that allow them to meet known and unexpected liquidity requirements. Sources of liquidity are:

- cash and cash equivalents;
- core deposits;
- reserve balances;
- assets available for sale that can be disposed of quickly and converted to cash;
- borrowing sources that include lines of credit that can be drawn on.

Essential to this analysis is that a bank has access to diverse sources of liquidity and can answer the following questions.

- Is there a stable base of core deposits, or is it shrinking?
- Is there reliance on short-term, volatile sources of funds to meet long-term obligations, or vice-versa?
- Is there ready access to money and capital markets in the event that additional funds must be raised?
- Does the bank have enough diversification among assets on its balance sheet that can be quickly converted to cash?
- Does management have enough policies and processes in place to evaluate its liquidity position funds management and contingency funding strategies on an ongoing basis?
- What picture is the cash flow statement presenting that will impact the bank's liquidity position?
- Is the loan-to-deposit ratio satisfactory? Calculated as Total loans and advances/Total deposits, this is a measure for assessing a bank's liquidity.

> If the ratio is too high, the bank might not have enough liquidity to cover unanticipated funding requirements; if the ratio is too low, the bank may not be earning as much as it could be.

Earnings

How Does a Bank Generate Net Income?

Banks lend money and accept deposits, invest excess funds, generate fee income, and pay bills. On the face of it, and through a quick perusal of a bank's income statement, the concept appears straightforward enough—generate a healthy net interest income and enough noninterest income to cover all noninterest expenses and then some. It is easier said than done, however.

The next sections describe the different components that go into the calculation of a bank's net income.

Net Interest Income

Managing and monitoring a large variety of interest-bearing assets and interest-bearing liabilities in a constantly changing interest rate environment is no easy task. When one thinks of the variety of interest-bearing assets (primarily investment securities and loan advances) that carry a multitude of interest rates (fixed rate or variable rates tied to indices such as Libor, Treasury rates, prime rates, bank rates) and a multitude of maturities, and the variety of interest-bearing liabilities (primarily customer and bank deposits and borrowings) that also carry a plethora of interest rates and span maturities from "on demand" to 10 years or more and everything in between, managing the balance sheet and interest rate risk is a challenging, complex, ongoing exercise.

> The proportion of noninterest income to total income speaks volumes as to the sources of revenues for a bank and its reliance on ancillary services versus traditional banking services.

Throw into the mix the vagaries of consumer and business demand for funds, national and world events that impact the financial markets and economies locally, nationally, and internationally, and a bank's ability to meet all of those demands while still generating income for its shareholders, and it becomes obvious that remaining financially healthy is a highwire act. Asset liability management, liquidity management, interest rate risk and sensitivity analysis, duration and maturity gap analysis are all inextricably intertwined.

The interest rate environment has been at historical lows these past few years. It has been especially challenging for banks to maintain consistently healthy net interest margins (NIM, measured by net interest income as a percentage of average interest-earning assets). Ideally, banks will strive for a NIM better than 3%.

Noninterest Income

To meet the objective of consistent net income and earnings per share (EPS), the other alternatives for banks have been either to generate as much noninterest revenue as possible through fees, service charges, and gains on sale of assets or to reduce operating expenses. Reducing provisions for losses and asset impairments is not a prudent option, particularly in a troubled world economy. To augment revenues from traditional banking services, more and more banks are generating fee and service revenue from private banking, trust and wealth management, financial advice, sale of nondeposit investment vehicles, insurance products, and other such ancillary services. The proportion of noninterest income to total income speaks volumes as to the sources of revenues for a bank and its reliance on ancillary services versus traditional banking services. It should help to focus an analyst's attention on the viability of these revenue sources for the bank.

Provisions for Impairment and Other Losses

Though all banks have lending and investment policies that purport to be prudent and establish parameters as to the types of loans, advances, and investments they will make and their relative concentrations, both as a proportion of the respective totals and of equity, it is difficult for any bank to accurately anticipate economic downturns and financial meltdowns (as have been experienced since 2007 and are continuing to impact several countries across the globe). These events are, to a fair degree, outside a bank's control, yet they have an adverse impact on the collateral value of loans and advances and the quality and collectability of its assets. Many banks across the world have experienced losses as a result of nonperforming loans, toxic investments, and other asset write-downs, particularly during the trough year 2009. Analyzing the carrying value of its assets is an ongoing risk management activity for every bank. This includes the valuation of goodwill and intangibles as well, some of which have suffered in the recent crises and been written down or charged off through profit and loss as being impaired.

Noninterest Expense

Most operating costs, with the exception of discretionary spending such as marketing and advertising, represent fixed costs that a bank must incur to operate its business efficiently. Depending on how internal and external factors impact other components of the financial statements, a bank may make strategic decisions to cut costs by divesting poorly performing branches, businesses, and subsidiaries and by outsourcing certain types of operations such as data processing, loan servicing, human resources, etc. Risk management techniques that include close monitoring of planned (budgeted) performance against actual results are another tool used by a bank to manage its financial performance. The efficiency ratio is a measure of how well a bank is controlling its operating costs. While there are variations in how banks compute the efficiency ratio, it is generally calculated as:

$$\frac{\text{Noninterest expense}}{(\text{Net interest income} + \text{Noninterest income} - \text{Gains on investment securities})}$$

The lower the efficiency ratio, the better the bank's performance. Ideally, banks will strive for efficiency ratios of 50–55% or less.

Net Income and Earnings per Share

Sustained positive earnings and earnings per share are among the planned primary objectives for any company's business plan—and no less so for a bank. Net income helps to build retained earnings, which in turn sustains healthy capital ratios. For a bank, maintaining better than minimum capital ratios (as we have already seen in this chapter) is the lifeblood for survival. Net income keeps stockholders happy by providing a source of continued dividends on their investment. EPS is a common measure of a company's profitability and is well known to anyone who invests in company stock.

In analyzing net income, however, it is important to understand which components of the income statement are major contributors to the net income or net loss—whether these be core operations, ancillary services, gains from investment securities sales or other asset disposals, or increases in noninterest expenses, or provisions for loan losses, or other asset impairments. Is net income or loss being generated by a one-time event that will not recur? Looking at the cause of changes in net income or loss over a period of time will help an analyst to focus on what events are shaping a bank's financial performance.

Summary

In summary, analyses of a bank's earnings encompass:

- the consistency, quality, and adequacy of earnings;
- sources and levels of earnings;
- the ability to bolster retained earnings and capital through earnings;
- levels of provision required for impaired loans and assets;
- net interest margins;
- the return on assets (ROA): Net income/Average assets;
- the return on equity (ROE): Net income/Average equity;
- the dividend payout ratio: Dividends/Net income.

Management Capability

This intangible measure encompasses the qualifications of board members, the level of participation of each, the level of collective oversight provided by board committees and the board over the critical operating, accounting, and financial reporting policies of the bank, as well as the qualifications of key members of management, their experience and capability in executing board-approved policies, and their oversight of the day-to-day operations of the bank.

Although it is difficult to quantify this measure, the annual reports of all public banks include discussion and disclosures related to board members, executive management, the level of shareholdings of each, the remuneration received, the qualifications, and the specific position each holds in relation to the bank. In addition, significant related party transactions—i.e. transactions that board members, executive management, or their affiliated interests have with the bank—will be disclosed. All of these disclosures point an analyst to the potential for conflicts of interest and the level of objectivity with which board members and executive management execute their responsibilities in protecting the interests of the bank, its customers, and its stockholders.

Risk Management

In this chapter we have alluded to varied risks in several aspects that must be managed in order to achieve positive financial performance. The typical risks listed below have direct or indirect effects on a bank's financial performance and should be addressed by all banks. Banks' annual reports detail the risk management activities that are applicable to the organization.

- *Credit risk*: Credit risk is addressed in the section "Asset Quality" above and encompasses more than the traditional definition associated with lending activities. Credit risk is found in all activities where success depends on counterparty, issuer, or borrower performance.
- *Interest rate and market risk*: Interest rate risk is addressed under "Net Interest Income" above. Market risk is the risk to a bank's financial condition resulting from adverse movements in market rates or prices, such as interest rates, foreign exchange rates, or equity prices. Changes in interest rates may have a significant effect on other areas of risk. For example, market risk can impair the bank's liquidity position.
- *Liquidity risk*: This is addressed under "Liquidity" above.
- *Operational and transaction risk*: Operational risk arises from the potential that inadequate information systems, operational problems, breaches in internal controls, fraud, or unforeseen catastrophes will result in unexpected losses. Transaction risk is pervasive to an organization. It is the risk to earnings or capital arising from problems with service or product delivery and may include potential financial losses from human error or fraud, incomplete information, and related decision-making or operational disruption.
- *Compliance and legal risk*: All banks must operate in compliance with a myriad of laws, rules, and regulations. Compliance risk arises from potential violations of or nonconformance with those laws, regulations, or prescribed practices which govern the bank's activities. Legal risk arises from the potential that unenforceable contracts, lawsuits, or adverse judgments can adversely affect the operations and financial performance of the bank.
- *Strategic risk*: Strategic risk results from adverse business decisions or the improper implementation of those decisions. Examples include the misalignment of business and technology strategic plans, improper market positioning (e.g. retail delivery strategies, geographic positioning, etc.) and pricing of products and services.
- *Reputation risk*: Reputation risk is the potential that negative publicity regarding a bank's business practices will cause a decline in the customer base, costly litigation, or revenue reductions, often as a result of poor earnings, regulatory censure, significant fraud or litigation, or failure to provide services or products in conformity with the local market. Reputation risk exposure is driven to a large extent by the bank's actions to manage other categories of risks.
- *Foreign exchange risk*: Tied to market risk above.
- *Technology risk*: Technology risk is the potential that the bank has an inadequate technology infrastructure and related technical support to properly process daily transactions, keep customer information private, and provide timely and accurate board and management information for key decision-making, thereby disabling the bank in the event of a catastrophe.

Critical Key Ratios: Risk-Adjusted Performance Measures (RAPMs)

We have seen that the safety and soundness of banks and the banking system are reliant on maintaining levels of capital that will see a financial institution through adverse periods and sustain it over the long run. Given the many tangible and intangible risks facing the banking industry today, protecting capital through risk-adjusted performance measures is of increasing importance. The most common RAPM is risk-adjusted return on risk-adjusted capital (RARORAC), which goes beyond the earnings measures represented by return on assets (ROA) and return on equity (ROE). RARORAC takes into consideration anticipated returns adjusted for expected future losses (credit losses, declines in interest income or noninterest income, contingencies, etc.). In addition, capital-at-risk represents not just equity (the difference between total assets and total liabilities) but the estimated funds required to protect against expected losses as well as unexpected losses—i.e. losses that could result from each of the risks identified in "Risk management" above. Hence, RARORAC is a marked change from traditional measures of return on equity not only with respect to computation, but also to measurement and complexity. RARORAC is measured as:

$$\frac{\text{Risk-adjusted return}}{\text{Capital-at-risk}}$$

Summary and Further Steps

Analyzing a bank's financial performance requires a holistic approach. It involves an understanding not only of the numbers that comprise the financial statements, but also of the various intangible or qualitative factors both internal and external to the financial institution that have a direct or indirect impact on the numbers. Banks are in a unique position in the world economy such that the performance of each can be significantly affected by external market forces, many of which are outside the banks' control. Like all other business organizations, however, internal risk management policies and the quality of management and board oversight that are within the organization's control have an impact on financial performance. An analyst needs to understand that there are interrelationships among all or many of the varied financial and performance indicators and the intangible factors that must be evaluated in concert in order to reach accurate conclusions.

More Info

Book:

Golin, Jonathan. *The Bank Credit Analysis Handbook: A Guide for Analysts, Bankers and Investors*. Singapore: Wiley, 2001.

Article:

Basel Committee on Banking Supervision. "Basel III: A global regulatory framework for more resilient banks and banking systems. Bank of International Settlements. Updated June 2011. Online at: www.bis.org/publ/bcbs189.htm

Websites:
Credit and Finance Risk Analysis: credfinrisk.com/bank.html
Federal Deposit Insurance Corporation (FDIC): www.fdic.gov
FitchTraining: tinyurl.com/ckh54pn

Appendix: Basic Bank Financial Statements

Balance Sheet

As with any business organization, a bank's balance sheet comprises assets, liabilities, and capital (stockholders' equity). The nature of these items reflects the uniqueness of the business of banking.

Assets

- *Cash*. The cash on hand (usually at various branch locations, in vaults, and in automated teller machines (ATMs)) and required reserves maintained with the respective central bank of the country.
- *Balances maintained with other financial institutions*. Includes short-term investments with original maturities of 90 days or less.

The above two balances are aggregated as "Cash and cash equivalents" (CCE).

- *Federal funds sold*. Temporary (often overnight) investments of excess funds with other banks.
- *Investment securities*. Debt or equity securities held for interest earnings, liquidity, or gains trading. There may be regulatory restrictions on the types of investment a bank can hold.
- *Derivatives*. Financial instruments whose price or value is dependent on the changes in value of other underlying assets, which may be stocks, bonds, currencies, commodities, etc. Banks generally use derivative instruments as a means of protecting themselves from interest rate or international currency exchange rate fluctuations. Due to the sophisticated nature of derivative instruments both from a risk and an accounting perspective, derivatives are typically entered into only by those banks that have the resources and expertise to handle them.
- *Advances or loans to customers*. Loans made to individuals, businesses, and other organizations for a whole plethora of reasons, ranging from buying a car to funding working capital for business organizations, construction projects, and the like.
- *Advances or loans to banks*. Typically, loans made by larger banks to other banks for a variety of reasons; accounted for in much the same manner as advances or loans to customers.
- *Property, plant, and equipment*. The bank's holdings of real estate (the bank's various locations may be leased or owned), furniture, fixtures, equipment, technology hardware, capitalized leases, or other similar assets that have an estimated useful life and which are used on an ongoing basis.

- *Goodwill and intangible assets*. Goodwill arises from the acquisition of another business where the consideration paid exceeds the assets acquired and the liabilities assumed. For a bank, intangibles usually represent items like loan-servicing rights, core deposit premiums, and customer lists, although trade names and computer software (purchased or internally generated) may also be included as intangible assets.
- *Deferred taxes*. These balances arise due to temporary differences in the carrying value of assets and liabilities for financial reporting purposes versus tax reporting purposes. Deferred tax assets represent temporary differences that will result in future tax benefits for the bank.
- *Other assets*. This could include a multitude of balances including accrued interest receivable, prepaid assets, investments in joint ventures, miscellaneous receivables, and repossessed assets.
- *Off-balance sheet items*. Includes items such as commitments, letters of credit, debt financing, off-balance sheet exposure to derivatives, etc.

Liabilities

- *Deposits*. These include deposits by customers (current or demand accounts, savings accounts, fixed deposits, also known as term deposit receipts or certificates of deposit) and other banks.
- *Borrowings*. These include short- and long-term borrowings from other banks, repurchase agreements, and federal funds purchased. Repurchase agreements are short-term arrangements to sell investment securities with an agreement that they will be repurchased at pre-set prices and in pre-set time frames. Federal funds purchased are temporary (usually overnight) borrowings of excess funds from other banks.
- *Debt securities issued*. These are generally longer-term borrowings for specific purposes and include trust preferred issuances and corporate bonds. The debt issuances of larger banks frequently trade on a regular basis and may be readily purchased and sold through investment brokers.
- *Derivatives*. See "Assets" section above for definition. Fair-value fluctuations may cause derivative instruments to be classified as liabilities.
- *Deferred taxes*. See "Assets" section above for definition. Deferred tax liabilities represent temporary differences that are currently taxable.
- *Accounts payable and accrued expenses*. Current liabilities arising out of the routine day-to-day operations of a bank such as bills payable, salaries payable, professional fees payable, etc.
- *Pension and retirement liabilities*. Depending on the type of employee benefits plans adopted by a bank, these may represent the actuarial valuation of future benefits payable.

Capital (or Equity)

- *Common capital (or stock)*. The par value of common shares issued and outstanding.

- *Surplus (share premium or additional paid-in capital)*. Excess over par of common shares issued and outstanding.
- *Other equity instruments*. Typically, different classes of preference (or preferred) shares.
- *Other comprehensive income*. This includes net income or loss for the current fiscal period. It also represents an account through which changes in fair values of certain items (e.g. investment securities that are classified as available-for-sale, derivatives that qualify for hedge accounting, foreign currency exchange rates, or actuarial valuations for certain types of deferred compensation plan) are recorded.
- *Retained earnings*. The cumulative amount of net income earned or loss incurred since the bank's inception, adjusted for cash or share dividends paid.
- *Reserves*. Banks in some countries are required to maintain statutory reserves as mandated by their regulators or central banks.

Income Statement

The presentation of a bank income statement varies widely from one country to another. Nevertheless, the components are generally the same.

- *Interest income*. Interest earned on all interest-bearing assets.
- *Interest expense*. Interest paid on all interest-bearing liabilities.
- *Net interest income*. The difference between interest income and interest expense.
- *Noninterest income*. Income from other sources such as service charges, fee income from the sale of trust services, wealth management services, etc., and gain on sale of investment securities, loans, or other assets.
- *Noninterest expense*. Operating expenses such as personnel costs, occupancy expenses, professional services, insurance, data processing, etc., and losses from the sale of investment securities, loans, or other assets.
- *Provisions for losses*. Losses such as loan losses, provisions for liabilities such as actuarial liabilities, and provisions for impairment losses such as investment or other asset impairment.
- *Net income or loss before taxes*. The excess of total income over total expense or vice-versa.
- *Provision for income taxes*. Current tax expense plus changes in deferred tax expense.
- *Net income or loss after taxes*. The excess of total income over total expense or vice-versa adjusted for tax expense or tax benefit.

Statement of Changes in Stockholders' Equity

The statement of changes in stockholders' equity comprises the activity during the year that resulted in changes in each of the components of capital (or equity) described under "Balance Sheet" above.

Cash Flow Statement

The cash flow statement gives a telling picture of how a bank's cash and cash equivalents changed during the year as a result of the cash inflows and outflows affecting each component of the balance sheet. The cash flow statement is segregated into three sections that indicate the bank's cash flows generated by or used in operating activities, investing activities, and financing activities. Focusing on the individual components in the cash flow statement gives the analyst an indication of the sources of the bank's business that are generating cash flows and those that are draining cash. Excessive cash outflows over cash inflows could have an adverse impact on the bank's liquidity position.

Notes to the Financial Statements

Basic financial statements for any business organization are accompanied by notes to the financial statements. Audited financial statements usually include an indicator that "the accompanying notes are an integral part of the financial statements." Each account balance on the financial statements is referenced to a note number. Notes to the financial statements usually lead with a summary of the bank's accounting policies as it relates to all key financial accounts. Thereafter, individual notes detail what comprises the account balance and how the carrying amount of the account came about.

Notes to financial statements contain all the relevant disclosures required by the Generally Accepted Accounting Principles (GAAP), such as International Financial Reporting Standards (IFRS), under which it is presented and enable a financial statement user to better understand the bank's financial condition and its operations. It is easy to access and read the audited financial statements of most banks across the world under the "Annual report" caption on their respective websites. An example would be www.hsbc.fr, where the annual report for HSBC France can be located by following the link "Informations financières."

Factoring Problem Loan Assumptions into Asset–Liability Management (ALM) Modeling

by Gary Deutsch

BRT Publications LLC

This Chapter Covers

- Traditional ALM modeling considers interest rate risk assumptions for loans based on new loan funding amounts and subsequent payments, prepayments, and maturing balances.
- However, it ignores modified payments, missed payments, and default issues such as impaired loans, repossessions, and foreclosures.
- It is these problem loan issues that are the subject of this chapter. Incorporating problem loan data and assumptions into ALM modeling is an evolving topic. This chapter provides guidance.

Introduction

An essential part of the interest rate risk (IRR) management process is the analysis and documentation of IRR assumptions. Since all methods used to analyze the rate sensitivity of financial instruments require estimates of the amount and timing of their cash flows, the embedded prepayment options found in many types of loans must also be estimated. These estimates must include the level and speed of prepayments for an expected rate environment. However, economic conditions may not always favor prepayments. Therefore, IRR assumptions should also include assumptions related to problem loans. For instance, late payments, restructured payments, and payments that will not be collected can have a significant impact on IRR assumptions, especially in more volatile economic times.

This chapter describes the types of assumptions related to problem loans that ALM managers should incorporate into the interest rate risk management process. Note that although the references in this chapter are to US Generally Accepted Accounting Principles (US GAAP), the IRR cash flow concepts should hold true for all financial institutions worldwide. For additional information on this topic, refer to the More Info section at the end of the chapter.

Industry Support

Including problem loan assumptions in IRR analyses is not a new idea, but it has not been widely adopted. Among the many post-Great Recession lessons learned is one that curiously few are discussing—the obvious need to better integrate credit risk assumptions with interest rate risk and liquidity risk in the asset and liability management process. According to Michael R. Guglielmo, managing director of the Darling Consulting Group in Newburyport, Massachusetts, the tools for ALM modeling often depend on the level of optionality embedded in an institution's balance sheet. He adds that asset and liability management committee (ALCO) activities that were once thought to be "nice to have" have quickly become "have to have." Among the long list of these activities is his belief that "credit and default-risk modeling will continue to migrate into ALM modeling."[1]

The PricewaterhouseCoopers (PwC) 2009 survey of the balance sheet management practices at 43 leading financial institutions across the globe[2] defines the four main areas of balance sheet management to be interest rate risk management, liquidity risk management, capital management, and management of discretionary investment portfolios. PwC concludes that the severe financial crisis in 2008 prompted banks globally to broaden their ALM perspective to include a more holistic view of their institution's balance sheet, but credit risk management is not on the list. Although balance sheet management is a good progression in the natural extension of ALM, the prospect of continued worldwide economic volatility should encourage more ALM managers to move in the direction of adding credit and default risk modeling to the IRR analysis process and to the ALCO decision-making agenda.

> Among the long list of "have to have" ALCO activities is the belief that "credit and default-risk modeling will continue to migrate into ALM modeling."

Case Study: Expanding the ALM Modeling Effort to Incorporate Problem Loans

Discount on a Retail Shopping Center Problem Loan Note

A common theme today is the selling of mortgage notes by banks that are in financial trouble or need to remove loans from their financial statements due to regulatory pressures. These deals are often opportunistic for banks, depending on market conditions.

Note-buyers will buy these mortgage notes at 40 cents in the dollar, often without alerting the business or investor who owns the property. For example, the value of a retail shopping plaza was appraised at US$3.6 million, and the owner borrowed US$2.80 million to purchase the center. The loan interest rate was fixed at 6%. The note was based on a 20-year amortization period but had a balloon payment due in five years of US$2,389,074.67. The US$2.80 million 6% mortgage note was sold to a note-buyer for US$1.12 million (40% of the borrower's original debt) with 24 months remaining on the note's original five-year maturity. When the note was sold, the outstanding loan balance was US$2,561,620.47 based on the original amortization schedule. However, the borrower had not made the four most recent payments, so the actual balance outstanding at the sale date was US$2,590,269.34 without considering any late fees or other charges. The bank also had to reverse four months of accrued interest at the time the note was placed on nonaccrual.

Over the three-year period that the loan was outstanding, the bank had accrued interest of US$483,782.99. However, since the borrower had not made payments for four months prior to the note sale, US$51,631.41 of this interest amount had to be reversed when the sale was completed.

When the note was sold, the bank charged off US$1,470,269.34, or the difference between the note's actual outstanding balance of US$2,590,269.34 and the note-buyer's offer of US$1,120,000. Of course, they had also reversed US$51,631.41 of interest income.

In the typical ALM modeling process, IRR assumptions include the regular payment stream of US$20,060.07 per month and the balloon payment in five years of US$2,389,074.67 for this amortizing loan. However, when the bank decided to sell the note at a substantial loss, the IRR assumptions had to be modified to avoid overstating future cash flows.

The impact of the note sale on IRR assumptions is set out below. All amounts are US dollars.

Original loan

- Monthly cash flow to reinvest = $20,060.07 for five years = $1,203,604.20.
- Balloon payment due in five years available for reinvestment = $2,389,074.67.
- Total cash flows available for reinvestment over the life of the loan = $3,592,678.87.
- Maturing rate for cash flows = 6%.
- Reinvestment rate for cash flows: this is set in the ALM modeling process.

Problem loan

- Monthly cash flow to reinvest = $20,060.07 for three years = $722,162.52.
- Balloon payment from note sale available for reinvestment = $1,120,000.00.
- Total cash flows available for reinvestment over the life of the loan = $1,842,162.52.
- Contractual cash flows not available for reinvestment = $1,750,516.35.
- Maturing rate for cash flows = 6%.
- Reinvestment rate for cash flows: this is set in the ALM modeling process.

The "Contractual cash flows not available for reinvestment" in the problem loan section represents the difference in total cash flows available for reinvestment over the life of the loan between the original loan and the problem loan. In practice, the contractual cash flows not available for reinvestment would be discounted to their present value at the contractual "maturing" interest rate.

As seen in the above example, problem loans can distort ALM modeling results unless problem loan assumptions are included in the IRR analysis process.

Problem Loans and Embedded Options

ALM modeling analyzes the reinvestment of cash flows from loan payments and payoffs. When borrowers cannot make payments according to their contractual agreement, there are lesser or no cash flows to reinvest. Furthermore, some borrowers that are having financial difficulties for legal or tactical reasons may choose to stop making payments until they can negotiate more favorable terms. From an ALM perspective, this represents an embedded option—the option to skip payments or to stop paying. If the bank chooses to modify a loan under the assumption that some payment is better than none, the bank is agreeing to realize a lower level of cash flows that will be available for reinvestment in the ALM modeling process.

> Some borrowers that are having financial difficulties may choose to stop making payments until they can negotiate more favorable terms. From an ALM perspective, this represents an embedded option to skip payments or stop paying.

Another type of option is the "event of default" included in loan agreements. An event of default determines when a bank can legally intervene and accelerate repayment from the borrower or guarantors. Prior to an event of default, banks must track past due payments, stop accruing interest, and determine whether the loan is impaired.

Expanding IRR Assumptions to Include Problem Loan Data

ALM modeling is the process of evaluating the extent to which changes in interest rates can increase or reduce a financial institution's net interest income. Since interest income is derived from balance sheet instruments (for example, loans and deposits) and off-balance sheet instruments (for example, unfunded loan commitments and hedges such as interest rate swaps), in ALM modeling it is necessary to project both changes in interest rates and changes in balance sheet and off-balance sheet instruments. For this discussion, the focus will be on balance sheet instruments.

To understand how changes in interest rates can impact a financial institution's net interest income, loans and deposit balances must be projected over the planning period, which is often a one- to three-year time horizon. Let us focus on loan balance projections, since loan losses are the topic of discussion in this chapter.

To project loan balances for ALM modeling, the institution's loan balances need to be separated into the following components.

First, the balance at the beginning of the planning period:

- *Less:* Projected loan payments (i.e. cash flows from principal and interest payments or interest-only payments);
- *Less:* Projected loan prepayments (e.g. payments received before the due date based on historical data from the institution's records or from a third-party source);
- *Less:* Projected loan maturities (e.g. loans with balloon payments due or loans that will be paid off due to financing obtained from another lending institution);
- *Plus:* Projected new loan balances (i.e. estimates from the institution's loan production planning process).

And second, the ending balance at the end of the period.

Each of these components represents cash inflows or outflows that will result in the balance at the end of the period being increased or reduced from the balance at the beginning of the period. When projected interest rates are multiplied by the beginning and ending balances to measure interest rate changes, it is the changes in the cash flow components that directly impact the increase or decrease in interest income.

However, the above cash flow components do not represent all of the factors that influence the dollar amount of the period-end balance. The missing factor is the projected cash flows that will not be received as a result of nonpayment of principal and/or interest. So a more complete listing of components to include in the ALM modeling process would be as follows.

First, the balance at the beginning of the planning period:

- *Less:* Projected loan payments (details as in previous list);
- *Less:* Projected loan prepayments;
- *Less:* Projected loan maturities;
- *Plus:* Projected new loan balances;
- *Less:* (New item) projected loan payments—i.e. principal and or interest—that will not be received.

And second, the ending balance at the end of the period.

Therefore, to more accurately project the cash flows that can impact loan interest income projections in the ALM modeling process, institutions need to project loan payments that they anticipate will not be received according to the loan's original or modified terms. This represents an expansion of the data requirements for ALM modeling. In the next section we elaborate on where to obtain and how to compile the data to use in preparing projections of loan payments that will not be received.

Obtaining and Compiling Problem Loan Data

To begin the process of identifying this new ALM assumption—of projected loan principal and/or interest payments that will not be received—ALM managers should coordinate with the credit function to obtain the information shown in Table 1 to use in developing IRR assumptions for problem loans.

Table 1. ALM data sources for problem loans

Problem loan timeline or event	Credit data source
Origination	Loan accounting system
Performing	Loan accounting system
Nonperforming	Loan accounting system
Nonaccrual	Loan accounting system
Impaired	Loan review function
Restructured	Loan review function
Foreclosed	Loan review function
Charged off	Loan review function
Sold collateral	Loan review function
Recovery	Loan review function

In the rest of the section we discuss each of these data sources and how the data can be used to create an IRR assumption for projected loan principal and/or interest payments that will not be received.

Loan Accounting System

A bank's loan accounting system (LAS) is the typical source of information on new loan balances and interest rates. For ALM models, these data are often grouped by type of loan, such as residential mortgage, consumer loans, commercial loans, and commercial real estate loans. The LAS should also be capable of tracking whether loans are performing or nonperforming (missing payments). When loans miss a predetermined number of payments (i.e. a loan has not paid for 90 days or more), the LAS should recognize that the loan should be placed on nonaccrual status and cease recording interest income for financial statement purposes.

Even if the LAS provides information about nonperforming and nonaccrual loans, this information is generally not in a format that can be used directly as an IRR assumption. For instance, the LAS should be a good source for delinquent loan payments and identifying those loans that have been placed on nonaccrual status. Missing from the LAS will be a projection of the loan payments that will remain in delinquent status and ultimately result in some portion of the loan being charged off. As was shown in the case study, the IRR assumption objective is to calculate the amount of the contractual loan payments that will not be received and to include this information in the ALM model as an early maturity at the contractual interest rate with no repricing opportunity.

Missing from the loan accounting system (LAS) will be a projection of the loan payments that will remain in delinquent status and ultimately result in some portion of the loan being charged off.

Using the calculation from the case study, loan payments totaling $1,750,516.35 would not be received as previously included in IRR assumptions when the loan was originated. The bank would also not accrue 6% interest on this amount for another two years, the remaining term of the loan, and the bank would not have $1,750,516.35 available to reinvest in another loan.

The case study example is for a single loan. There is more discussion of the assumptions for single loans in the "Loan impairment" section below. However, when dealing with groups of homogeneous loans[3] (as is the case for most loans to consumers), IRR assumptions for problem loans cannot be derived directly from the LAS because data on charge-offs and recoveries need to be associated with loan balances to analyze historical loss trends. Most loan accounting systems provide the raw data for this analysis, but the data typically must be compiled and analyzed outside of the LAS to develop meaningful IRR problem loan assumptions. Therefore, banks need to adopt a methodology that can be used to develop these assumptions. One approach is to work with the credit function that develops the allowance for loan and lease loss estimate.

In the United States, Generally Accepted Accounting Principles (GAAP) and banking regulatory guidance has resulted in an allowance for loan and lease losses (ALLL) estimation process that involves two components: impairments recognized on individual loans; and losses inherent in groups of homogeneous loans. A complete discussion of this estimation process is beyond the scope of this chapter. However, briefly stated, the estimation process for the second component—losses inherent in groups of homogeneous loans—relies heavily on a study of historic loss rates with adjustments to these loss rates to recognize the impact of current economic volatility and market conditions.

> Financial institutions that follow International Accounting Standards would look to future economic events as well as current events to compile their ALLL estimate.

Table 2 provides an overview of the data that are used to estimate losses inherent in groups of homogeneous loans. Notice that the estimation method for commercial and commercial real estate loans is listed as both "Individual" and "Risk pool." Some of these loans will be analyzed individually for impairment, as discussed below, while others will be included in the risk pool analysis. Also, residential mortgages and consumer loans are estimated using risk pools except when they are involved in a troubled debt restructuring. In the United States, GAAP requires these loans to be analyzed individually for impairment because of the modification of their debt terms. Only the allowance estimate related to risk pools is included in Table 2.

Table 2. Problem loan data estimation worksheet as of December 31, 20XX

	Commercial	Commercial real estate: construction	Commercial real estate: income	Residential mortgages	Consumer
Allowance estimation method	Individual/ risk pool	Individual/ risk pool	Individual/ risk pool	Risk pool except TDR	Risk pool except TDR
Balance	$8,000,000	$23,000,000	$12,000,000	$35,000,000	$5,000,000
Weighted loss	0.85%	1.46%	0.66%	1.45%	2.90%
Risk pool loss estimate	$68,000	$335,800	$79,200	$507,500	$145,000
Past due	1.10%	3.25%	1.60%	2.10%	4.85%
Past due payments	$88,000	$747,500	$192,000	$735,000	$242,500
Nonaccrual	0.60%	0.95%	0.45%	0.65%	1.05%
Nonaccrual interest	$48,000	$218,500	$54,000	$227,000	$52,500

TDR: Troubled debt restructuring.

The data in the Table 2 worksheet can be used to develop IRR assumptions for problem loans. For instance, in column 1 (Commercial), the weighted loss of 0.85% is multiplied by the outstanding commercial loan balance of $8,000,000 to generate a loss estimate of $68,000. This $68,000 risk pool loss estimate is cash flow that will not be received and therefore cannot be reinvested in the ALM model simulation. Without this loss estimate, the ALM model would assume that the $68,000 will be reinvested and income would be overstated accordingly. The same thought process holds true for "Past due payments" and "Nonaccrual interest." Estimates of cash flows that will not be received from principal and interest payments or interest-only payments must be factored into ALM simulations to produce more accurate income calculations as well as to more accurately represent asset or liability sensitivities.

Table 3 includes the ALLL estimate for one of the risk pools from Table 2. The Table 2 ALLL estimate for commercial real estate construction loans is used in the "Base" case ALM model simulation. Table 3 also includes a "Recovery" case and an "Extended recession" case for use in the ALM model. These cases are stress tests of the IRR assumptions.

For each simulation alternative, the worksheet includes a column for "Months of coverage" that reflects the estimated time required for commercial real estate (CRE) construction loans to move through the workout cycle. The last column includes the average ALLL estimate per month for CRE construction loans. This number represents the dollar amount of principal and interest that will "mature" and not be available for reinvestment each month over the months of coverage period. This number is an estimate of the more precise calculation available for individual loans (i.e. comparing the agreed upon present value of cash flows with the present value of cash flows when the borrower experiences financial difficulties) as discussed in the case study earlier in this chapter.

Table 3. Monthly ALLL estimate worksheet

Simulation	ALLL estimate for CRE construction risk pool	Months of coverage	Average ALLL estimate per month
Base	$335,800	12	$27,983
Recovery	$200,000	10	$20,000
Extended recession	$800,000	16	$50,000

ALLL: allowance for loan and lease losses; CRE: commercial real estate.

A worksheet similar to Table 3 should be prepared for each risk pool. This process should include an analysis of the amount of time a loan takes to move through the workout process for that particular type of loan included in the specific risk pool under analysis. The workout process involves monitoring borrowers through their financial difficulties and potentially accepting amendments to loan agreements, restructuring debt terms, or accepting payoffs in amounts less than borrowers owe under loan agreements. In cases where the loan relationship cannot be saved, the bank may have no choice but to liquidate collateral to repay the loan. Any or all of these situations comprise a loan workout process and ultimately result in the bank settling for less money than it is owed. The "Months of coverage" column in Table 3 shows estimates of the time it takes for this process to arrive at the point where the bank and the borrower have reached a final agreement to settle the debt.

It should be noted that for loans that are not involved in a workout process, the data in Table 2 for past due payments and nonaccrual interest can be used as is for input into the ALM model. For instance, past due payments for commercial real estate construction loans total $747,500. These should be the same data that are available through the LAS except that the LAS may not provide the data by risk pool. Since a risk pool can include various loan types, the calculation of past due payments using a summarized past due percentage for the loan types included in the risk pool may be the only practical way to gather these data for the ALM model. In this example, the $747,500 represents the amount of past due payments as of December 31, 20XX, that may not be collected in the future. Here again, these are payments (cash flows) that cannot be reinvested in the ALM model. Further reading on this topic is provided in the More Info section.

Nonaccrual interest also represents a portion of the payment that may not be collected. These data do not have to be included in the ALM model if past due payments are already included. However, preparing a worksheet similar to Schedule 2 each month or quarter for nonaccrual interest can provide trend data that could be useful to the asset and liability management committee (ALCO) in reviewing the impact of varying economic and market conditions.

Another aspect of the worksheets in Tables 2 and 3 that is not shown is the "maturing" interest rate. Since the methodology used to estimate the payments that may not be received in Table 2 involves aggregating and analyzing LAS data, interest rates associated with the risk pool loans should be aggregated and averaged as well, if possible.

Loan Review Function

Table 1 lists the data sources for problem loans that can be used to develop IRR assumptions. These sources are divided between data that can generally be extracted from a bank's loan accounting system (LAS) and data that are only available through loan files. The data that are only available through loan files are often entrusted to a loan review function. Loan review is typically responsible for evaluating areas such as credit quality, the sufficiency of credit and collateral documentation, proper lien perfection, proper approval by an account officer and/or committee, adherence to loan agreement covenants, compliance with internal policies and procedures, laws and regulations, and the appropriateness and timeliness of inclusion as a classified loan. This function must remain independent of the loan production process to ensure objectivity when evaluating these areas.

> Given this broad perspective related to lending and the direct exposure to problem loans, the loan review function is often an excellent source for the types of IRR assumption data that are needed.

Loan Impairment

According to US GAAP, loans are impaired when, based on current information and events, it is likely that a bank will be unable to collect all amounts due according to the contractual terms of the loan agreement, including both principal and interest.

In most cases, US banks will be required to measure an impaired loan using a present value calculation based on the following guidance.[4]

> - The estimates of expected future cash flows should be based on reasonable and supportable assumptions and projections.
> - All available evidence should be considered in developing the estimate of expected future cash flows, including estimated costs of selling the collateral if those costs are expected to reduce the cash flows available to repay or otherwise satisfy the loan.
> - The weight given to the evidence should be commensurate with the extent to which the evidence can be verified objectively.

As shown in the case study, loan impairments should be used as IRR assumptions to reflect loan "maturities" that cannot be reinvested.

Changes can occur in the assumptions that are used to determine impairment. For cash flow assumptions under US GAAP, if after the initial measurement of impairment there is a significant change (increase or decrease) in the amount or timing of an impaired loan's expected future cash flows, or if actual cash flows differ significantly from the cash flows previously projected, a bank should recalculate the impairment by applying the present value procedures to the revised cash flow estimates and adjust the valuation allowance for the revised impairment estimate.

Because of the potential for changes to impairment amounts, banks should use the most current impairment numbers in their IRR model assumptions.

Restructured Loans

When faced with a problem loan, lenders will frequently try to restructure the credit to ease the situation. In a troubled debt restructuring, the bank, for economic and legal reasons related to the borrower's financial difficulties, grants a concession to the borrower that it would not otherwise have granted. Restructuring may involve extending payment schedules, reducing interest rates, reducing the amount of principal or the amount of accrued interest due, granting additional credit, or having property transferred to the bank in full or partial satisfaction of the debt.

The following are examples of how to account for loans that have experienced a modification of terms or a settlement under US GAAP.

- *Modification of terms.* US GAAP requires a bank that modifies debt terms for a borrower to calculate the impairment related to this modification and establish a valuation allowance. This valuation allowance, which becomes part of the bank's allowance for loan and lease loss estimate, represents loan payments that may not be received in the future. Therefore, the amount of the impairment should be used as an adjustment to the ALM model cash flow assumptions.
- *Collateral transfer/exchange of assets.* In the United States, the substitution of a new borrower for a current borrower is treated as a collateral transfer or debt settlement through establishing a new loan. Therefore, according to US GAAP, the receipt of a loan from a new borrower is accounted for as an exchange of assets. The asset received (the new loan) is recorded at fair value. Although in a modification of terms impairment is recorded through a valuation allowance, a settlement results in a new loan that is recorded at fair market value and a loss is recognized and charged to the allowance for loan and lease losses (ALLL) balance.

In these restructured loan examples, the impairment amounts should be used as IRR model assumptions according to the discussion in the section on loan impairment as well as the case study. When an exchange of assets takes place, the exchange will often result in a charge-off. In the United States this charge-off is deducted from the ALLL balance, so the charge-off amount is not used as an IRR assumption. The amount charged off is already included in an impairment analysis or in the risk-pool ALLL calculations from Tables 2 and 3. This is because charge-offs are estimated and added into the ALLL balance at the end of each accounting period. So, when a loan charge-off actually occurs, it is deducted from the ALLL. Therefore, for IRR modeling, the estimated charge-off is used and not the actual charge-off to provide for a more timely recognition of possible changes in cash flows.

Foreclosures, Charge-Offs, and Sale of Collateral

Foreclosures, charge-offs, and sale of collateral (the actual impairment or risk-pool ALLL calculations from Tables 2 and 3), are also sufficient for IRR model assumptions. When collateral is taken to pay off past due payments, IRR assumptions related to the past due payments have already been factored into the ALM model, as noted in the discussion related to Table 2. The collateral taken becomes an asset on the bank's balance sheet and the loan balance is eliminated. Once this transaction takes place, credit risk has been realized and no further IRR assumptions are needed. With foreclosed assets there is risk related to the liquidation of the assets and the amount that will ultimately be recovered. However, this is a different sort of risk that falls outside the context of the discussion of problem loans in this chapter.

Coordinating ALM Policies with Loan Policies and Procedures

A bank must establish written policies and procedures for its loan portfolio. The guiding principle in establishing such policies is achieving profitable returns from the lending process while managing risks that are inherent in any loan portfolio. Some of the more common risks that a bank manages within its lending portfolio are:

- credit risk;
- collateral risk;
- concentration of credit risk;
- interest rate risk;
- operational risks.

This list of the common risk characteristics is based on the lender's perspective. The ALM manager and the ALCO should adopt a similar approach to coordinating interest rate risk with the credit, collateral, and operational risks that lenders must manage, monitor, and mitigate. Ideally, the interest rate risk described in asset–liability management policies will be expanded to include the maturity and repricing characteristics of loans from the lender's perspective. ALM managers already evaluate contractual loan payments and prepayments. They should also add modified payments, missed payments, and credit default issues such as impaired loans, repossessions, and foreclosures to their model simulations.

In larger banks with more complex operations, ALM policies should contemplate using a credit default risk model to determine the probability of default and loss given default for impaired loans. For these larger banks, IRR assumptions could incorporate the probability-based results of a credit default model instead of inputting data related to modified payments, missed payments, and credit default issues such as impaired loans, repossessions, and foreclosures into model simulations. The More Info section at the end of the chapter provides further information on this approach.

Credit Risk Modeling

There are many well-researched applications that deal with the pricing of securities and the valuation of portfolios of assets sensitive to market risk. However, the integration of interest rate risk and credit risk in a common framework is still undeveloped territory.

Current IRR modeling relies on having a normal distribution of returns based on interest rate assumptions. A normal distribution is possible because the primary uncertainty in the analysis process is the yield curve, which already factors in credit risk. For the United States the credit risk assumption has been zero, although this may change in the years to come.

When factoring in credit risk related to bank borrowers, there is no yield curve equivalent available to use in default probability analyses. Instead of a normal distribution as used in interest rate risk analyses, the distribution of credit losses is based on non-normal and heavily skewed distributions, such as a large probability of small loan returns and a small probability of large loan losses. There are many causes of these losses that require more sophisticated modeling approaches.

Credit risk models deal with the lack of normal loss distributions in various ways. Some start with a normal distribution and develop ways to identify probabilities that fall out of the normal range. Others may assess credit risk due to default losses only. Ideally, this type of model would consider market information such as the loan's credit quality rating and the term structure of credit spreads.

Models relying on "default events" base their analysis on expected historical default rates, similar to the more manual approach used in Table 2. This approach enables the modeler to calculate the loss distribution using the historical default rates. However, this approach does not enable the modeler to value loans at current market prices for mark-to-market equity-at-risk analyses.

Alternatively, mark-to-market models enable modelers to calculate the present value of a portfolio of credit risk-sensitive assets dependent on credit risk only. From an ALM modeling perspective, interest rate risk is not incorporated into the mark-to-market models.

These credit risk models serve an important purpose in large banks with complex loan portfolios. However, more work needs to be done to integrate interest rate risk with credit risk. Whether this is accomplished through the credit risk model vendors listed at the end of the chapter or through ALM model vendors (or both) remains to be seen.

In smaller banks, the more manual analytical approach discussed in this chapter can more readily provide for the integration of credit risk (problem loans) with interest rate risk. Here again, this effort is in its very early stages, and continued economic volatility may provide the incentives to further develop this integrated modeling capability.

Summary and Further Steps

The focus of this chapter has been on expanding ALM modeling to include assumptions about problem loan interest rate risk related to modified loan payments, missed payments, and default issues such as impaired loans, repossessions, and foreclosures. The learning points that are intended in this chapter can be summarized as follows.

- There is some industry support for incorporating problem loan data into IRR assumptions, but much more work has to be done to bring credit risk into routine ALM modeling exercises.
- Problem loan impairment analysis provides a good example of how to identify appropriate data for inclusion in IRR assumptions.
- When expanding IRR assumptions for all types of problem loans, banks need to source data from their loan accounting system and loan review function.
- IRR assumptions using data from the loan accounting system can be compiled using methodologies found in the allowance for loan and lease losses (ALLL) estimation process.
- IRR assumptions using data from the loan review function can be compiled using impairment analysis methods discussed in the chapter.
- Banks working to integrate problem loan data into their IRR assumptions should begin by coordinating their ALM policies with their loan policies and procedures.
- Interest rate risk modeling is based on a normal probability distribution, whereas credit risk modeling is based on non-normal and heavily skewed probability distributions, making these two risk issues somewhat difficult to reconcile.
- An important next step for banks is to embrace the idea that problem loan data should be incorporated into IRR assumptions and the ALM modeling process. As more banks take on this challenge, there will hopefully be further development of methodologies to address the combined impact of interest rate risk and credit risk on the earnings, equity, and safety and soundness of the banking industry. Additional resources are listed below to assist banks in this effort.

More Info

Credit Risk Models and Research

Baer, Tobias, Venkata Krishna Kishore, and Akbar N. Sheriff. "Best practices for estimating credit economic capital." McKinsey working papers on risk no. 11. April 2009. Online at: tinyurl.com/89yz32y [PDF].

CreditManager (based on the CreditMetrics methodology developed by the RiskMetrics Group and formerly JP Morgan): tinyurl.com/7gbvke7

CreditPortfolioView (from McKinsey): www.mckinsey.com

Credit Suisse First Boston. "CreditRisk+: A credit risk management framework." 1997. Online at: globalriskguard.com/resources/credit/creditrisk.pdf

Martin, Richard. "Credit portfolio modeling handbook." Credit Suisse First Boston, October 29, 2004. Online at: tinyurl.com/74n5l77 [PDF].

Portfolio Manager (from KMV): www.moodyskmv.com

Task Force of the Market Operations Committee of the European System of Central Banks. "The use of portfolio credit risk models in central banks." Occasional paper series no. 64. European Central Bank, July 2007. Online at: www.ecb.int/pub/pdf/scpops/ecbocp64.pdf

ALM: Credit Risk Research Studies

Jobst, Norbert J., Gautam Mitra, and Stavros A. Zenios. "Dynamic asset (and liability) management under market and credit risk." Brunel University, Centre for the Analysis of Risk and Optimisation Modelling Applications (CARISMA) technical report. June 2003. Online at: tinyurl.com/7lloamy [PDF].

Jobst, Norbert J., and Stavros A. Zenios. "Extending credit risk (pricing) models for the simulation of portfolios of interest rate and credit risk sensitive securities." Wharton Financial Institutions Center working paper 01-25. July 2001. Online at: knowledge.wharton.upenn.edu/papers/1179.pdf

ALM Modeling and Training Companies

Darling Consulting Group: www.darlingconsulting.com

Fiserv (ALM model was formerly ips-sendero): www.riskandperformance.fiserv.com

Kamakura Corporation (integrated risk solutions for capital risk, credit risk, market risk, operational risk, and liquidity and interest rate risk): www.kamakuraco.com

SunGard; see link to Ambit Risk and Performance Management product: tinyurl.com/7879blj

Notes

1. Guglielmo, Michael R. "Asset/liability management in a new era of regulatory scrutiny: Preparing for the 'new normal.'" *Bank Accounting and Finance* (October 2010). Online at: tinyurl.com/7vshvpv [PDF].
2. PricewaterhouseCoopers. "Balance sheet management benchmark survey: Status of balance sheet management practices among international banks—2009." 2009. Online at: tinyurl.com/7tna9q2 [PDF].
3. Relative to commercial loans, homogenous loans are smaller balance loans made to consumers. Consumer loan products include residential real estate loans, auto loans, personal loans, credit cards, etc.
4. Other data that US GAAP suggests as a basis for measuring impairment include the market price of the loan or the fair value of the collateral supporting the loan. However, market prices are often not available for loans, and the fair value of the collateral approach should only be used when the borrowers and or guarantors cannot or will not be making any further payments on the loan.

Product Taxonomy: A Key Tool for Understanding Risk–Return Within the Banking Framework

by Markus Krebsz

Subject Matter Expert

This Chapter Covers

- An introduction to products and taxonomy, product taxonomies for financial institutions, and the structure of a taxonomy.
- Applications of product taxonomies in a financial setting and the objectives in using them.
- Regulatory developments after the credit crunch.
- A guide to developing and implementing a product taxonomy for financial institutions.
- A practical approach to taxonomy for financial institutions.
- Principles for the development of a product taxonomy.

Introduction: Products and Taxonomy

What does a callable, daily, dual-currency range accrual with quanto features have in common with a sugar-free, hazelnut-flavored, soya milk decaf cappuccino? The answer is that both are products.

Dealing with "products" (whether coffee or financial) requires an understanding of:

- what their features are;
- how to determine or measure their value;
- the type of customers who would be interested in buying them.

It is also important to understand and manage the risks related to the products and to have the capability to drill down into their underlying components (in the case of the coffee, for example, to find out if the hazelnut-flavored syrup contains nuts).

If you are working with coffee it is relatively easy to drill down into underlying components and present the information to the customer. This is achieved by having a menu showing available products (cappuccinos, espressos, lattes, frescatos, etc.) together with product-specific features (semi-skimmed or soya milk, sugar-free, fair-trade, flavored, etc.), and trade-specific features (drink in or takeaway, short, tall, grande, venti, etc).[1]

But what about the capital markets? How do you classify a certain interest rate product that has an observable asset class, product class, underlying(s), optionality, call features, different coupon types, is inflation-linked, and has a high degree of market volatility? What are the risks of originating or trading such a financial instrument, how much capital does your firm need to put aside to manage it, and how will you need to report to your shareholders and to the regulator? What do you call it?

How can firms classify financial products in a meaningful way and tick most of the information requirement boxes of the consumers of such information—i.e. front office, middle office, quants, model certification, legal and compliance, finance and accounting, regulatory reporting, product control, risk management, and asset and liability management? The answer is simple: by having an appropriate product taxonomy in place that can support all those functions.

This chapter aims to provoke thought on this topic and to equip you with some pragmatic pointers about how to establish such a taxonomy.

Product Taxonomies for Financial Institutions

Taxonomies are not only used as part of scientific methodologies, they also play a hugely important role for many, if not all, corporations. For instance, think of a grocery store and how they manage their product inventory. Their taxonomy becomes obvious and easily visible when one shops for groceries online; you, as a consumer, can follow the supermarket's taxonomy by clicking through the products on its website and you may be able to recognize an imposed, path-dependent tree structure that is representative of the grocery store's product taxonomy.

Similarly, we can ask what financial institutions are dealing with. Of course, with financial instruments—i.e. products. The added complexity in the case of most of these instruments is that, unlike a shopping basket full of groceries, they cannot be visibly "seen" and hence are not that easily recognizable (apart from the legal documentation or piece of paper that represents the product, such as a banknote, mortgage documentation, or a bond term sheet).

Given that on a global scale there are probably many hundreds of different financial products that are being dealt with on a daily basis, you may think that many, if not all, financial institutions have a well-developed and clearly articulated methodology that enables them to properly manage these products. And as financial institutions' bread and butter is dealing with financial products that represent both assets and liabilities, one may think that a product taxonomy plays an important, if not a central, part in firms' asset and liability management (ALM) function.

Surprising as it may sound, many financial institutions have only relatively recently discovered the need for a firmwide product taxonomy and, even more concerning, many firms currently do not even have one.

The Structure of a Taxonomy

The word "taxonomy" originates from two ancient Greek words:

- τάξις, *taxis*, meaning "order" or "arrangement;" and
- νόμος, *nomos*, meaning "law," "science," or "method."

More generally speaking, taxonomy can be understood as a classification system based on a controlled vocabulary. Each term in the vocabulary carries an embedded hierarchy, and taxonomic terms are closely related to each other.

The taxonomy's embedded hierarchy is based on broader and narrower terms. These terms themselves contain equivalent or synonymous relationships, and the intrinsic relationships of the taxonomic components impose a naturally occurring topical tree structure.

The tree structure of the taxonomy consists, quite literally, of the taxonomic "root," branches or "nodes," and "leaves." Most importantly, these taxonomic components are connected and interlinked via a unique path.

Similar to the leaves of a tree that are connected via (smaller and larger) branches to the tree's stem and roots, each taxonomic "leaf" is connected to the taxonomic root via a path-dependent structure that connects it through the nodes of the taxonomy (Figure 1).

Figure 1. Generic root–node–leaf structure and unique path-dependent sequence of a taxonomy

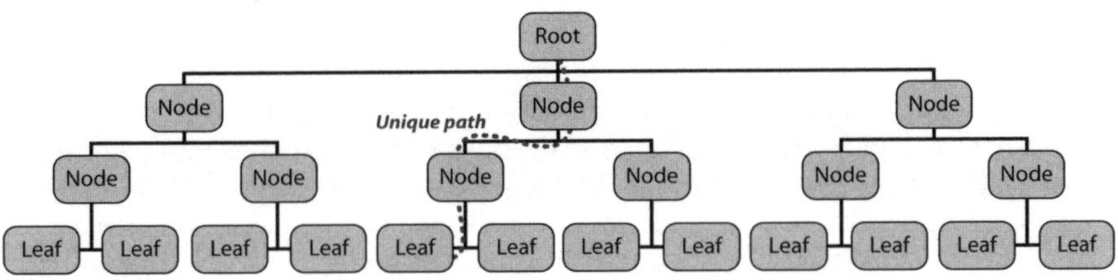

Applications of Taxonomy

Taxonomies are frequently used as classification systems in scientific frameworks. One of the better-known taxonomies is probably the classification of biological organisms, also known as "alpha taxonomy."

Product Taxonomy—A Key Tool

Generally, firms dealing with financial instruments—no matter how simple or complex—are required, by law and for the sake of their stakeholders, to handle these products properly. More specifically, this means that banks and other financial institutions must capture, book, price, value, report, govern, risk manage, bookkeep, and account for the instruments they buy, hold, and sell—or, in some unfortunate cases, make provision for losses resulting from dealing with such products. In simple terms, firms need to manage their assets and liabilities appropriately and have robust functions and methodologies in place that can support their ALM function.

None of these activities, however, can be easily, or indeed at all, addressed without having an adequate and firmwide product taxonomy. This has been one of the particularly painful realizations following the credit crisis (for more on this see the case study in the next section). Consequently, many financial institutions have realized the need to establish a solid product taxonomy as a key tool for identifying asset-liability mismatches as well as understanding and managing their day-to-day operations and the risk–return profile of individual trades as well as of whole (product) portfolios.

Case Study

Understanding Risk–Return

Take a typical fixed-income trader: as he or she is trading nonlinear structured rates instruments, he or she captures the trade. However, in the absence of a firm wide product taxonomy the trading system that handles these instruments offers the trader maximum flexibility in describing the particular trade. There will be certain observable trade facts, such as the notional amount, the maturity, the underlying asset or index, and call options, etc., that are features of the particular deal, expressed maybe in a term sheet and not leaving much room for interpretation.

Next, there is the "product name," which is a free text field. Hence, the trader enters what he or she thinks is most appropriate for the particular deal's product name. In our example, let us say that the trader enters "vanilla swap."

The deal is priced as a "vanilla swap" and passed through from the trade capture via trade booking systems to the firm's analytics platform. The risk of this so-called vanilla swap is modeled and valued by the firm's finance department. If we assume that this was a sizable transaction totaling $250 million with an AA-rated counterparty, the trader's account now shows a nice healthy profit contribution of $15 million for the deal.

There's just one minor problem: the lack of any product taxonomy, with the whole risk assessment and valuation process based on the product name itself—in this example what appeared to be a vanilla swap with an AA-rated counterparty. However, if it takes a closer look at the particular transaction, ignores the product name that was assigned to the deal by the trader, and instead investigates the observable facts or attributes of the actual trade, the firm may be unpleasantly surprised.

It turns out that the trade in question is in fact not a "vanilla swap" at all, but the purchase of an AA-rated collateral debt obligation of asset-backed securities (or a CDO of ABS), whereby the underlying is in fact 85% residential mortgage-backed securities (RMBS) comprising mainly US subprime loans. Oops!

A CDO of ABS is hardly a standard product, and the risk–return profile of such an instrument is fundamentally different from that of an actual vanilla swap of, say, a three-month Libor to six-month US dollar with an AA-rated counterparty.

While the case study is an extreme example, similar misclassifications based purely on the name of a traded product and subsequent misrepresentation of the trade as part of the risk management, financial accounting, and regulatory reporting happened regularly at many firms prior to and during the credit crunch—and not once or twice, but quite frequently—often on a systemic level. More worryingly, misinterpretation of trades, with a potentially detrimental impact on firms' ALM efforts, is likely to continue until firms adopt and implement robust, firmwide product taxonomies.

Taxonomy in the Banking Framework

So what are the typical problems in a banking framework, and how can a clearly articulated, robust and firmwide product taxonomy address and help to overcome these issues?

The first summary list below provides an overview of common problems experienced by firms as a result of the lack of a clear product classification. It shows how key gaps in a financial institution's product control and governance framework and related processes may result in financial losses and increased regulatory and reputational risks.

Key Control Gaps

- *Model usage and performance*. Inability to map pricing, risk measurement, and valuation models to products. There is a significant risk of models incorrectly calculating risk or valuation numbers, particularly for those models that rely partially on unobservable input parameters or introduce nonstandard risk.
- *Product mandate compliance*. Inability to confirm systematically that front-office trading desks/risk classes are compliant with product mandates—i.e. front-office traders are only dealing instruments within their mandated brief.
- *Business product ownership*. Inability to confirm systematically that all products, as booked within the underlying risk systems, have unique business owners of the risks related to trading in such products.
- *Client entitlements*. Inability to monitor client entitlements at a sufficient level of granularity, specifically in relation to client type/product mix and complex trade approvals.
- *Risk analysis and reporting of specific trade types*. Nonstandard product-naming conventions across risk systems, and inability to report systematically on specific product features.
- *Management information*. Impaired decision-making, risk transparency, and risk measurement/management.

The Beneficial Impact from Both Having a Product Taxonomy for a Range of Business Operations

Optimization of risk-weighted assets (RWA), improved financial resource allocation, and greater ALM accuracy:

- *Market risk*. The mapping of position to value-at-risk (VAR) time series is compromised by the lack of consistent and granular product typing, resulting in erroneous trade capture.
- *Credit risk*. The quality of product definition at trade capture has a direct bearing on the quality of the RWA calculations that drive the financial institution's capital.
- *ALM*. Clearer product definitions and robust classification increase understanding and measurement of how good (or bad) potential asset vs. liability mismatches actually are, enabling firms to employ more targeted remedial actions if necessary.

Operational risk and operational efficiency:

- *Right first time and read only*. Better data quality whenever correct product identification is required at the entry point of the trade (i.e. right first time) and keeping manual intervention to an absolute minimum (read only of trade information).

- *Finance/risk-integrated reporting*. The lack of a product standard limits return on investment in a firm's end-of-day risk aggregation. Integrated profit and loss and risk reporting streams all require a consistent treatment of identical product types.
- *Single product master*. If multiple product listings are used across the organization, each needs to be maintained and mapped/reconciled to other product lists to support cross-functional control and reporting requirements (i.e. risk and finance reconciliation, etc.).

A product taxonomy gives a competitive edge and enables the speedy delivery of new product-related initiatives by:

- *Reducing the time needed to market new products*. Supports a product being defined once as part of an on-boarding and new product approval process and being linked centrally to the required reporting hierarchies.
- *Facilitating validation and quality assurance*. Results in cheaper delivery of control system initiatives.
- *Providing a shareable corporate resource*. Helps to identify which new or enhanced systems or processes can be utilized going forward.

These lists are by no means exhaustive, but even so they constitute a strong business case for the adoption of product taxonomies at banks and other financial institutions.

Regulatory Briefs

Overview

Following the credit crunch, regulators united and discussed globally how the articulation of risk appetite, the management of risk, and prudence in the valuation of financial firms can be considerably improved.

Apart from increased transparency and investor due diligence, more stringent regulatory capital requirements, and ongoing stress-testing of banks, some regulatory voices have recently been much more centered around product control, model risk, and prudent valuation.

All these areas, however, are very closely related to the availability of an appropriate product taxonomy. How else can firms understand and control the products they are dealing with? And how can firms make sure that they use the appropriate models to manage the risks posed by certain products? Models will never be a true reflection of reality and consequently will always constitute a simulated environment. However, this is not being helped by the use of inadequate models altogether because there is no clear understanding of the particular financial instrument whose risk is being modeled.

Coming back to the coffee example, what's the point of modeling the risk of coffee connoisseurs burning themselves when pouring iced latte over their hands? Or, in financial terms, of using an interest rate model that uses three-month US dollar interest rate curves to model the risk of a single-range accrual that is based on Swiss francs? The answer is simple: firms can only model and value products robustly if they know what the financial instruments they are dealing with are. While this seems fairly obvious, during and after the credit crunch regulators have grown increasingly suspicious of firms that do not come across as capable of determining their own products.

The next section provides a brief overview of current global regulatory initiatives in the product taxonomy space—and we can expect more of these in the next few years.

Bank for International Settlements (BIS): Financial Stability Board

In December 2010 the BIS Financial Stability Board's senior supervisors group published a white paper entitled "Observations on developments in risk appetite frameworks and IT infrastructure." It stated the following: "Significantly, firms with a single firm-wide data taxonomy, as described above, can facilitate the integration of disparate systems and platforms with the firm's existing architecture. Thus, development of this taxonomy will directly improve firms' ability to address the otherwise difficult task of integrating legacy systems." (BIS, 2010).

The white paper is well worth closer examination. It would appear that the senior supervisors' approach tabled in the white paper has further triggered national regulators' individual responses, some of which are briefly discussed in the following paragraphs.

The UK Financial Services Authority's Stance on Model Risk and Prudent Valuation

Here in the United Kingdom, the Financial Services Authority (FSA) is currently working on several initiatives around model risk, prudent valuation, and product taxonomy that are worth mentioning, and we can expect to see more in 2012/13. Its initiatives in this space date back to August 2008, when the FSA sent a "Dear CEO" letter entitled "Valuation and product control" to financial institutions in the United Kingdom (Sants, 2008). The letter outlines concerns about control failings that had led to several mismarking incidents as well as drawing attention to valuation uncertainty and regulatory prudent valuation.

It also stated that "The complexity of firms' trading operations has been continually increasing over the last ten years. ...firms must be prepared to take extra steps to deal with the incremental risks associated with less liquid, complex and/or modelled products. The increased *valuation uncertainty* that can be associated with these products is likely to precipitate the need for increased focus on the regulatory principles on prudent valuation, which are an important component of the overall regulatory capital framework for the Trading Book. Adjustments to *Tier One capital are required where prudent value is assessed as being materially below fair value...*" (emphasis in last sentence mine) and furthermore that "by developing better frameworks for the measurement of residual valuation and model risks after the application of IPV, model validation and other processes, firms would be better placed...to deliver a control framework consistent with the *prudent valuation principles*."

In other words, with this letter the FSA demonstrates that it is actively contemplating adding further regulatory charges to the tier one capital for firms that fall behind in terms of prudent valuation and, intrinsically, model risk and product classification. That's one way to incentivize firms to clean up their act. Another, which the FSA has used and continues to use, is to establish temporary trading restrictions on specific products. Although not widely publicized, this has been done on several occasions, and some of the remedial actions that have been employed by firms to lift these regulator-imposed restrictions are to put robust product taxonomies in place and subsequently to provide assurance to the FSA that they are now capable of robustly assigning models to related products and hence are modeling risks appropriately.

Furthermore, the FSA has implemented a new assessment framework for prudent valuation to promote a more systematic approach to the assessment of valuation uncertainty and prudent valuation. Since 2011, on a quarterly basis, firms have been required to report initial prudent valuation adjustments along with policies and procedures defining the firms' approach to and framework for valuation uncertainty. The FSA reviews and formally assesses each firm's prudent valuation framework and methodologies through comprehensive reviews and meetings with individual firms. Most importantly, *from the perspective of product taxonomy, the FSA assesses granular judgmental analysis by firms at product level.*

US Commodity Futures Trading Commission and the International Swaps and Derivatives Association

In light of forthcoming regulatory changes around central counterparties (CCP) and centralized clearing houses (CCH), the US Commodity Futures Trading Commission (CFTC), together with other market associations and trade bodies such as the International Swaps and Derivatives Association (ISDA), have recently started initiatives around unique product identifiers (UPIs).

This is with a view to establishing a market infrastructure for standardized over-the-counter (OTC) derivative products enabling electronic execution and central clearing similar to other securities markets and ultimately aims at increasing post-trade transparency. A recently published white paper entitled "Product representation for standardized derivatives" (ISDA, 2011) examines how such a new infrastructure for OTC products can be achieved, considers the implementation of a centralized derivatives product registry, and discusses the benefits of a product registry and UPIs.

A Brief Guide to Developing and Implementing a Product Taxonomy for Financial Institutions

After defining the product taxonomy, discussing its benefits for understanding risk–return in the banking framework, and indeed simply realizing the need to have a product taxonomy in light of the further regulatory changes on the horizon, the big question for many financial institutions is Where do we go from here?

The next section provides some pointers and practical guidance. You may find the following two tools particularly useful, and I am hoping that you will find them equally valuable when planning to develop, or when actually developing, a bespoke product taxonomy for your institution.

The Taxonomy Development Process

Every project has several stages, and the development of a firmwide product taxonomy can easily amount to a major project. For instance, one US investment bank developed and adopted a robust, well thought-through product taxonomy—but altogether it took them close to seven years to complete it.

However, this hardly comes as a surprise if you know that a trade or product lifecycle stretches across the whole range of a bank's functional areas, starting with trade capture and booking systems in the front office, through the traders' pricing, valuation and risk systems, and last but not least the trade population in the firm's end-of-day risk aggregation, finance, and regulatory accounting systems. Depending on the size of the financial institution and the nature of its business, you are potentially looking at anything between 50 and up to 250 systems—in some extreme cases, even more.

Hence, it's important to come up with a generic schema for the development of a taxonomy, but bear in mind that any taxonomy is likely to be firm-specific and, therefore, somewhat bespoke. This means that although conceptually the development schema shown in Figure 2 may prove useful, you should not shy away from amending it to ensure that it is fit for your particular purpose.

Figure 2. Generic schema for development of a taxonomy. (*Source*: Adapted from Whittaker and Breininger, 2008)

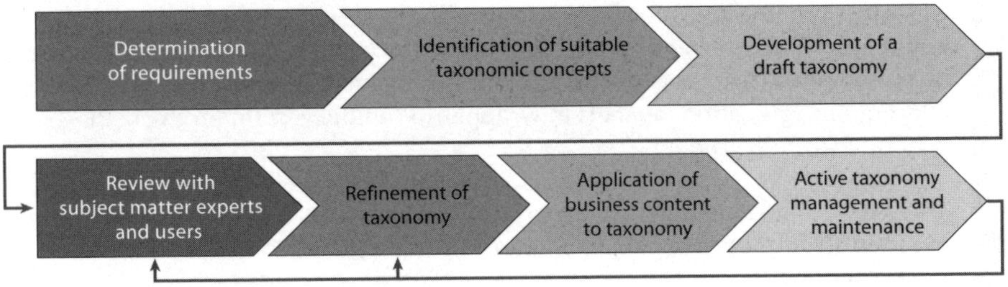

Typically, the development and implementation of a taxonomy encompasses the following phases.

1. Determination of requirements
   - *Scope*: Which business division and functional areas are to be covered by the taxonomy?
   - *Purpose*: What is the key purpose of the taxonomy?
   - *Type of content format*: Is there a particular format, and are there sound industry practices that can serve as an example?
   - *Target audience and users*: Who is going to use the taxonomy and how?
   - *Business objective*: Why do we need a taxonomy?

Output and tools: Business case and requirements document; statement of scope; project plan; terms of reference; risks, assumptions, issues, and development (RAID) log; key project contacts list.

2. Identification of suitable taxonomic concepts
- Where and what is the content and which products are to be classified by the taxonomy?
- Perform product inventory analysis with the aim of producing a draft product list:
  - What exists already?
  - Where is it located?
  - How many source systems are involved?
  - How broad will the coverage be?
  - How much variety exists in the source systems?
- Conduct user interviews

Output: Identify a current product list for each business function and system—and, equally important, how they are mapped to each other.

3. Development of a firm's draft product taxonomy
- General design consideration: What is an optimum level of nodes/hierarchies? A two-level structure seems to work well.
- Start broad, not deep.
- Approaches: Top-down and/or bottom-up approach.
- Develop upper taxonomic levels (see next section for an explanation):
  - Major product features (i.e. mandatory nodes).
- Develop lower taxonomic levels (see next section for an explanation):
  - Product-specific features (i.e. product-specific nodes).

Output: Common rules for format of taxonomic terms, taxonomic structure, and relationship between core nodes (mandatory and product-specific features), noncore nodes (instance-specific and function-specific nodes), and possible additional aggregation layers (i.e. wrapper to bundle certain products to generate strategy trades).

4. Review with subject matter experts and users
- Identify appropriate subject matter experts to validate the proposed draft taxonomy.
- Sound practice here suggests:
  - Avoid overthinking.
  - Avoid developing unnecessary sections.
  - Avoid overengineering the taxonomy.

Output: Sound validation of the proposed taxonomy that answers the following questions:
- Does the structure of the taxonomy make sense?
- Does the taxonomy go too deep?
- Have all major products been included?
- Are there any gaps that need to be addressed at this stage?

5. Refining the taxonomy
- Refining of a product taxonomy is mainly an iterative process covering:
  - Analysis of the results of feasibility studies.
  - Incorporation of changes.
  - Addressing user feedback.

- Taxonomies tend to be living/growing tools, i.e. they are never finished.
- Refinement should stop when the taxonomy is "good enough," i.e. fit for purpose.
- Refinement of a taxonomy should always observe a balance of value vs. detail.

6. Application of the taxonomy to the business content
- In the context of banks or financial institutions the application of taxonomy to content would mean products to cover certain divisions (for instance investment bank or retail banking).
- Integrate with existing applications (i.e. trade capture, trade booking, valuation, risk in the front office and end-of-day risk aggregation, ALM tools, and finance valuation engines).
- Associate taxonomy terms with products.
- Address links to other firmwide concepts:
  - Trader mandates.
  - Model inventory and certifications.
  - Internal and external taxonomies.
- Provide guidelines for use, application, and training for users.

7. Active taxonomy management and maintenance
- Establish ownership of taxonomy.
  - Who owns and maintains taxonomy? Documentation.
- Establish governance process.
- Establish change control process.
  - Review, approval, and implementation of change; version control.
- Periodic review to establish if the product still "fits" its purpose and objectives.

A Practical Approach to Taxonomy for Financial Institutions

This section provides a practical approach to taxonomy for financial institutions. Although largely a conceptual representation of a taxonomy, this concept has been applied and tested and is one of several approaches that have been proven to work. Again, it is, however, important to realize that any product taxonomy must be fit for purpose for the firm that builds, adopts, and uses it.

Coming back to the root–node–leaf-imposed tree structure discussed earlier, one possible way to implement a product taxonomy at a financial institution is by choosing a root–node-based map approach to product features that will apply to all products the firm is dealing with.

The major components of such a taxonomy are:

- core nodes;
- noncore nodes;
- an aggregation layer or layers.

Mandatory Nodes

Core nodes may comprise mandatory nodes, which represent the root of the taxonomic classification and are relevant to all products and functions. The following lists a sample of such possible mandatory nodes and suitable valid values for each node.

- *Asset*: Equities, rates, credit, foreign exchange, etc.
- *Product*: Swap, option, forward, etc.
- *Underlying*: Interest rate, single currency, currency pair, common stock, etc.
- *Market*: Listed, OTC, exchange-traded, private placement, etc.
- *Complexity*: Simple, exotic, complex, etc.

Product-Specific Nodes

In contrast, product-specific nodes capture attributes that define the specific product type, and hence will not necessarily apply to all products. Following is a list of examples of product-specific nodes and valid values for each of these.

- *Currency treatment*: Single currency, dual currency, quanto, etc.
- *Exercise feature*: Callable, puttable, etc.
- *Exercise type*: European, American, Bermudan, autocallable, etc.
- *Time operation*: Asian, min/max, lookback, lock-in, ladder, etc.
- *Underlying structure*: Single, basket, rainbow, etc.
- *Early exercise condition*: Target, barrier, elimination, memory touch, etc.
- *Performance type*: Cliquet, escalator, swing, etc.
- *Conditional payoff*: Kick-in, kick-out, etc.
- *Barrier features*: Up, down, continuous, discrete, etc.
- *Coupon types*: Fixed, floating, inflation-adjusted, zero-coupon, etc.
- *Funding status*: Cash, synthetic, etc.
- Etc.

Noncore nodes may comprise instance-specific nodes that capture attributes for the particular instance of that product type and they are complemented by function-specific nodes, which represent extensions of the taxonomy created for different functional areas (i.e. finance, risk, and regulatory reporting).

An aggregation layer (or layers) then further enhances this taxonomy by providing an aggregation logic which may be used to link and combine individual products in a holistic fashion—for example "Structured investment wrapper," "Deals by combining several strategies," "Strategies that combine several traded products," and so on.

Figure 3 is a graphical representation of this root–node-based approach and the relationship of the different taxonomic levels or layers.

Figure 3. Root–node-based approach, node relationships, and product aggregation

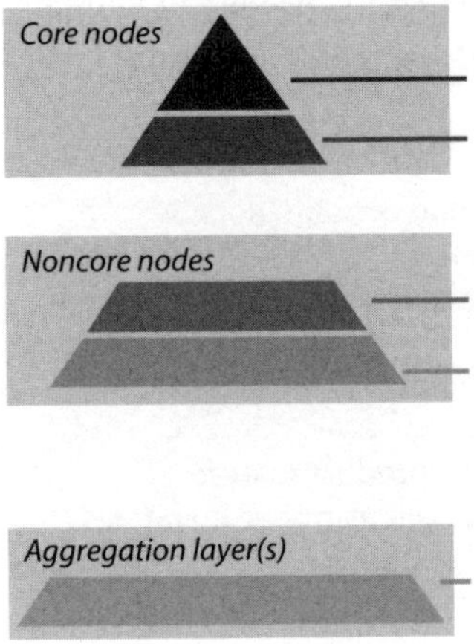

Core nodes comprise:
Mandatory nodes = root of the taxonomic classification and relevant to all products and functions.
Product-specific nodes capture attributes that define the specific product type (not always applicable).

Noncore nodes comprise:
Instance-specific nodes capture attributes for the particular instance of that product type.
Function-specific nodes are extensions of the taxonomy created for different functional areas, e.g. risk management, financial reporting, regulatory reporting, etc.

Aggregation layer(s):
An aggregation logic that may be used to link and combine individual products, e.g. structured investment wrappers, deals by combining several strategies, strategies that combine several traded products, etc.

Other Considerations

As part of a product taxonomy framework, the following specifics may apply.

Product Identification

- Via a product taxonomy rule-based approach (through trade capture, valid values, and business rules).
- Content values for mandatory nodes must be defined for all products classified by the taxonomy.
- Optional specifiers for various product characteristics of product-specific nodes.
- Additional instance- and function-specific nodes can be populated on the basis of rules specific to the product type identified (i.e. via product-specific templates).

Additional Features of a Taxonomy

- Links to trader mandates, model inventory, and model and/or product certifications.
- Product aggregation layers to manage the risks of complex instruments.
- Easily maintainable and extendable for new products.

Principles of Taxonomy Governance

- Governed by a cross-functional working group (business and control).
- Driven by control and reporting requirements.

Principles for the Development of a Product Taxonomy

When developing a firmwide product taxonomy, it is also worth keeping in mind the following principles.

The product taxonomy:

- is driven by control and reporting requirements that contain globally authorized business definitions, terms, and codes;
- will define the global data standard for global products, enabling consistent understanding;
- enables front-to-back product representation by applying consistent, cross-functional design principles;
- contains the product code, product name, and key product features;
- will link to other internal and external concepts, such as trader mandates, model inventory, and certifications and other hierarchies;
- overarches two key product concepts that support product control and reporting requirements, as set out in the next two lists.

Product classifications:

- consist of a set of product-classifying attributes that are used to classify but not to describe the product;
- are used to group products with similar features;
- *are not data dictionaries of all product attributes* but are restricted to attributes required for reporting purposes;
- need to be easily maintainable and extendable in order to cater for new products.

Product lists:

- are a single master list of products;
- contain a unique product code, name, and description;
- define the primary product key within the firm's rule set;
- define the minimum product features needed for general control and reporting requirements;
- define products' business owners and internal entitlements;
- need to be easily maintainable and extendable for new products.

Conclusion

Product taxonomy, and setting up such a taxonomy, is certainly not one of the easiest topics, and much more could be written on it. Hopefully, you will find this chapter to be a useful introduction into an often overlooked, yet fundamentally important and crucial area for financial institutions.

Additional information on feasibility studies and asset class definition, particularly in the structured finance space, can be found in Krebsz, 2011.

More Info

Book:

Krebsz, Markus. *Securitization and Structured Finance Post Credit Crunch: A Best Practice Deal Lifecyle Guide*. Chichester, UK: Wiley, 2011. Online at: www.structuredfinanceguide.com

Articles:

Bank for International Settlements (BIS) Financial Stability Board. "Observations on developments in risk appetite frameworks and IT infrastructure." December 23, 2010. Online at: www.fsa.gov.uk/pubs/other/ssg_2010.pdf

Bennett, Mike. "Financial securities ontology." Hypercube Ltd. May 2007. Online at: www.hypercube.co.uk/docs/ontologyexploration.doc

International Swaps and Derivatives Association (ISDA). "Product representation for standardized derivatives." White paper, April 14, 2011. Online at: tinyurl.com/6sxtmnw [PDF].

International Swaps and Derivatives Association (ISDA). "Implementation plan for unique product identifiers." June 30, 2011. Online at: tinyurl.com/d3ta9xa [PDF].

Sants, Hector. "Dear CEO: Valuation and product control." Financial Services Authority, August 13, 2008. Online at: www.fsa.gov.uk/pubs/ceo/valuation.pdf

Whittaker, Mary, and Kathryn Breininger. "Taxonomy development for knowledge management." Presented at World Library and Information Congress, 74th IFLA General Conference and Council, Quebec, Canada, August 10–14, 2008. Online at: tinyurl.com/74yuqau [PDF].

Website:

Enterprise Data Management (EDM) Council's "Semantics Repository": www.edmcouncil.org/sec_semantics.aspx

Notes

1. For a coffee-related product taxonomy that illustrates the coffee examples further (and is to be taken with a pinch or two of salt), please refer to the following link: www.quicksilverweb.net/sbucks/sbcharts.htm

Tools for Measuring Interest Rate Risk

by Steven V. Mann

Moore School of Business, University of South Carolina, USA

This Chapter Covers

- The two dimensions of interest rate risk: level risk and curve risk.
- The two approaches for measuring interest rate risk: duration/convexity and full valuation.
- The valuation of any security involves determining the present values of expected cash flows and figuring out how much the embedded options are worth.
- Four attributes govern a bond's response to a yield change: the remaining term to maturity, the level of the coupon rate, the level of the yields, and the presence of embedded options.
- Duration can be defined as the average percentage price change for a 100 bp movement in the reference yield curve.
- Convexity measures the magnitude of the error of linear approximation by duration of the price–yield relationship.
- The full valuation approach performs a full valuation of a bond (or bond portfolio) for each of the chosen interest rate scenarios.

Introduction

One can understand risk intuitively as the chance of an unpleasant surprise. Financial institutions must be able to manage their exposure to risk. To accomplish this task, they must be able to identify the risks to which they are exposed and measure that exposure. Numerous types of risk put a financial institution in harm's way. One major exposure is to interest rate risk. Interest rate risk has two dimensions—*level risk* and *curve risk*. Level risk is the chance of an adverse movement in the price of a bond owing to a parallel shift in the reference yield curve. Curve risk is the prospect of an adverse movement in the price of a bond owing to a change in the shape (i.e. slope and curvature) of the reference yield curve. To manage their exposure to interest rate risk, financial institutions must be able to measure both level and curve risk. The purpose of this chapter is to introduce the tools for measuring both types of interest rate risk. Most of the time will be spent discussing level risk, while curve risk will be covered to a lesser extent.

We will discuss two approaches for assessing the interest rate risk exposure of a bond or bond portfolio. The first approach entails the computation of measures that approximate how a bond's price or the portfolio's value will change when interest rates change. The most commonly used measures are *duration* and *convexity*. We will discuss duration and convexity measures for bonds and bond portfolios. The second approach is the *full valuation approach*, which involves selecting possible interest rate scenarios for how interest rates and yield spreads may change and then revaluing the bond position.

Why Do Bond Prices Change?

Any security can be thought of as a package of one or more cash flows. A complicated security is a package of cash flows with one or more options attached. The option attached to the security gives its owner (either the holder or the issuer) the right to alter the security's cash flows at an optimal time. That said, the valuation of any security involves determining present values and figuring out how much the embedded options are worth.

To determine present values, a discount rate is employed. Simply put, a discount rate is an exchange rate across time. A discount rate translates the value of a set of cash flows scattered across time and with different exposures to risk into a single sum. In general, discount rates are driven by two factors—a default-free benchmark interest rate and a risk premium. A default-free benchmark interest rate reflects the risk-free interest rate. Even in a world without risk, interest rates are positive. The reason is that human beings would prefer to consume now as opposed to later. Interest rates are bribes designed to quell our impatience to consume. Correspondingly, risk premiums are bribes that are designed to neutralize our risk-aversion. As a general description of how human beings behave, we operate under the assumption that investors are risk-averse. Risk-aversion does not mean that investors shun risk, merely that one must compensate them for taking it. The risk premium is the spread over the risk-free rate required to induce an investor to hold a risky security as opposed to a safe one. For a given level of risk, the risk premium is time-varying. The size of the risk premium depends on both the level of interest rates and investors' willingness to bear risk.

Given this background, we can now address the question of why bond prices change. First, any factor that results in a change in the bond's required yield will result in a change in the price of an option-free bond in the opposite direction. Second, the mere passage of time will push all bond prices to the par values. Bond prices that trade at a premium will be pulled to par without any change in required yield. Although we are cognizant of the second factor, our focus in this chapter is the first factor—specifically, the immediate response of the bond price to an instantaneous change in the bond's required yield.

The Price–Yield Relationship of a Bond

Figure 1 depicts the relationship between the price of a default-free, option-free bond and its required yield. Here, 30-year, 10-year, and five-year US Treasury notes were chosen as examples of such bonds, paying coupons of 4.375%, 3.375%, and 1.5% respectively.[1] Note the features that all three curves in Figure 1 have in common—namely, each relationship is downward-sloping and curved (more or less). The downward slope is courtesy of the inverse relationship between bond prices and their required yields. As for the curvature, it is a byproduct of the mathematics of the bond-pricing formula. The relationship is said to be convex as it bends toward the origin and out toward the horizontal axis. Bond market participants use the term "positive convexity." It turns out that the slope and curvature give us important information about the exposure of a bond to interest rate risk.

Figure 1. The price–yield relationship

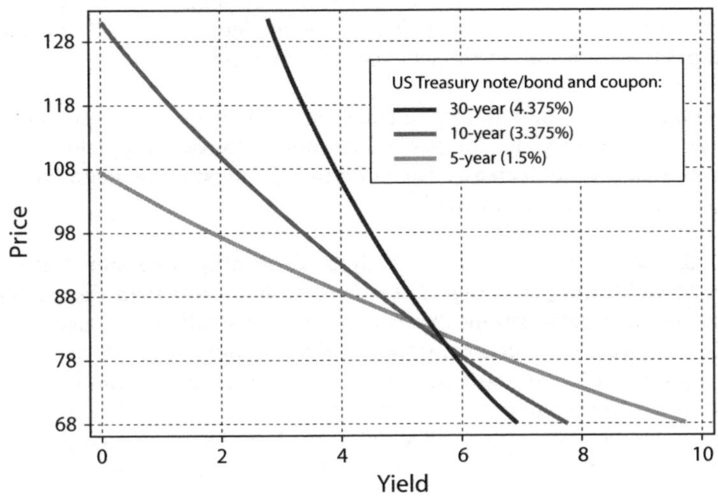

A bond has four attributes that impact its response to a given change in required yield:

- the remaining term to maturity;
- the level of the coupon rate;
- the level of the yields;
- the presence of embedded options.

These four attributes affect the slope and curvature of the price–yield relationship.

The price–yield relationship for an option-free bond is downward-sloping and curved. A bond's interest rate risk depends on the slope of this relationship and the degree of the curvature.

Four Observations About the Shape of the Curve

The first observation we put forward is that the percentage change in price, given a change in yield, is not the same for all bonds. Looking back at Figure 1, this certainly rings true. The price–yield relationships for the three Treasury notes/bonds have different slopes and curvatures, so equal yield changes of, say, 100 bps will evoke different percentage price changes.

The second observation is that, for small changes in yield, the percentage price change for a particular bond is approximately the same whether the yield increases or decreases. Let us demonstrate this with some numbers. Consider a 30-year, 10% coupon bond priced to yield 10% so that the bond trades at par. Now we reprice the bond at yields one basis point higher and lower. At a yield of 10.01%, the price falls to 99.9054. At a yield of 9.99%, the price rises to 100.0947. The dollar value of a 1 bp change if the yield increases by 1 bp is 100 – 99.9054 = 0.0946. The dollar value of a

1 bp change if the yield decreases by 1 bp is 100.0947 – 100 = 0.0947. These changes are almost exactly the same in absolute value. For small changes in required yield, we can treat the curved price–yield relationship as if it were linear. As a result, the amount that the bond price rises or falls is almost exactly the same.

The third observation states that for large changes in yield the previous result no longer holds. For large changes in yield, the percentage price change for a yield increase is different from that of a yield decrease. The curvature influences the magnitude of the price changes for larger changes in yields.

The fourth and last observation takes the third observation one step further. For large changes in yield, the percentage price increase is greater than the percentage price decrease. We will demonstrate this result with some numbers. Once again we employ our 30-year, 10% coupon bond initially priced to yield 10%. We now consider dramatic changes in the bond's required yield. First, let us reprice the bond at 8%, which represents a 200 bp reduction in yield. The resulting price is 122.6235, which reflects a percentage change in price of 22.6235%. Now let us reprice the bond at 12%, which represents a 200 bp increase in yield from the initial yield of 10%. The resulting price is 83.8386, which reflects a percentage price change of –16.1614%. Note that the percentage increase (22.2635%) when yields fall is greater in absolute value than the percentage price decrease (–16.1614%) when yields rise. This result is attributable to positive convexity. Indeed, these four observations can be explained by the convex shape of the price–yield relationship.

We turn now to the question of which attributes affect a bond's sensitivity to a change in yield. In other words, what attributes explain the slope and curvature of the price–yield relationship? Consider the four hypothetical bonds with an initial yield of 8% in Table 1—two five-year notes with coupons of 7% or 10% and two 30-year bonds with coupons of 7% or 10%. The first column shows the different levels of required yield in increments and decrements of 50 bps, with the initial yield being 8%. Accordingly, each cell in the table represents a percentage change in price for a given level of required yield.

Table 1. Percentage change in bond price for a given level of required yield

	Note/bond and coupon			
Yield (%)	5-year, 7%	30-year, 7%	5-year, 10%	30-year, 10%
6.0	8.67	28.36	8.28	26.69
6.5	6.42	20.15	6.13	19.02
7.0	4.23	12.75	4.04	12.06
7.5	2.09	6.06	1.99	5.75
8.0 (initial)	0.00	0.00	0.00	0.00
8.5	–2.04	–5.51	–1.94	–5.24
9.0	–4.02	–10.52	–3.84	–10.03
9.5	–5.96	–15.08	–5.69	–14.42
10.0	–7.85	–19.26	–7.50	–18.45

We see two factors at work here. First, when yield and maturity are held constant, the lower the coupon, the greater the sensitivity of the bond price to a given change in required yield. Coupon payments lessen the impact of a given change in required yield. As we move in Table 1 between the two five-year bonds, we see that for the higher-coupon bond all the percentage price changes are lower in absolute value. The same pattern is evident when one compares the percentage price changes of the two 30-year bonds. The second factor at work is the impact of maturity when yield and maturity are held constant. Other things being equal, the longer the maturity, the greater the impact of a given change in required yield. The reasoning is straightforward: cash flows more distant from the present are affected more dramatically by a given change in required yield.

Introduction to Duration

In general, duration measures the sensitivity of the price of a bond (in percentage terms) to a change in yield. Here we are trying to measure the slope of the price–yield relationship at a particular point on the curve. Let us introduce the following notation:

Δy = Change in the bond's yield (decimal)

P_+ = Bond price if the yield increases by Δy

P_- = Bond price if the yield decreases by Δy

P_0 = Initial price of bond (per $100 of par value)

> Duration is a linear approximation to the price–yield relationship, which is nonlinear. If the change in rates is considerable or the price–yield relationship is more curved, the linear approximation will be less reliable.

We develop the duration measure under the assumption that the reference yield curve is flat and moves by way of parallel shifts. As a result, the yield for all maturities changes by the same number of basis points.

The duration measure that we will develop is a linear approximation to the current price–yield relationship. To obtain the slope of a line we need two points. The first point is the percentage price change for a 1 bp increase in yield, which is given by the expression

$$\frac{P_- - P_0}{P_0(\Delta y)100}$$

Similarly, the second point is the percentage price change for a 1 bp decrease in yield, which is given by the expression

$$\frac{P_0 - P_+}{P_0(\Delta y)100}$$

These two numbers are close to each other in absolute value but are not exactly the same because the price–yield relationship is a curve. Suppose that we wanted to know the average percentage price change for a 1 bp movement in the yield regardless of the direction. We would simply add the percentage price change expressions together and divide by two:

$$\frac{1}{2}\left[\frac{P_- - P_0}{P_0(\Delta y)100} + \frac{P_0 - P_+}{P_0(\Delta y)100}\right]$$

Simply put,

$$\frac{P_- - P_+}{P_0(\Delta y)100}$$

This expression tells us the average percentage price change for a 1 bp movement in the reference yield curve. Duration gives us the average percentage price change for a 100 bp movement in the reference yield curve. To move from the expression we have to the expression we want, simply multiply by 100. Duration can be computed using the following formula:

$$\text{Duration} = \frac{P_- - P_+}{2P_0(\Delta y)}$$

Example

Let's put the formula through its paces. Consider a 10%, 30-year bond priced to yield 8%. We need to choose a value for Δy in order to compute P_+ and P_-. The bigger the value of Δy, the greater the difference between P_+ and P_-. It turns out that the choice for Δy is somewhat arbitrary as the duration computed is almost exactly the same regardless of the value of Δy chosen. The important point to remember is that the choice of Δy does not affect the interpretation of the formula. Duration is the average percentage price change for a 100 bp change in the reference yield curve. Let Δy be 20 bps. We reprice the bond at a yield of 7.8% and a value for P_- of 125.3646. Perform the same operation with a yield of 8.2% to obtain a value of 119.9815 for P_+. Inserting these values into the duration formula results in

$$\text{Duration} = \frac{125.3646 - 119.9815}{2(122.6235)(0.002)} = 10.97$$

That is, when the reference yield curve shifts by 100 bps, we would expect this bond to change in value by approximately 10.97% in the opposite direction.

The advantages of duration being a linear approximation are manifest. We can easily approximate how much the bond value will respond to different interest rate shocks. If the reference yield curve shifts by 200 bps, the bond value will move by twice the duration's value in percentage terms. If the reference yield curve shifts by 50 bps, the bond's value is projected to change by half the duration, and so on.

Our next task is to expand our tool duration to three specific applications. First, what if we are dealing with expected dollar price changes as opposed to percentage price changes in response to interest rate shocks? Second, how does one compute the duration of a portfolio of bonds? Third, how does one extend the notion of duration to a bond with one or more embedded options?

Dollar Duration

When a financial institution is managing its exposure to interest rate risk, it is often useful to think in terms of dollar changes in value as opposed to percentage changes in value. For example, suppose that a trader wants to hedge the interest rate risk of a short position in a bond which he or she believes to be overvalued. The trader is concerned with offsetting adverse changes in the value of the position rather than percentage price changes. This brings us to dollar duration. Duration tells us the approximate percentage price change for a 100 bp shift in the reference yield curve.[2] Two bonds with the same duration will not experience the same dollar price change. The approximate dollar price change for a 100 bp shift in the reference yield curve is given by the expression

Dollar price change = Duration × Bond price × 0.01

Portfolio Duration

Investors almost always hold a portfolio of bonds as opposed to a single bond. Thus, we are interested in measuring the interest rate risk exposure of a portfolio. A portfolio's duration is simply the weighted average of the durations of the individual bonds that comprise the portfolio. Each portfolio's weight is the proportion of the portfolio that is attributable to each security. Consider the hypothetical three-bond portfolio detailed in Table 2.

Table 2. Portfolio duration example

Bond	Full price	Duration	Portfolio weight
A	100.6555	1.886	0.489
B	101.5119	7.518	0.394
C	60.1730	9.421	0.117

The portfolio duration is 4.987. The question arises as to how this number is to be interpreted. A portfolio duration measures the approximate percentage change in the portfolio's value if the yield for each of the bonds changes by 100 bps.

Effective Duration

The approximation formula for duration assumes that the bond's cash flows are invariant to parallel shifts in the reference yield curve. For an option-free bond this condition holds. A parallel shift in the reference yield curve does not engender a change in the expected size and timing of an option-free bond's cash flows. For bonds with embedded options, the cash flows are interest rate-dependent. Simply put, when interest rates change, the cash flows change. Duration (as calculated above) is not an appropriate measure of interest rate risk sensitivity for bonds with embedded options: callables, putables, structured products, etc. The presence of the embedded call option changes the convexity of the price–yield relationship.

Figure 2 shows the price–yield relationship for an option-free bond and a callable bond. The curve labeled *a–a′* is the price–yield relationship of an option-free bond. Correspondingly, the price–yield relationship for a callable bond is given by the curve *a–b*. An embedded call option causes the price–yield relationship to bend back the opposite direction (curve *b–b′*) relative to an option-free bond. The reason for this effect is that as yields fall the value of the embedded call option increases. The bondholder is short the call option, so the increase in its value causes the callable bond's price to appreciate at a decreasing rate.

Figure 2. Price–yield relationship for option-free bond and callable bond

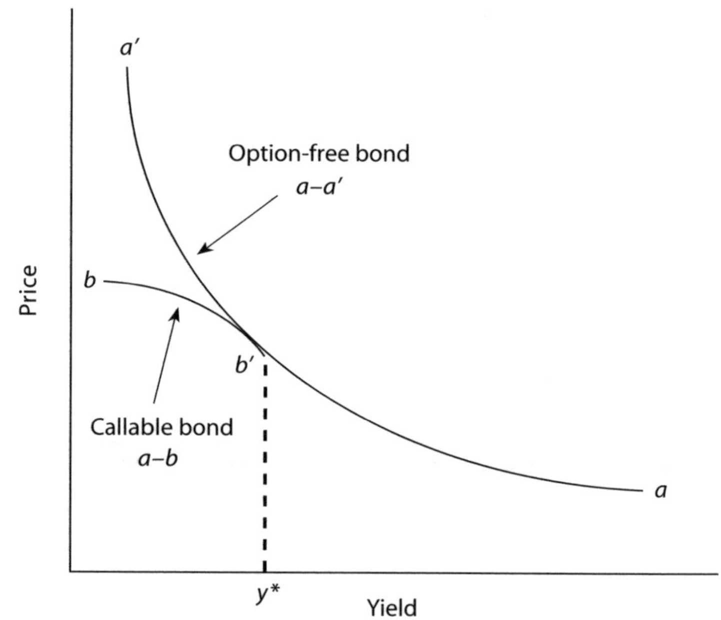

To account for embedded options, analysts often employ a so-called *effective* or *option-adjusted* duration using our approximation formula developed earlier. The only difference is in how P_- and P_+ are computed. These terms are computed using a valuation model that is designed to incorporate the impact of the shift in the reference yield curve on the cash flows of a bond with an embedded option. Thus, the interest rate dependence is incorporated directly into the calculation of P_- and P_+. Many analysts believe that the duration and effective duration of option-free bonds should always be the same. This is strictly true only when the reference yield curve is flat and moves with parallel shifts. The reason for this is that the par and spot curves do not shift by the same amount except when the yield curve is flat.[3]

Introduction to Convexity

Duration is a linear approximation to the relationship between bond prices and yield, which is inherently nonlinear (see Figure 1). The question is under what conditions this linear approximation is viable. To answer this question, we need to be able to measure the curvature of the price–yield relationship. Using the same notation as before, we employ the following formula to approximate the curvature or convexity of the price–yield relationship:

$$\text{Convexity} = \frac{P_+ + P_- - 2P_0}{P_0\,(\Delta y)^2}$$

We will use the approximation formula to compute the convexity of a 30-year US Treasury principal STRIPS valued at 25.088 and yielding 4.692%.[4] Assume that y is 20 bps, as before, and reprice the bonds at lower and higher yields. The following are the inputs to be inserted into the formula:

$\Delta y = 0.002$

$P_+ = 23.669$

$P_- = 26.594$

$P_0 = 25.088$

The convexity is computed as follows:

$$\text{Convexity} = \frac{23.669 + 26.594 - 2(25.088)}{23.088(0.002)^2} = 870$$

> Duration and convexity are complements, not substitutes. One either uses duration alone when interest rates are stable, or duration and convexity together when interest rates are volatile.

This number, 870, represents the degree of curvature of the price–yield relationship. Larger convexity values represent greater curvature. A larger curvature translates into a larger error from using a linear, duration-based approximation to estimate a nonlinear relationship. Convexity is used to measure the magnitude of that error. Duration provides a first approximation of a bond's sensitivity to change in yield. Convexity gives a finer, second approximation. The approximate percentage change in price due to convexity, or the so-called convexity correction, is given by the expression

$$\text{Convexity correction} = 0.5 \times \text{Convexity} \times (\Delta y)^2$$

Let us return to our Treasury STRIPS to illustrate. If the yield increases from 4.692% to 7.692%, what is the percentage price change due to convexity?

$0.5 \times 870 \times (0.03)^2 = 0.3915$

Thus, the percentage price change due to convexity is 39.15%. This is the error due to using duration alone. Now let us put duration and convexity together.

The duration of this Treasury STRIPS is 29.157. The percentage change in the bond price predicted using duration alone is computed as follows:

Percentage change = –29.157 × 3 = –87.47%

This is the price change predicted using duration, which is a linear approximation. The convexity correction adjusts the linear approximation to take into account the effect of the curvature of the price–yield relationship. The approximate percentage change in the bond price using both duration and convexity is summarized as follows:

Linear approximation estimated by duration:	–87.45%
Convexity correction:	+39.15%
Total:	–48.30%

The convexity correction adjusts for the error from using duration alone. The correction will be larger when the convexity is large and interest rates are volatile.

Case Study

You are given the task of demonstrating that the proper method for approximating a portfolio's internal rate of return is through the use of dollar duration weights and not market value weights. Dollar durations are simply the product of a bond's full price and its duration. Consider the following hypothetical spot rates out to two years:

Maturity (years)	Spot rate (%)
0.5	3.0
1.0	3.30
1.5	3.55
2.0	3.85

Treat this coupon note as if it were a portfolio of zero-coupon securities which should be discounted using Treasury spot rates. Use these spot rates to price a 4% coupon, two-year note and answer the following questions.

- What is the yield to maturity of the note?
- What is the market value-weighted yield of a portfolio of zero-coupon bonds with identical cash flows that replicates the two-year note? Assume that there is no arbitrage.
- What is the dollar duration-weighted portfolio yield?

The Full Valuation Approach

An alternative method to measure the interest rate risk exposure of a bond position or a portfolio of bonds is to revalue it assuming different hypothetical yield levels. For example, a manager may want to measure the interest rate exposure to instantaneous shifts of 50, 100, and 200 bps in the reference yield curve. This approach comprises the valuation of a bond or bond portfolio for multiple interest rate scenarios and is referred to as the *full valuation approach*. It is sometimes referred to as *scenario analysis*.

> The full valuation, or scenario analysis, approach is the most flexible method for assessing a portfolio's exposure to curve risk because any change in the reference yield curve can be simulated.

To illustrate this approach, suppose that a portfolio manager has a US$50 million par value position in US principal STRIPS (i.e. a zero-coupon investment) that matures on May 15, 2041.[5] The price is 26.7928, with a corresponding yield of 4.471%. The market value of the position is US$13,396,400. Since the manager has a long position in this issue, he/she is concerned with a rise in yields since this will reduce the position's market value. To assess the portfolio's exposure to a rise in yields, the manager decides to examine how the STRIPS' value will change if yields increase instantaneously by 50, 100, 150, and 200 bps—i.e. four scenarios. Because this zero-coupon bond is option-free, valuation is straightforward. The STRIPS' price per US$100 of par value and the market value of the US$50 million par position are shown in Table 3. Also presented are the change in the market value and the percentage change.

Table 3. Illustration of full valuation approach to assessing the interest rate risk of a bond position for four scenarios. (Adapted from Fabozzi and Mann, 2010, p. 331)

Scenario	Yield change (bp)	New yield (%)	New price	New market value (US$)	Change in market value (%)
1	50	4.971	23.1650	11,582,500	−13.540
2	100	5.471	20.0355	10.017,750	−25.221
3	150	5.971	17.3349	8,667,450	−35.300
4	200	6.471	15.0035	7,501,750	−44.002

Current bond position: US principal STRIPS maturing May 15, 2041.
Price: 26.7929; yield to maturity: 4.471%; par value owned: US$50 million; market value of position: US$13,396,400.

The full valuation approach can also handle scenarios where the yield curve does not change in a parallel fashion. Here, the scenario analyzed is for a change in the slope of the yield curve combined with changes in the levels of the yields. As a result, the portfolio manager can measure the exposure of a portfolio to yield curve risk.

A common question that often arises when using the full valuation approach is which scenarios should be evaluated to assess exposure to interest rate risk. For some regulated entities specified scenarios are established by regulators. For example, it is common for regulators of depository institutions to require entities to determine the impact on the value of their bond portfolio for 100, 200, and 300 bp instantaneous changes, both up and down, in interest rates. Risk managers and highly leveraged investors such as hedge funds tend to look at extreme shocks to assess exposure to interest rate changes. This practice is referred to as stress testing.

Of course, in assessing how changes in the yield curve can affect the exposure of a portfolio, there are an infinite number of scenarios that can be evaluated. The state-of-the-art technology involves using a complex statistical procedure[6] to determine a likely set of yield curve shift scenarios from historical data.

In summary, we can use the full valuation approach to assess the exposure of a bond or portfolio to interest rate shocks, assuming that the manager has a good valuation model to estimate what the price of the bond will be in each interest rate scenario. Moreover, we recommend use of the full valuation approach for assessing the position of a single bond or a portfolio of a few bonds. For a portfolio with a large number of bonds and/or bonds containing embedded options, the full valuation process may be too time-consuming.

Summary and Further Steps

- Interest rate risk is one of the most important risks with which a financial institution must contend.
- The slope and curvature of the price–yield relationship of a bond determines the exposure to interest rate risk.
- Duration is a first (i.e. linear) approximation to the price–yield relationship.
- Convexity is a finer second approximation that takes into account the degree of curvature of the price–yield relationship.
- The full valuation approach is the most general, accurate, and flexible approach for measuring interest rate risk.

More Info

Books:

de La Grandville, Olivier. *Bond Pricing and Portfolio Analysis: Protecting Investors in the Long Run*. Cambridge, MA: MIT Press, 2001.

Fabozzi, Frank J., and Steven V. Mann. *Introduction to Fixed Income Analytics: Relative Value Analysis, Risk Measures, and Valuation*. 2nd ed. Hoboken, NJ: Wiley, 2010.

Fabozzi, Frank J., and Steven V. Mann (eds). *The Handbook of Fixed Income Securities*. 8th ed. New York: McGraw Hill, 2012.

Fabozzi, Frank J., Steven V. Mann, and Moorad Choudhry. *Measuring and Controlling Interest Rate and Credit Risk*. 2nd ed. Hoboken, NJ: Wiley, 2003.

Golub, Bennett W., and Leo M. Tilman. *Risk Management: Approaches for Fixed Income Markets*. New York: Wiley, 2000.

Ilmanen, Antti. *Expected Returns: An Investor's Guide to Harvesting Market Rewards*. Chichester, UK: Wiley, 2011.

Notes

1. Currently, the only difference between US Treasury notes and bonds is the initial term to maturity.
2. Dollar duration for a 1 bp change in yield is to all intents and purposes the same as the dollar value of a 1 bp change in yield.
3. For more on this issue see Golub and Tilman (2000).
4. A 30-year US Treasury principal STRIPS is a zero-coupon security created by dealers from the principal payment of a 30-year bond. STRIPS is an acronym for "separate trading of registered interest and principal of securities."
5. A principal STRIPS is a zero-coupon bond created from a bond's principal payment.
6. The procedure used is principal-component analysis.

Understanding and Applying Funds Transfer Pricing

by Hovik Tumasyan

PricewaterhouseCoopers, Canada

This Chapter Covers

- The role funds transfer pricing plays in a bank.
- Mechanisms used to perform funds transfer pricing, illustrated through numerical case studies
- The methodological aspects of defining the transfer price rates for typical asset and liability instruments.
- Reflections on the current state of affairs for funds transfer pricing frameworks.

Introduction

In its simplest form funds transfer pricing (FTP) is the process whereby the treasury of a bank (its funding center) aggregates funds centrally and then redistributes them throughout the business units, balancing funding resource excesses and shortages and thus creating an internal market for liquidity. If there is still a deficit for funds, the treasury raises more funds from the capital markets, and if there is an excess of funds, treasury invests them in capital markets or lends in the wholesale markets.

FTP has been an integral part of bank management for more than three decades. It traces its origins to the 1970s and the deregulation of interest rates in the United States, when it was developed as a tool for managing the interest rate risk in banks.[1]

Fundamentally, the purpose of FTP remains the same as it was when it was developed: to aggregate the interest rate exposure of the whole bank into a central location for its effective management. In doing so, FTP generates a few other results that sometimes are quoted as the main purpose of FTP:

- by transferring the interest rate risk into a central location, it makes the booked income of business units immune to interest rate fluctuations;
- by charging for such transfers, it effectively determines the net interest income of business units;
- because banks acquire interest rate exposure in the process of funding their balance sheets, FTP is perceived as the mechanism of charging for funding costs and as a tool to manage the liquidity risk of the bank.

It has to be noted, however, that equating the management of interest rate risk to allocating the costs for funding can be an oversimplification in today's banking organizations. The simplistic and directional view that higher interest rates increase the costs of funding, and that this risk needs to be managed against, seems to be reminiscent of times when all the loans (mortgages) in the banking books were fixed-rate (as far back as the 1970s and 1980s). Today, banking books have almost as much in the form of variable-rate loans indexed to a variety of alternative indices (which creates basis risk) as they have of fixed-rate loans. Moreover, interest rate management transactions are sometimes carried out between a banking unit (like retail) and a swap desk in the capital markets division, while the treasury charges a fixed rate for an overall use of resources.[2]

In the aftermath of the recent financial crisis, FTP has regained its prominent role as the key tool in measuring and managing the liquidity risk in banks.

In this chapter we will follow the funding cost allocation side of the FTP and will acknowledge the interest rate exposures *en passant*, distinguishing between the two in examples.

How Does It Work?

The Mechanics of Funds Transfer Pricing

The mechanism of FTP is dictated by the very nature of the banking business. In the course of their day-to-day business, banks either lend or take deposits independently. As a result, business units end up either being short of funding for lending or in excess and looking to invest. The treasury of the bank owns the process of transferring the funds internally from businesses that have the excess to those that need the funding. In the process, treasury charges a rate for the funds provided to, and pays a rate for funds purchased from, the business units (the FTP rate). This results in a decomposition of the net interest margin (NIM) of the bank into three components—the lending business NIM, the deposit business NIM, and the treasury NIM. Figure 1 illustrates the FTP process and a decomposition of the NIM.

Figure 1. The mechanics of FTP—no interest rate or liquidity risks

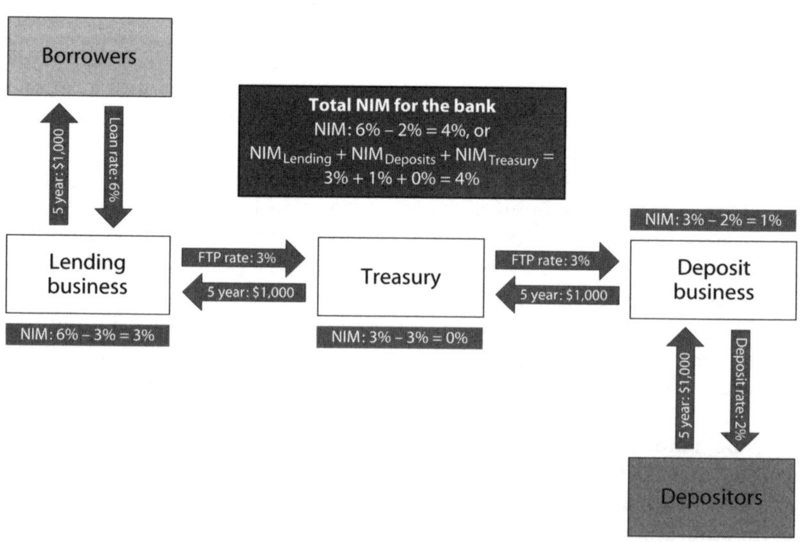

In this example the treasury (the bank's funding center) has purchased \$1,000 at a FTP rate of 3% to fund a loan of the same amount, passing the FTP rate paid for deposits to the lending unit as an interest expense. In this transaction neither the bank as a whole nor the units involved (including the treasury) have taken interest rate or liquidity risks, as reflected in the 0% NIM of the treasury. Note that the bank NIM of 4% is composed of the three NIMs:

$$NIM_{Lending} + NIM_{Deposits} + NIM_{Treasury} = 3\% + 1\% + 0\% = 4\%.$$

Figure 1 represents the simplest of the situations that can occur in a bank. Normally, the deposits are of shorter terms than the loans. So there is a maturity mismatch that creates both interest rate and liquidity risk exposures. An example of this is shown in Figure 2.

Here the same five-year loan of \$1,000 is funded by purchasing \$1,000 raised from depositors through a two-year deposit at 1%. First, note that the bank in this scenario generates a greater NIM of 6% – 1% = 5%. To achieve this, the bank exposes itself to the risk associated with being able to roll the two-year deposit until the loan is repaid (liquidity risk) and the risk of paying higher rates for the one-year deposits if the interest rates go up in the process (interest rate risk).

As can be seen from Figure 2, the FTP process has moved both risks into treasury, plus the extra 1% NIM for assuming the responsibility of managing these risks.

Figure 2. The mechanics of FTP, with interest rate and liquidity risks aggregated to the treasury

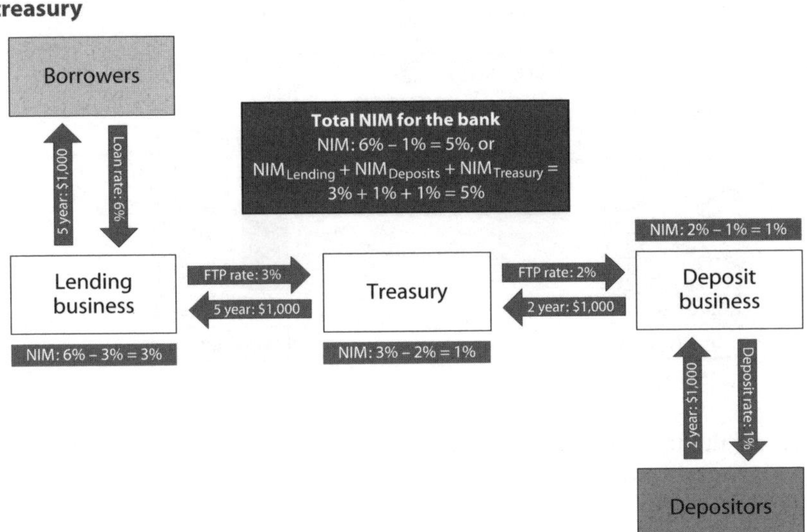

To develop the discussion further, we will maintain the business structure described in Figures 1 and 2: a lending unit, a deposit unit, and the treasury. We will also assume that the treasury owns a funding center, which runs a FTP book that lists all the transfer-priced assets and liabilities of the bank.

So, how does the treasury decide how much to pay and how much to charge for the funds it acquires and redistributes? Treasuries employ three main approaches to determine the FTP rate applied to business units and the funding center—*the single-pool approach*, the *multiple-pool approach*, and the *matched-maturity approach*.

Pool Approaches

In the simplest case the FTP center nets the excesses of some business units with the deficits of others. The central pool lends to deficit units and purchases the excesses from others and uses the same rate for both. This procedure is known as the *single-pool approach* (Figure 3). It is a simple approach, but it does not meet any of the goals of a FTP framework as formulated in the introduction.

First, since the assets and the liabilities are matched at the business unit level before identifying the shortfalls and excesses of funding resources, FTP does not know the maturity profile of the pools and will operate on an average-rate basis. As such, it will always leave both interest rate exposures and funding costs unmatched. Furthermore, since it has no control over the business unit operations, the maturity mismatch profile of the excess pool and the funding required are not known to the FTP center *a priori*.

Figure 3. Single-pool approach to funds transfer pricing

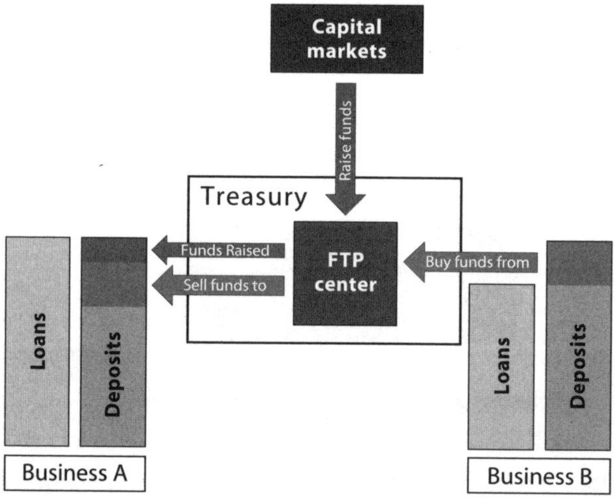

The size of the unknowns and the success of such a simplistic framework depend on how homogeneous are the products of respective business units and how trivial is the interest rate environment. In today's banking environment products are increasingly structured, come with embedded contingent cash flows and the interest rate environment is anything, but trivial.

> With today's products in financial institutions and financial markets the single-pool approach is an oversimplification.

The next level of sophistication moves in the directions of the shortfalls of the single-pool approach and is referred to as a *multiple-pool approach*. This approach acknowledges the maturity structure during the netting of the assets and liabilities of the business units and produces pool-specific FTP rates. Pooling may be based on the maturity structures of the products and the repricing indices, as well as on other specifics like behavioral patterns.

While a clear enhancement, the approach still suffers from dependencies on pool averages and assumptions about the acceptable level of granularity of the pools—i.e. how many pools adequately reflect the maturity mismatch profile and the funding costs of the bank as a whole.

The approach that is recognized today as the most adequate for achieving the goals of a FTP framework is known as *matched-maturity transfer pricing*. Under this approach, FTP rates charged for the use of funds and rates credited for providing funds are based on matching the rate on the cost-of-funds curve to the maturity of the asset or the liability instruments. To do so, all the assets and the liabilities are first "transferred" into a central book, referred to as the "FTP book." This is structurally different from the pool approaches, as shown in Figure 4.

Figure 4. Matched-maturity approach to funds transfer pricing

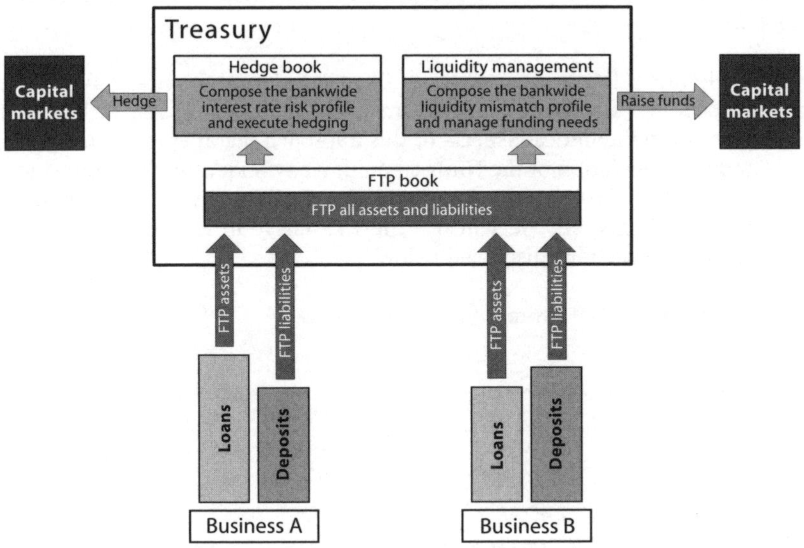

This approach serves both goals of FTP: allocation of the cost of funding and construction of the interest rate risk exposure for structural hedging (both for structural interest rate and foreign exchange risks).

There are variations on the setup shown in Figure 4. For example, pools could still be formed after all the assets and liabilities have been transferred into a FTP book transaction by transaction. However, this is counterproductive since it loses the level of granularity that generates the precision in assessing the liquidity profile and interest rate risk.

Experience shows that the moment banks move to multiple-pool approaches, the incremental effort to make the switch to maturity-matched transfer pricing becomes smaller and smaller, and banks usually adopt the latter as an approach for the whole balance sheet.

For this reason, the remainder of this chapter will elaborate on funds transfer pricing using the matched-maturity approach.

Matched-Maturity Funds Transfer Pricing

A matched maturity of funds approach to FTP is currently considered to be the most adequate approach by many practitioners. As mentioned before, under this approach rates charged for the use of funds and rates credited for providing funds are based on matching the maturity of the asset and liability instruments to the FTP rate that corresponds to that maturity on the cost-of-funds curve (an example of such a curve is shown in Figure 5). After this rate is identified, shadow interest expense (credits) to assets and shadow interest income (debits) to liabilities of the business units are created following a double-entry accounting mechanism. Simultaneously, mirror positions of these shadow entries are created in the FTP book.

We will first follow a few key examples to illustrate the mechanics of funds transfer pricing of assets and liabilities using the matched-maturity approach. We then will explore some of the theoretical aspects of this approach. Parallel to the assigning of a FTP rate and the calculation of the NIMs created, we will identify the interest rate risk exposures for each of the cases discussed and plot the maturity mismatches according to the liquidity risk created. We will use the FTP curve in Figure 5 as our working example for the transactions discussed below.

Figure 5. Example of a FTP curve

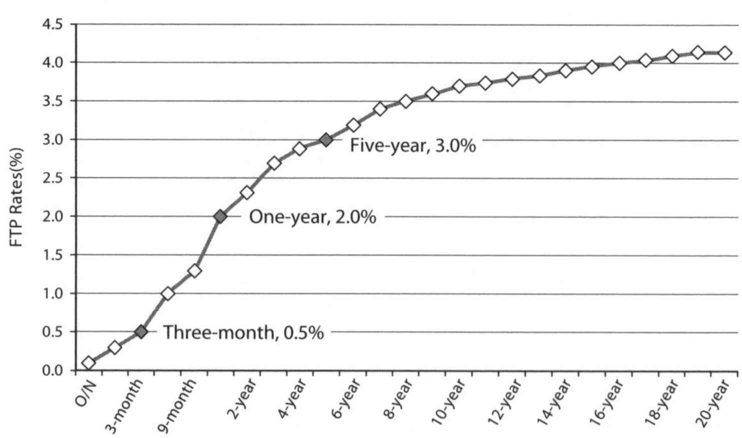

Transfer Pricing of Assets

Consider a five-year loan that pays 6% annual interest. In this example the FTP book reflects the matched-maturity funding of the loan, where the FTP rate of 3% is picked from the five-year point on the cost-of-funds curve (Figure 5) of the bank and is passed through to the lending unit as an interest expense. Such a transaction fixes the net interest margin across the whole bank at 3%.

Figure 6. Transfer pricing a fixed-rate loan

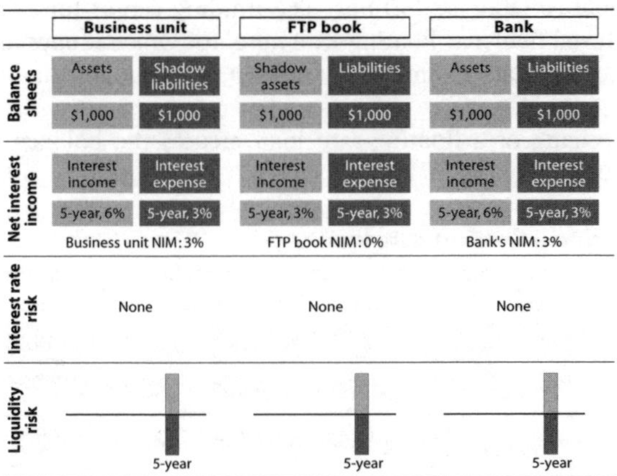

The transaction above does not create either an interest rate exposure or a liquidity risk, since both interest rates are fixed and principal cash flows are matched in time. The only risk that the loan carries for the bank at this point is the default risk of the borrower, management of which is the main competency of the business unit.

The next example, shown in Figure 7, illustrates how interest rate exposure and liquidity risk are acquired for the same transaction due to variations on this simple picture that result from taking a view on either liquidity risk or the interest rates.

Figure 7. Transfer pricing a fixed-rate loan with views

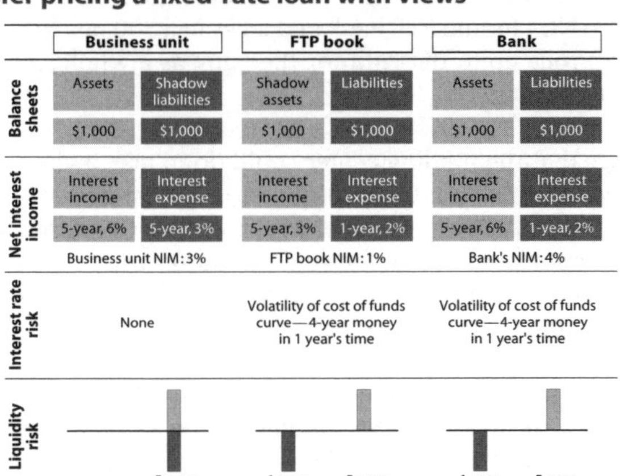

In this example, the funding center (which runs the FTP book) is of the view that wholesale markets are liquid enough and it will be able to roll the wholesale funding position at the end of the first year either for another year or borrow at more beneficial four-year rates at that time. The funding center has created an extra net income margin of 1% in the FTP book and has enhanced the bank's NIM overall, albeit by taking liquidity and interest rate risks.

Consider now the same five-year loan that instead pays an interest indexed to one-month Libor and equal to Libor + 350 bps. The funding center funds the loan with a one-month Libor-indexed five-year floating-rate note, for which it pays one-month Libor plus 50 bps. The 50 bps spread is sometimes referred to as the *liquidity premium.*

The funds transfer pricing of a floating-rate loan creates the balance sheets and net interest margins shown in Figure 8.

Figure 8. Transfer pricing a floating-rate loan

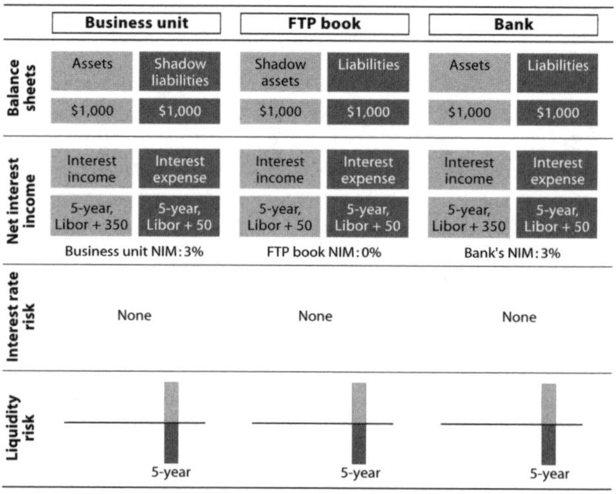

Again in this example we have matched the interest rate index (and its tenor) explicitly, which generates a zero NIM for the FTP book and locks in a 300 bps NIM for the business unit, which in its turn rolls up to the NIM for the bank as a whole. No interest rate or liquidity risk has been acquired.

There are a few things that the funding center could do to take a view in this situation: create exposures to liquidity risk (maturity mismatch); take interest rate risk (by funding at a fixed rate or on different terms); or generate a basis risk (by mismatching the index or its tenor). All of these actions create the same situation where the funding center is taking risks (different risks and different mechanisms, but the same outcome) and has to provide return on the capital allocated to these risks.

We illustrate in Figure 9 just one of these cases, where liquidity risk exposure is created by a maturity mismatch. In this case the funding center takes a view that the bank-specific asset swap spreads will tighten (and hence the liquidity premiums will decrease).

Accordingly, the funding center is funding the five-year floating-rate loan with a one-year floating-rate note indexed to the same interest rate. Figure 9 shows the balance sheets and net interest incomes of the business unit, funding center, and the bank as a whole.

Figure 9. Funds transfer pricing a floating-rate loan with a view

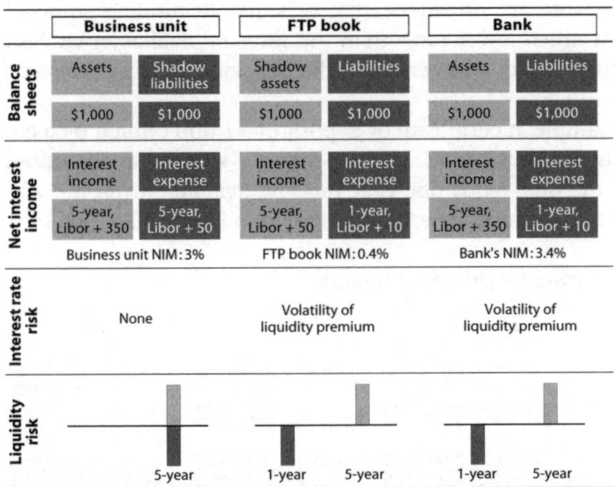

This of course creates the liquidity risk of not being able to roll the one-year note in one year's time or issuing a four-year note on the same terms. It also exposes the bank to the volatility in asset swap markets, with the risk of spreads widening at the short end of the term structure.

It should also be mentioned that in the examples above principal cash flows were arriving at maturity. This is usually not the case, and when principal cash flows come with a certain schedule they need to be matched to their time of arrival, not the maturity of the transaction. This creates a principal cash flow-weighted FTP rate to be assigned to the whole transaction. An example is shown in Figure 10.

Figure 10. Principal cash flow-weighted FTP rate calculation

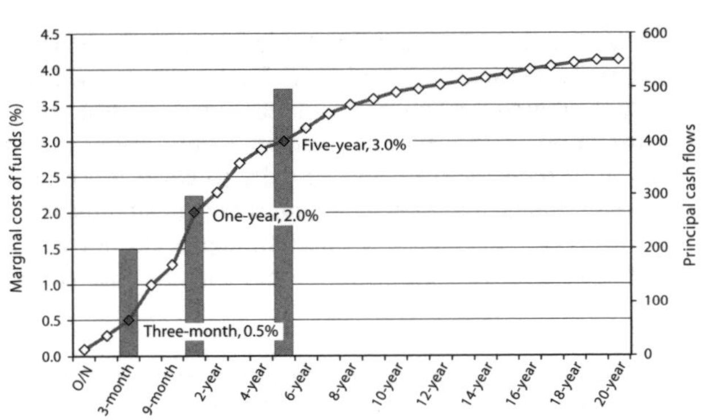

Principal cash flow-weighted FTP rate =
(200/1,000) × 0.5% + (300/1,000) × 2.0% + (500/1,000) × 3.0% = 2.2%

Here the FTP rate is 2.20%—not 3.00%, as it would have been in the case of a single principal cash flow at the maturity point (five years).

Transfer Pricing of Liabilities

As the banking industry was reminded during the recent financial crisis, deposit-collecting businesses are providers of very valuable funding sources. Because banks offer deposits at much lower rates than the rates on available wholesale funding, FTP allocates this opportunity cost benefit to the deposit-collecting units.

Consider, for example, a certificate of deposit of $1,000 offered by a bank that pays 1% to the holder in one year's time. The deposit unit sells the funds raised to the treasury at the price of the analogous one-year funding available from the wholesale markets, which is 2% at that point in time. This is shown in Figure 11.

Figure 11. Funds transfer pricing deposits

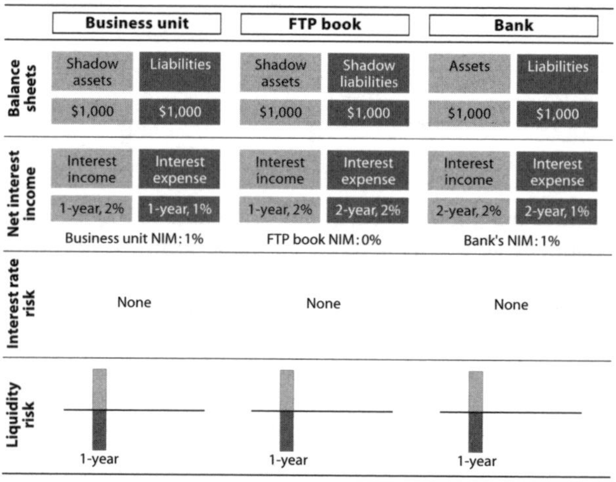

This transaction does not create any interest rate or liquidity risk, because the terms of both sides of that particular transaction are matched.

The funding raised is usually invested in banking assets, which have much longer maturity terms than the deposits. So, inevitably, funding loans with deposits creates the negative maturity mismatch for banks, thus constituting their liquidity risk profiles. Such a direct interpretation of the deposit contract would imply that banks have to refinance some portion of their deposits almost daily to cover these negative maturity gaps. Therein, however, hides the real value of the deposit businesses for a bank that many deposit businesses feel that FTP methodologies do not give enough credit for, when the matched-maturity approach is implemented as mechanically as it appears above.

Deposit products at a high level can be divided into two main categories, term and non-term, and both can be interest-bearing or not. The truth of the matter is, however, that deposits hardly ever behave as they are contracted to.

For example, customers with term deposits may decide to roll forward (sometimes even with increased balances), rather than withdraw the expired deposit contracts. On the other hand, a deposit instrument with no stated maturity contains no penalties for withdrawing the whole balance on the account with no or little notice (a no-cost put option in the contract design).

So, to understand the behavior of the deposits from the standpoint of the behavior of principal cash flows and the associated "liquidity value," one has to view them in bulk and with respect to the macro environment (interest rates, economics, and other collective behavioral specifics).

In bulk, deposit balances demonstrate stable patterns or "stickiness," with liquidity life characteristics resembling those of a term debt. This is of course of fundamental economic benefit to the banks, and as such should be reflected in the FTP methodologies to create the right incentives in the business growth of deposit business lines.[3]

Despite the fact that banks have ample quantities of historical data (or at least they should), the development of a single, well-understood approach to constructing the maturity profile of the deposit portfolios remains little more than an artisanal craft in many banks today.

One of the two widely used approaches is the tranching approach, whereby the analysis determines a portion or "tranche" of a pool of appropriately chosen deposit products as "core" or long-term stable tranche, based on historical analysis of past cash flow patterns in balances. This tranching continues until some amount is apportioned to a "non-core" or volatile tranche, and is assigned a very short term maturity. Accordingly, the stable or core tranche of the deposit pool has a long-term FTP rate matched to it, while the non-core tranche is assigned a short-term FTP. The two together determine a blended FTP rate for the pool of deposits under analysis.

The second, simulation-based approach models both the balances and the interest rates on deposit products through factor models with stochastic terms.[4] The types of factors used are usually split into two groups—the interest rate and the macro-environment (current rates offered, competitor rates, and fees, etc.) and the pool-specific factors (levels of service and convenience, customized products, customer mobility, local demographics, etc.). The simulation allows the forecasting of the maturity profiles of deposit pools which can be used to assign maturity-matched FTP rates. The resulting maturity profile in this approach is considerably more granular and lends itself to more flexible and proactive deposit pricing and/or liquidity management.

A third methodology uses a replicating portfolio approach,[5] whereby the historical cash flow behaviors of the deposit pool are replicated by a portfolio of risk-free instruments (both cash and derivatives). Unfortunately, as with any replicating portfolio approach, the resulting liquidity profiles and FTP rates tend to be extremely sample-dependent and unstable in time. Consequently, this approach has struggled to achieve as wide an acceptance as the first two.

In the aftermath of the recent financial crisis and the acute dependence of banks on more stable and diversified funding sources, banks have found themselves in need of more comprehensive study and model-building for their deposit pools.

Methodological Aspects of the Matched-Maturity Approach

First, let us note that in all the cases considered in previous sections funds transfer pricing mechanisms achieved the following goals:

- the liquidity and interest rate risks were aggregated into a central point in the bank;
- business unit P&Ls did not carry interest rate exposures;
- the liquidity risk and interest rate exposure of the FTP book, as well as its P&L for those exposures, matched that of the bank as a whole;
- the views on liquidity risk and expectations about the interest rates were taken at the appropriate point in the organization, where those risks can be measured and managed;
- they help to answer the question where risk capital for the (structural) interest rate risk exposure of the bank should be allocated.[6]

Because banks lend and borrow through hundreds of transactions a day, a functioning and self-consistent FTP framework, built on solid theoretical fundamentals, is required to allow the implied views on liquidity and structural risks in a bank's balance sheet to be revealed.

There are a few structural elements that form the methodological foundations for calculating the funds transfer pricing rate in the matched-maturity FTP approach. However, the most central is *the choice of the benchmark cost-of-funds curve* (like that in Figure 5). The choice of such a curve reflects (or implies) both the "philosophy" and the approach to management of liquidity and structural interest rate risk on the balance sheet of a bank. Usually, once this curve has been chosen, banks have a few "add-on" spreads to it that range from bank-specific direct and indirect operating costs to spreads for optionalities embedded in the transfer-priced instruments (for example prepayments in mortgages or putable deposits, etc.) and costs for holding the portfolio of liquid assets.

From a microeconomics standpoint, it can be shown that the optimal price for the transfer of an intermediate good between two business units is its opportunity cost.[7] Furthermore, if the units are free to determine their own outputs[8] and the market for the intermediate commodity is competitive, then the optimal transfer price for an intermediate good is its marginal cost in the market. In the case of funds transfer pricing, where the intermediate commodity is the funds from depositors, the choice for the benchmark cost-of-funds curve becomes the curve for the marginal cost of funding for the bank in the wholesale markets. For banks that have active access to funding in the wholesale markets, this curve has been the AA curve, which simply reflects the ratings of almost all wholesale market participants.

For more than a decade, however, this curve has been practically replaced by the swap curves, reflecting the short-term nature of funding of bank balance sheets that kept the spread between the two curves hovering around 10 bps for a very long time. The recent financial crisis, however, showed that this spread is as volatile as the curves themselves and that it can have a nontrivial term structure. FTP methodologies should capture both the size of this spread and its term structure.

This spread appears in FTP parlance as the *liquidity premium*. In some organizations there is a cultural misconception that being charged this premium is "a punitive measure." Sometimes this can be traced to a methodological misconception that "matched term" means matching the tenor on the index of a variable-rate loan, rather than its maturity term, overlaid with the expectation that the loan can be funded by rolling a short-term funding. In contrast, of course, if one matches the actual term of the variable-rate loan, the rate index has added to it a spread equal to the cost of the funding spread for the bank for its variable-rate funding. While it is true that these spreads have a liquidity premium embedded in them, the latter is more what is known as the *market liquidity premium*, rather than a *funding liquidity premium*.

Another methodological misconception is around the choice of a single or multiple benchmark cost-of-funds curve. For example, banks may select a mortgage curve to transfer price mortgages while using the institution's wholesale funding curve for all remaining assets and liabilities. Mortgages are especially appealing candidates for separate benchmarks, since these assets have counterparts, such as mortgage portfolios and mortgage-backed securities, which are traded in financial markets. While this may make the multiple curves option seem reasonable at first glance, the actual consequences turn out to be contrary to what a FTP is trying to achieve—i.e. inaccurate hedging, incorrect measurement of treasury/funding center performance, and misguided product pricing.[9]

> An inadequate FTP methodology or a biased FTP framework will send the wrong signals one transaction at a time, over time creating an unintended balance sheet structure in the form of a disproportionate mix of asset portfolios on the asset side (e.g. the size of subprime loans and trading portfolios), and/or liquidity holes on the liability side (e.g. Northern Rock).

Transfer Pricing Equity Capital

Maintaining high ratings is a cost of doing business for a bank. The presence of an amount of equity capital adequate to the asset risks allows banks to borrow at favorable rates in capital markets. As a result, all assets on a business unit's balance sheet are funded by debt capital, with only few exceptions where the actual equity capital of the bank is used for funding. Generally, equity capital gets allocated to the individual business activities as risk capital to cover potential losses and perform risk–return and portfolio analyses.

The costs of capital that should be charged for these two cases — equity funding and risk capital allocation — are different.[10] In the first case it is the full cost of equity capital equal to the required return on equity[11] charged to the business unit as a transfer price for the equity capital, while in the second case it is the full cost of equity *less* the return on a risk-free investment (it is the risk-free rate that goes into the estimation of the cost of equity capital using the Capital Asset Pricing Model (CAPM)).

This netting of the cost of equity capital with a risk-free rate happens in the form of an '*equity credit rate*', credited to the business unit's P&L.

When and how much of such a credit should be applied, has a wide variety of interpretations and calculation methodologies throughout the banking industry[12]. The industry practice seems to revolve around two main candidates for the equity credit rate – a long-term rolling average FTP or a risk-free rate, both calculated top-down in most cases and often with some misguided reference to the duration of the equity.

The case for which the FTP rate becomes the equity credit rate arises when an asset is partially funded with equity capital, but the FTP system has booked it as a fully debt-funded asset.[12] In such cases the equity credit rate becomes a '*blended rate*'. The FTP rate is credited back to the business unit P&L applied to the equity-funded portion of the asset and simultaneously the cost of equity capital is charged to the P&L as the cost of funding for that portion. The whole transaction then is charged the transfer price for the allocated risk capital in the form of the netted cost of equity capital as described above. Thus the equity credit rate becomes a weighted average rate between the FTP rate and the risk-free rate (see for example, Note 10).

A Summary and Strategic View on FTP

To increase their relevance and stature, internal audit departments should increase the frequency of their analysis and incorporate a data-driven approach in assessing and reporting on risk. This can be accomplished through the following steps.

- transfer liquidity and interest rate risks from the business units into a central point in the bank;
- by charging for such transfers, effectively determine the net interest income of business units;
- by transferring the interest rate risk into a central location make the booked income of business units immune to interest rate fluctuations;
- serve as the mechanism for charging for funding costs and as a tool for managing liquidity risk.

However, in the environment of very low interest rates that preceded the recent financial crisis cost of liquidity has not been a constraint in growth strategies of banks. Consequently, FTP frameworks have remained underfunded and underdeveloped; infrastructures for charging for liquidity have remained overly simplistic, lacking scalability and responsiveness in times of stress.

More importantly, a foundationally sound, functionally robust, and structurally scalable FTP framework can perform far-reaching strategic functions. Advancing analytical capabilities of FTP methodologies from the "costing" paradigm in management accounting to "*risk pricing and transfer*" in risk capital management can redefine and expand FTP's role to encompass the task of adequately reflecting all hedgable risks that come embedded in booked assets and liabilities.

This is a far-reaching and strategically essential role that transfer pricing is functionally well placed to play in bank balance sheet management. Such an expanded role will not only attend to the traditional FTP role of fixing the value created by commercial units at the booking point, but will also enable aggregation of all the hedgable risks into one central unit for management and risk capital allocation. The strategic importance of the latter is easy to acknowledge since, hedgable or not, all financial risks that banks take require risk capital, financed by the most expensive form of capital—common equity.

Furthermore, stripping out these hedgable (or passive) risks allows banks to:

- free up risk capital to finance more of value-creating risk-taking in areas where the bank has commercially meaningful competitive advantage;
- create a natural environment for executing optimal hedging strategies;
- provide financial agility for adjusting to the changing macro-environment and competitive landscape.

Implementation of such proactive FTP frameworks requires a strategic view on FTP's role sponsored by the senior management of the bank.

Moreover, FTP has become a regulatory requirement.[13,14] Regulators expect banks to be able to demonstrate how their FTP frameworks are aligned to best-practice principles for liquidity management.[15,16]

In many respects an effective FTP function is the first line of defence for a bank's balance sheet and its business model.

In many respects an effective FTP function is the first line of defence for a bank's balance sheet and its business model

More Info

Books:

Adam, Alexandre. *Handbook of Asset and Liability Management: From Models to Optimal Return Strategies*. Chichester, UK: Wiley, 2007.

Esch, Louis, Robert Kieffer, and Thierry Lopez. *Asset and Risk Management*. Chichester, UK: Wiley, 2005.

Matz, Leonard, and Peter Neu. *Liquidity Risk Measurement and Management: A Practitioner's Guide to Global Best Practices*. Singapore: Wiley, 2007.

Murphy, David. *Understanding Risk: The Theory and Practice of Financial Risk Management*. Boca Raton, FL: Chapman & Hall/CRC, 2008.

Van Deventer, Donald R., Kenji Imai, and Mark Mesler. *Advanced Financial Risk Management: Tools and Techniques for Integrated Credit Risk and Interest Rate Risk Management*. Singapore: Wiley, 2005.

Notes

1. A selective history of these events can be found in Van Deventer, Imai, and Mesler (2005).
2. Although there can be a few things that can go wrong with such a setup, the two more significant ones seem to be the conflict of interest in the positioning of the swap desk and the practical infeasibility of forming an aggregate view of the interest rate exposure for the bank as a whole. Nevertheless, such practices are too widespread to be ignored.
3. See McGuire, W. J. "Indeterminate term deposits in FTP: Quantified solutions at last!" *Journal of Performance Management* (May 2004): 14–26, and references therein; and Turner, Steve. "Funds transfer pricing: Cracking the code on deposit valuation." Novantas White paper series. November 2008. Online at: novantas.com/articlepdf/69.pdf
4. See Cornyn, Anthony. G., Robert A. Klein, and Jess Lederman (eds). *Controlling & Managing Interest-Rate Risk*. New York Institute of Finance, 1997, for a review of such models; Dewachter, Hans, Marco Lyrio, and Stan Maes. "A multi-factor model for the valuation and risk management of demand deposits." Working paper 83. National Bank of Belgium, 2006. Online at dx.doi.org/10.2139/ssrn.1689550. See Van Deventer, Imai, and Mesler (2005) for discussions.
5. For an example see Kalkbrener, Michael, and Jan W. Willing. "Risk management of non-maturing liabilities." *Journal of Banking & Finance* 28:7 (2004): 1547–1568. Online at: dx.doi.org/10.1016/S0378-4266(03)00131-6
6. This has implications for the question whether the FTP book should be a profit or a cost center. In the most general case it can be a profit center in terms of the NIM, but a cost center with respect to economic profit or on a required return-on-equity basis. The size of this cost center (together with other contributing factors) can help to determine the level of the risk tolerance for interest rate and liquidity risk for the bank as whole.
7. See for example Brickley, James, Clifford Smith, and Jerold Zimmerman. "Transfer pricing and the control of internal corporate transactions." *Journal of Applied Corporate Finance* 8:2 (1995): 60–67. Online at dx.doi.org/10.1111/j.1745-6622.1995.tb00288.x; Hirshleifer, Jack. "On the economics of transfer pricing." *Journal of Business* 29 (1956): 172–184; and Ford, G. "Internal pricing in financial institutions: Issues" in Tom Valentine and Guy Ford (eds). *Readings in Financial Institutions Management*. Sydney: Allen and Unwin, 1999.
8. For example, how much the lending business lends does not affect how much deposit is taken in, and the imbalances in divisional outputs can be met in the external market.
9. See Shih, A., S. Wofford, and D. Crandon, "Transfer pricing: Pitfalls in using multiple benchmark yield curves." *Journal of Bank Cost & Management Accounting* 13:3 (2000): 56–66.
10. See Tumasyan, H. "Credit where equity is due." Social Science Research Network. April 21, 2011. Online at: dx.doi.org/10.2139/ssrn.1818003
11. The required return on equity for a bank is usually measured as *risk-free rate + beta of the bank × equity premium* using a CAPM approach.
12. Kipkalov, Alexander. "Transfer pricing capital." *Journal of Performance Management* 22:2 (May 2009): 38–46; and Shih, A., and A. Tavakol. "Making sense of the transfer pricing of equity." *Bank Accounting and Finance* 10:4 (1997): 47–52.
13. Committee of European Banking Supervisors. "Guidelines on liquidity cost benefit allocation." European Banking Authority, October 2010; and Financial Services Authority. "Dear treasurer: Funds transfer pricing." July 2010. Online at: www.fsa.gov.uk/pubs/international/ftp_treasurer_letter.pdf
14. See also the report by Grant, Joel. "Liquidity transfer pricing: A guide to better practice." Australian Prudential Regulation Authority Working paper, March 2011. Online at: tinyurl.com/74aaecj
15. See also Institute of International Finance. "Principles of liquidity risk management." March 2007. Online at: www.iif.com/download.php?id=tv/yzuHHXJ0=
16. See Basel Committee on Banking Supervision. "Basel III: International framework for liquidity risk measurement, standards and monitoring." December 2010; and Basel Committee on Banking Supervision. "Principles for sound liquidity risk management and supervision." September 2008.

Index